new world **kitchen**

ecco

An Imprint of HarperCollins*Publishers*

new world kitchen

Latin American and Caribbean Cuisine

PHOTOGRAPHS BY TIM TURNER

Norman Van Aken

with Janet Van Aken

Also by Norman Van Aken

Norman's New World Cuisine

Norman Van Aken's Feast of Sunlight

The Great Exotic Fruit Book

NEW WORLD KITCHEN: LATIN AMERICAN
AND CARIBBEAN CUISINE.
Copyright © 2003 by Norman Van Aken.
Photographs copyright © 2003 by Tim Turner.
All rights reserved. Printed in the United States of America.
No part of this book may be used or reproduced in any
manner whatsoever without written permission except in
the case of brief quotations embodied in critical articles
and reviews. For information, address HarperCollins
Publishers Inc., 10 East 53rd Street, New York, NY 10022.

HarperCollins books may be purchased for educational,
business, or sales promotional use. For information please
write: Special Markets Department, HarperCollins
Publishers Inc., 10 East 53rd Street, New York, NY 10022.

FIRST EDITION

Designed by Marysarah Quinn

Library of Congress Cataloging-in-Publication Data

Van Aken, Norman, 1951–
New World Kitchen : Latin American and Caribbean
Cuisine / Norman Van Aken, with Janet Van Aken.—1st ed.
p.   cm.
Includes bibliographical references.
ISBN 0-06-018505-8 (hc.)
1. Cookery, Latin American.   2. Cookery, Caribbean.
I. Van Aken, Janet.   II. Title.

TX716.A1 V294 2003
641.598—dc21
2002027158

03 04 05 06 07 ❖/QBF 10 9 8 7 6 5 4 3 2 1

This book is dedicated to Mama.
You lit the candles that keep us seeing
the beauty of this amazing journey.
—Norman and Janet

contents

Acknowledgments

First and always, this book wouldn't have been possible without the love and support and hard work of my wife, Janet. Truly this book is as much hers as mine. Fortunately for me, she is mine also.

My gratitude goes to our son, Justin, who was born here in Florida and has more to do with his father's life's work than any other man, in that I want him to be happy knowing that work can be a form of love.

I'd also like to thank the people of Florida, my adopted state, for sharing its rich diversity of cultures, foods, traditions, and natural beauty.

My deep thanks go to my partner in our restaurant, Carl Bruggemeier, for giving so generously of his strength, his expertise, and his energy, keeping our restaurant on the straight and narrow as I put this book together. Of course, I want to thank Carl's wife, Debi, for her patience and good humor.

I also want to acknowledge and express my appreciation to the entire team at NORMAN'S. Some have gone on to other things, and many have remained to help fulfill our vision. Special thanks to my assistant, Anna Elena Pedron; our chefs, Craig Petrella, Arthur Artiles, and Frank Ferreiro; pastry chef Todd Mueller; and Fan Fan Noel. I'd like to thank the wine experts Rodrigo Martinez and Proal Perry.

Thanks to our recipe testers Paola Gaitan and Lisa Neuwirth. Thanks also to my Latin and Caribbean friends who helped keep a Midwestern born chef's Spanish and New World food history on the up-and-up. They include Viviana Carballo, Omar Prunera, Gianna Bergonzini-Pedron, and Libardo Salazar.

The vision and support of the esteemed Daniel Halpern at Ecco was fundamental in making this book, as he was the first to see that it was time to give birth to this endeavor. Thanks to Mitchell Kaplan, who brought Dan to dinner at my restaurant in the very beginning, and who always brings me great authors to feed. To my editor, Lisa Chase, whose attention to detail and passion for excellence make for fine company in any project seeking truth and clarity. To Tim Turner, who is the world's finest food photographer and one hell of a man to ask to illuminate your dreams.

One of my primary mentors in writing this book was Mr. Luis Zalamea, whose historical and cultural input were crucial. He is a gentleman of the old school, and that is something we need in an era that reveres speed more than beauty. Technically, he hails from Colombia, but really he is a man of the world. Though we are longtime friends, I simply cannot call him Luis. He might prefer it, but for me he is Mr. Z. I attach the formality out of humility. He's helped me immeasurably, and his words and mine form at times a type of palimpsest. I'd have been lost without him in many of these places.

I've included a bibliography of books that have inspired me, but I specifically would like to thank several of the founding visionaries in the melding of Latin and Caribbean cooking who were so instrumental in my education. Among them are Elisabeth Lambert Ortiz, Betty Fussell, Douglas Rodriguez, Stephan Pyles, Dean Fearing, John Sedlar, Mark Miller, Robert Del Grande, Anne Lindsay Greer, Diana Kennedy, Rick Bayless, Jean Andrews, Maricel Presilla, Jessica Harris, and Raymond Sokolov.

I'd like to thank my brother Charlie Trotter for his unwavering friendship.

I'd also like to thank some of the giants of our extended restaurant family, who've been very kind to us over the years: Daniel Boulud, Emeril Lagasse, Nobu Matsuhisa, Jim Clendenen, Tony Soter, Alice Waters, Tetsuya Wakuda, Wolfgang Puck, Lulu Peyraud, Mireille Guiliano, Ruth Reichl, Caroline Stuart, Michael and Ariane Batterberry, Barbara Kafka, and Johnny and Betsey Apple.

Several professional organizations and publications have been a mainstay in supporting my work over the years. To mention all of them would be impossible, but in particular I'd like to thank the James Beard Foundation, the American Institute of Wine and Food, and the International Association of Culinary Professionals.

I'd also like to thank the people in our industry who've helped me with finding the sources for ingredients from around the world. Their contributions and names appear in the Source Guide (page 310).

Dear family and friends who help us remember that while we are cooks who must perform, we are people too who need to chill, include Pam and Steve, Proal and Connie, Brian and Gina, the entire Amsler family, Russ Alba, Daniel Gill, Steve Greystone, and my sisters, Bet and Jane, and my brother, Buddy.

Finally, in memoriam: Raji Jallepalli, Jean-Louis Palladin, Barbara Tropp, and Jamie Shannon. Sometimes the lights go out early, but through love like theirs, we still can see.

Anthony Bourdain

You probably know Norman Van Aken as the James Beard Award–winning chef of NORMAN'S in Coral Gables, Florida, the founding father of the legendary "Mango Gang" of Southeastern chefs, and one of the originators of such trends—often mentioned in conjunction with his name—as "fusion," "Pan-Latino," "Nuevo Latino," and "Floridian" cuisines. The general consensus is that he's the Big Dog when you're talking about that part of the country—that he has made a whole swath of territory, an entire spectrum of flavors and ingredients, his own. If you are lucky enough to have eaten in his restaurant, you know how good he is.

Like all too few great American chefs who can trace their roots back to the frontier days of new American cooking—the wild seventies and eighties—Norman Van Aken came up the old-school way, the hard way: learning on the ground and in the trenches. He learned not just the intricacies, strategies, and challenges of the professional kitchen and dining room but what makes food work. Starting with his humble beginnings as a teenage busboy and dishwasher, and continuing through years of bouncing around from restaurant to restaurant as a cook, sous-chef, and chef, he saw and learned not only which dishes were likely to succeed and be popular but what about them would please and excite people. This is valuable information. The knowledge and ability that distinguishes great from ordinary chefs is a close familiarity with the roots of pleasure, the quantification of the cook's strange and terrible power to titillate, tease, inspire, seduce, satisfy, and nourish. This is wisdom missed by many of Norman's school-taught, classically trained contemporaries, for whom "this is how to make a demi-glace" is all too often accompanied by "you cannot do this" and "this is not done." While much of the Western cooking world petrifies in the smothering grip of the old European masters, Norman Van Aken remains, while a respected elder statesman of American cuisine, something of an outlaw.

It is only appropriate that Norman has succeeded so famously in "fusing" ingredients generally associated with other countries and other cultures. He is generally credited with having coined the term "fusion" to describe this type of cuisine, and at NORMAN'S, he continues to combine creatively—even fiendishly—elements of the Old World and the new in ways that are dazzling and that, when admired up close, smelled, tasted, and savored, make perfect sense.

I'm a New Yorker, largely unfamiliar with the foodways of South America and the Caribbean, a dinosaur Francophile, deeply and instinctively suspicious of strange, new-sounding ingredients. On my first visit to NORMAN'S, his eponymous restaurant, I was frankly intimidated by the exotic-sounding juices, spices, and tubers, many of them foodstuffs that wouldn't likely pop up on my own Eurocentric prep list. I should not have been concerned. Unlike so many practitioners of fusion, Norman Van Aken, rather than creating tiny, gorgeous yet sterile monuments to his own brilliance, regularly creates dishes that speak to the soul. As you will learn in these pages, few of his ingredients are "new" or "foreign" at all, but vital parts of cultures and traditions that have been with us all along. His cooking, like his writing, reveals that most rare

and wonderful attribute in a chef: a deep, heartfelt knowledge and understanding of human nature and cultural history, of the shared need to be nourished.

New World Kitchen: Latin American and Caribbean Cuisine takes on very traditional home and hearth dishes from all over the Caribbean and Latin America, as well as celebratory treats for special occasions, and makes abundantly clear that fusion has been going on all around us for centuries. It is the traditional way that hungry people everywhere found over time to create magic and sorcery with what was available at the time. The same engine that drove the creation of classical French and Italian cuisines, the same process of incorporating new ingredients from the New World into the old to solve very real problems of preservation, availability, the needs and desires of capricious overlords, which brought us confit and salt cod and escargot bourguignon, also brought us the tortilla, *ceviche*, and *feijoada*. *Feijoada* (a terrific recipe is included) is perhaps the perfect example of the original fusion: a classic stew created in Brazil by African slaves, using the scraps and leftovers of their cruel Portuguese masters, incorporating influences from Africa, the indigenous Indian population, and the heavily Arab and spice route–influenced Portugal (already a melting pot). Eating *feijoada* in Rio, or the spicy Bahían fish stew, *vatapá,* in Salvador—the glorious mix of flavors and cultures employed in the service of pleasure—one sees a natural affinity between what has always gone on throughout history and what goes on nightly in Norman's kitchen.

So fear not fusion. New World cuisine is a better description of what Norman Van Aken

is up to, anyway. Like the original visitors to the New World—who arrived in unfamiliar places, changing and being changed by what they encountered—you can and will bring something back. There will be an exchange. But, as this book makes clear, the dishes described are inspired, principally, by nothing more daunting than good home cooking. And that's the best kind there is.

Before you bring out a dull, stainless steel meat ax and your iodized salt and start opening cans of oversalted, MSG-laden broth to serve as stock, take the time to read the section on ingredients and their handling—the items you should buy, or have, or understand before diving in. Everything begins with good ingredients. If the glossary frightens you with unfamiliar names and terms, know that just about anywhere you may live in America, someone nearby is using them right under your nose.

Delve deeply into Latino and Asian markets, which you will find everywhere from New York to Minneapolis, from Houston to San Francisco. You will discover not only food to eat but also food for thought—your own new world, not too far from your own. This book can serve as a concise and satisfying guide into its myriad delights.

Norman Van Aken learned his craft by eating, by reading, by experimentation, and through years of trial and error in professional kitchens. He has kindly spared you, the reader, the necessity for much of that experience. He did not become a renowned figure of international reputation through enthusiasm alone. His technique, his adoption of what have come to be known as European methods of knife handling and cooking processes—sauce making, stock and glace preparation and presentation—adds a degree of sophistication, finesse, and eye appeal one is unlikely to find on the street. Popular South American street foods like *empanadas* and *acarajé* may be ubiquitous and workmanlike in appearance, but tweaked by Norman, prepared with love and attention, these familiar dishes can be a revelatory surprise. For instance, *ceviche,* a standard hangover remedy for many Colombians, can be a cup full of raw fish, spicy sauce, and chiles. But with a sprinkle of austere Asian sensibility and an appreciation of pristine seafood, the dish can become elegant, even sublime. Nothing heretical about blending Japanese and South American, of course. Hundreds of thousands of Japanese have been living in Peru and Brazil for years. Chinese, Indonesian, and Indian influences have been well represented in the Caribbean for centuries—hence the New York standard, Comida China y Criolla. Anyone familiar with basic French techniques for braising and stewing should feel right at home with *mojo* curry chicken and arroz con pollo. If you like French and Italian "Mama" classics, there's nothing here that should slow you down.

Norman's persistent love of chile peppers and garlic transfigures the ordinary. His use of fresh fruit juices with funny-sounding names is an invitation to learn, to experience, to explore—discovering not only what is great about this big, bad, sometimes cruel, almost always beautiful world we live in but also what is good about our own enduring heritage.

A revealing detail of Norman Van Aken's early career is that he spent so much time on Key West—a refuge for sensualists, madmen, geniuses, beach bums, artists, smugglers, hustlers, fishermen, and cooks. That he kicked around the conch shacks, fish houses, Cuban snack bars, and beaches of that island before making his bones in the big city is a clue to his true nature. Above the clean white apron that you will inevitably see him wearing on the jacket, beats the heart of a true Parrothead, a man who knows in his bones that food tastes best when there's sand between your toes, when there's a palm tree nearby, when someone's playing samba music, or tropicale, or soca, or mariachi somewhere in the distance. Drums are involved. He knows that food is first about pleasure. And while it is also about place, you can now bring a little bit of that place home with you, wherever you may live.

If you were looking for what's missing from so much of contemporary food—a respect for the past coupled with a bold willingness to innovate—then relax, pop a Red Stripe or a Corona, put Bob Marley or Jorge Ben or Tito Puente or Jimmy Buffet, I guess, on the stereo, and get ready to cook.

It's all here.

introduction

Two powerful forces fueled my passion for cuisine and culture. The first was my mother. Her name was Ruth and she was a woman who loved the restaurant business as much as she loved a good adventure. During World War II she'd gone as a young single woman from her hometown of New York City out to Long Beach, California, to work in a shipyard. It was just the first of many roles in a life she embraced with dazzling fearlessness.

Over time my mother became a waitress, met my father, and married. And after we kids were old enough, she went back to the restaurant life she so adored and became a hostess, a cashier—whatever it took to get the work done. "You're not carrying that tray right. Let me show you how to do that," I remember her saying over and over to the waitresses who worked with her in the various restaurants over the years. Many of the "kids" she taught became like her own children. She loved the constant stream of diners coming in, and the cultures to which the food she was serving could lead her.

We lived in a tiny northern Illinois town called Diamond Lake, a place of Irish-German-Polish stock, but every year more and more Mexican families settled there and took jobs as domestic workers and gardeners at the wealthy homes of nearby Chicago's North Shore. They, like so many immigrants, brought with them their traditions and the flavors of their homeland. I still remember the first time I accompanied Mama into the little store a Mexican family opened across the lake from us, where they sold chipotles and chorizo, tamales and *masa*. La Bodega, the place was called.

Curiosity drew her there, with me in tow, where we encountered vivid colors, exotic implements, tempting smells, and another gastronomic language—all foreign to our Anglo-Saxon palate. I remember seeing portraits of JFK and Jesus on the wall, discovering *molcajetes* (grinding stones), and marveling at my first piñatas. But Mama was as comfortable in La Bodega as she was walking the aisles of the A&P. "The world's my home," she used to say with complete confidence, and I like to think that she passed on that way of living to me. Surely, her enthusiasm for food and her amazing interest in people of all nationalities have influenced my cooking and my explorations of the flavors, fragrances, and textures of the cuisines of the Caribbean and Latin America.

There was such a simplicity to life then. Every winter in the early and mid-fifties we were on a Delta Airlines jet to Miami Beach for Christmas vacation. My parents weren't rich, but I still remember vividly waking up in the back of whatever convertible they'd rented, thinking, *This* is the life.

As soon as I was nineteen, old enough to do what I wanted, I hitched down to South Florida. Oh, there were a couple of detours along the way—a moment of college in Hawaii, a bit of manual labor in Colorado and Kansas, work as a short-order cook in an Illinois diner—before I made my way to Key West and settled into cooking as a vocation for good. It was the early seventies, and I was exposed daily to the cuisines of the Caribbean and Latin America, which soon became, after my mother's lasting influence, the other culinary influence in my life as a chef.

When I eventually decided to become a professional chef, however, I naturally gravitated to classic French cuisine—that was what one did. Back in the seventies regional American cooking had few proponents (it would be ten years before Alice Waters and Paul Prudhomme kindled *that* fire). Though I didn't have the money to attend cooking school, I did have the will to teach myself. One by one I bought the books that would form the foundation of my education. I read them like a jailhouse lawyer, sensing they were my only hope of escaping the rough lives of the cooks I encountered during the wild and wooly days and nights in the first kitchens I knew.

Originally, I was deeply influenced by France's three-star chefs—Roger Vergé, Alain Chapel, Alain Senderens, the Troisgros brothers. Yet my day-to-day eating experience was of vibrant New World flavors—West Indian chutneys and Central American plantains, Bahamian conch salad and Cuban steak *a la parilla*—in the cafés and open-air market stalls of Old Key West. Slowly but surely the magic of those foods and their special language came to define me as a chef.

There was, in fact, a defining moment in my decision to become the chef that I am today; it was one morning in 1987, as I sat on the deck behind Louie's Backyard. At this point I'd cooked in a lot of joints, and I use that word purposely. I'd been frying eggs and barbecuing ribs even as I was venturing into the Cuban and Bahamian shacks and cafés around Key West for lunch or a *café con leche*. By the eighties I had become a chef and I was running Louie's, long considered one of the best restaurants in Key West. Louie's is situated where the Gulf of Mexico meets the Atlantic Ocean. I was studying a stack of cookbooks—French, Middle Eastern, South-western, Italian—in pursuit of dishes for my menus, when I looked up to see a sailboat drifting southward. I too drifted with it for some time, wondering where it might be going and what the sailors would see, touch, and taste when they got there.

And just like that, I realized that it was time for me to put away my books on the dishes of other places. It was one of those moments of complete clarity: As much as I had drawn from the wisdom and artistry of hundreds of years of European cuisine, it was now time for me to express where and what I was living—and that was Florida. South Florida, in particular.

I thought about how North America's music had evolved, how its literature and architecture and dance were amalgamations of cultures bumping up against one another. Key West was a place where Spanish, African, and Anglo influences converged, yet the foods we were eating (including at my own restaurant) seemed almost frozen in time. No one had yet imagined what kind of fusion cuisine—a phrase I coined—might result if food expressed those cultures the way the cuisines of New Orleans, California, and the American Southwest gastronomically expressed those who inhabited these places. Latin America and the Caribbean are guided culinarily by a vast range of histories and cultural influences—and an ever-shifting present tense. And like us, they take great pride in their differences. Perhaps the biggest revelation for me in writing this book was learning firsthand just how significant a role food plays in every culture.

My moment of clarity then became one of resolve. I closed up my books and put away my

notes. The sailboat was beyond the horizon now. I could *feel* Cuba just ninety miles away. The answer had been around me all along. I ate it and drank it almost every day. My new teachers were going to be in the cafés and homes of South Florida, not in the books of France.

In the following weeks and months I went back to some of the same joints I'd eaten in many times since I had settled in Key West in 1973. I went to a restaurant called B's and another called La Lechonera, to El Cacique and some places that had no names at all. I sat on stools at counters and ordered the Cuban-Bahamian fare. I pestered cops and fishermen and house painters and housewives about what they were having. Often I asked them if they wouldn't mind translating a menu item for me. I earned the suspicion of many a waitress as I quizzed them and took notes on a little spiral pad. It got very exciting—I felt like I was cracking a case or solving a puzzle. I envisioned how each meal was cooked and how I would adapt it to the dishes I loved from my own life experiences.

Less than a year after my epiphany on Louie's deck, I opened up an addition to Louie's Backyard. It was on the second story and we called it, simply, The Café. Underneath that name we made up a sign that said NUEVO LATINO CUISINE. Inspired by The Café at Chez Panisse in Berkeley, California, I wanted an informal restaurant. But instead of Alice Waters's rustic, delicious Mediterranean-style food, I was offering unheard-of constructions like "*Mojo* Marinated and Roasted Chicken with Saffron Rice and *Rioja* Essence" and "Seared Tenderloin of Beef on a Bed of Crispy *Vaca Frita*" and "Grilled Florida Snapper with *Mojo Verde* and Plantain Curls." Diners at Louie's would come up when they heard I was now cooking at The Café, eye the menu, and typically head right back down the stairs to the more "cosmopolitan" food I had created in the original restaurant. Before they departed, however, they offered their opinions, and for a long while they went something like this: "What, are you *crazy*? I'm not paying twenty bucks for black beans and yellow rice."

That was then, and we not only survived but in the words of William Faulkner: *We prevailed.*

Choosing and creating the recipes for this book was necessarily different from what I do in my restaurant. The cooking there is a per-formance, staged to create an experience more for diners than cooks. I don't expect the recipes in this book to be presented to the table in a series of courses; we rarely eat that way in our homes. It's the food of homes and families that I want to bring to you.

But I want to state for the record that my dishes are not fully re-created "authentic" dishes. I use history as a logical point of entry, but I cook with twenty-first-century openness. The best analogy I can think of is how the musician Ry Cooder approached his work with the Cuban musicians in the beautiful *Buena Vista Social Club.* Mr. Cooder is a talent who admires talent. He respected those men and women so much that he went down to their world to make great music. He played *with* them. That's how I like to feel about my approach to Caribbean and Latin cuisine. I'm not simply playing their music; we're making music together.

Happily, America's foods, eating habits, and cooking methods have evolved and diversified more in the last twenty-five years than in the previous 175. Think back to the shelves of any midsize supermarket in the seventies. Most stores catered to what could be called the meat-and-potatoes diet. Simplicity dominated the menus of the day; variety was virtually nonexistent. Radicchio, arugula, and fresh herbs were unheard of in American cooking. No meat, fish, or produce was imported from abroad. Witness the same shelves today, filled with exotic foods, spices, and ingredients from the earth's far corners: salmon from Chile, prawns from Ecuador, steaks from Argentina, wild mushrooms from Italy, lamb from New Zealand, rare cheeses from France. The list is nearly endless.

This revolution in our food habits is equally dramatic when it comes to eating out. Writers such as Elisabeth Lambert Ortiz and Diana Kennedy have schooled chefs and fine home cooks for decades with their valiant work. This has led to restaurants like Patria and Chicama in New York, Pasión in Philadelphia, Topolobampo in Chicago, and Ciudad in Los Angeles. Yet this explosive interest in Latin-Caribbean foods is not confined to fine dining; it has traveled the distance to fast food as well. America has always been all about assimilation. My friend Luis Zalamea tells me a story I find intriguing. In the forties, during his prep-school days, a sophisticated classmate took him to the Italian district fringing Greenwich Village to a hole-in-the-wall food stand, the only place in New York where you could sample a new delicacy just introduced from Naples: pizza. To think how quickly pizza has become the number one snack in the world, with sales in the billions (and yet to recall its humble beginnings in America), is to fathom the capacities of the food revolution in this country.

The reality is that we can expect over 50 percent of North America's populace to be comprised of people of Latin descent by the year 2050 or earlier. Our understanding and appreciation of the true nuances of these countries should not be swept aside by the simplification of the fast food mentality. In this book I have attempted to illustrate the sophistication and adaptive brilliance of the people of Latin American and the Caribbean with the same energy I'd bring if I were writing a book on Italian or French cuisine.

You begin to understand that to speak of the cuisines of the New World in generic terms would be like reducing France's many unique culinary traditions to "French cooking." The origins of New World cuisine, as I like to call it, are in pre-Columbian cultures, especially those of Peru and Mexico; in Africa, particularly in the Caribbean and Brazil; in Asia and the Pacific, an influence felt throughout the Americas in subtle yet significant ways; and, of course, in Europe.

Brazil is certainly an epicenter of New World cuisine, divided, like Gaul, into three parts: the indigenous tribes, the African slaves, and the Europeans who subjugated them. Peru is another nexus of New World foods, blessed as it is with a vertical geography, from its coastline, supplied by the Humboldt Current with abundant fish and seafood, to the tropical fruits of the Amazon Basin jungles, to the tubers growing below its snowcapped peaks. These unique features have favored the development of a varied and opulent cuisine, dating back at least six thousand years. Peruvian cuisine is like a wide channel fed by many tributaries: pre-Incan and Incan, European (Spanish, Italian, French), plus Polynesian, Chinese, and Japanese.

The vocabulary of this cuisine is not one most readers will have grown up with, but that is certainly part of its allure. I find delicious the very sounds of these words: *acarajé* [ah-cahr-ah-zhay], *xinxim* [sheen-sheem], *mojo* [mo-ho], and *chifa* [chi-fa]. To prepare for the pronunciation of many of these words, you may first want to try my Caribbean *carnivale*. My Spanish-speaking friends kindly congratulate me for even trying some of these words, as they gently prompt me to get them right. That's all I'm asking of you. Take it one day at a time and let the flavors and sounds of the names of these foods connect you to the New World of Latin American and Caribbean cooking.

To write this book I interviewed hundreds of people. I asked them where they shopped, which ethnic foods they loved, and what their parents and grandparents ate. The elements of the recipes here come from more than twenty countries. What this process confirmed for me is that despite our growing food sophistication, we know almost nothing about Latin American cooking in North America, even as it exists in many humble but excellent restaurants that keep transplanted Latin Americans connected to their homelands. My sincere hope is that this book, in which I always endeavor to give the context for a dish or ingredient, will enlighten you, even as the foods delight you.

Perhaps it's only fitting that my mother, a woman born in New York City, one of the most democratic, crosscultural places in the world, would lead me to my path of cooking and the cuisines of the New World, even though I took a few forks in the road. My own twenty-one-year-old son is now working as a *barista* in a Colorado coffee shop. He swears he'll never be a chef. But I can sense the start of something.

preparation tips

I often surprise people when I tell them that I never went to cooking school. I probably would have been booted out because of my disdain for rules that I felt to be unnecessarily restrictive and chauvinistically Eurocentric. But I do have a number of basic guidelines, tips, and how-to suggestions that I present to you here.

Butter I use only unsalted butter, because I want to control how much salt goes into a dish and because adding salt to butter is an inexpensive way for manufacturers to extend its shelf life. This is somewhat ironic, as butter was originally prized for its inherent sweetness.

Salt I always use kosher salt. I like that it is less forceful in its saltiness; table salt is aggressive and doesn't play well with the other flavors I'm seeking to bring out in food. I also like the way I can control kosher salt: I add its granules to my dishes with my fingertips. I hold my hand well above whatever I'm seasoning, because that way it showers down and is nicely distributed. Try that with table salt, and you'll likely get a downpour on one small area of whatever you are making. Finally, kosher salt dissolves nicely on the tongue and on the food itself.

Garlic and Chiles You may notice that I routinely add garlic and chiles to my skillet or pot before I add other vegetables such as carrots, onions, and celery, and you may wonder why I don't just add them all in one step. Let me explain by giving you an analogy: it is like the recipe for a good party. You can count on your best friends to show up first, before the rest of the guests. Garlic and chiles are two of my best friends: vivacious, somewhat bawdy, very attractive. When they are the first to start the party, their mood and conversation set the tone for the room, so that by the time the other guests arrive, the m.o. of the night has already been established. You wouldn't achieve that if you rushed everyone into the room all at once. It's just the way energy works. So, if the garlic and chiles get their first, they make the dish livelier as you progress through the recipe.

Roasting Chiles and Bell Peppers

Roasting chiles and bell peppers is one of the best techniques for bringing out their intense flavors. When I call for roasted chiles or peppers, I'm assuming that you have prepared them as I describe here.

I use different methods for roasting and peeling bell peppers and chiles. I roast lightly oiled bell peppers on a grill; their thick, meaty walls do not break down the way the thin walls of most chiles do. Alternatively, you can grill them on a wire rack over a gas burner; the aroma they will create in your house is like heaven.

Most chile peppers, on the other hand, are best when shocked out of their thin skins. I heat plenty of vegetable oil to 365 degrees in a deep-fryer or heavy saucepan, then carefully submerge the chiles in the hot oil. (You can get the job done in less oil if you turn the chiles from time to time.)

Once the bell peppers or chiles have blistered all over, transfer them to a large bowl lined with paper towels and cover the bowl tightly with plastic wrap. Allow them to steam for about 5 minutes. If preparing chiles, protect your hands by wearing rubber gloves. Take the peppers out of the bowl and delicately pull off their skins, using your fingers or a small knife.

Tropical Fruits Among the most loved foods in Latin and Caribbean cultures are tropical fruits and their juices. Fortunately for the rest of us, even the most exotic of them are increasingly available throughout the world, thanks to the wonders of overnight shipping.

note: You should assume that whenever I call for fruit juices, I mean that it should be freshly squeezed or obtained from a juice bar, where they squeeze it for you.

Plaintains Unless you are working with very dark ripe (*maduro*) plaintains, you'll need to know how to peel them; peeling a plantain at the green or yellow stage is not like peeling a banana. The starchiness of the fruit makes the peel stick to it. To remove the skin easily, prepare a large pot of warm water. Cut off the ends of the plantain and make three to four slashes through the peel, cutting end to end, and let the plantain soak in the water for 30 minutes or so. The skin will peel off much more easily. Some people like to lightly oil their hands to guard against the stickiness of the fruit, but I rarely do this.

Beans Cooking beans is not hard at all, but it's difficult to give general guidelines for cooking times, as these vary considerably depend-

ing on the type and age of the beans. The best way to get fresh dried beans is to shop in markets—Latin and Caribbean markets come to mind—where there is a population that is likely to guarantee a brisk turnover in the inventory.

In general, follow these rules of thumb: Let the beans soak overnight before you boil them. Cook them until they are just tender. Depending on the age of the beans, this will take anywhere from 1 1/2 to 3 hours. Do *not* add salt to them until they cooked; adding salt during cooking will toughen the beans. Furthermore, beans are often cooked with bacon or ham hocks, which will imbue them with some saltiness—so when you do salt them, taste first.

Tomatoes The French term for peeling and seeding tomatoes is *concasser,* which means "to break up." The technique is a way to remove the less flavorful skin, seeds, and water and leave you with pure tomato flavor. To do so, core ripe tomatoes, cut an X in the bottom of each and lower them, a few at a time, into a pot of boiling water. Count to ten, then, using a slotted spoon, retrieve the tomatoes and delicately drop them into a bowl of ice water; this stops the cooking. As soon as the tomatoes are cool, transfer to paper towels to drain for a minute. Then, working on a cutting board, peel away and discard the skin. Cut the tomatoes crosswise in half. Using a small spoon, remove the seeds, and gently squeeze out the liquid. Many of the recipes in this book call for "tomatoes, peeled, seeded, and chopped"; in these, I intend for you to chop the flesh into small cubes.

Marinating and Smoking Marinating and smoking meats and fish have been vital techniques in New World cuisine since, well, since there was a New World.

It is wrong to think that a marinade will make a tough food miraculously tender; that can be achieved more effectively by slicing, grinding, or pounding the meat or fish. (This is one of the ways we deal with the mollusk known as conch, which is typically ground.) However, since pre-Columbian times, people in Mexico and Central America have wrapped meats and fish in papaya leaves, taking advantage of an enzyme in the leaves that helps tenderize the surface of whatever is wrapped. Even more effective are the pickling mediums that these peoples developed over time. Though pickling does not dramatically tenderize, it can dramatically affect the flavor of foods. In Latin America and the Caribbean, the most famous examples of pickling are *ceviches* and *escabeches.*

As for smoking, there are two basic methods: hot-smoking and cold-smoking. At home, the first is easier to accomplish. A barbecue grill can be turned into a smoker simply by using wet wood chips, placing the food as far away as possible from the fuel, and covering the grill. The smoke flavors whatever you are cooking. I generally cook the food all the way through when I am hot-smoking it, but I sometimes smoke the food for a shorter period of time and then finish cooking it on the open grill or in the oven.

Cold-smoking is classically used for salmon and other rich fish, and it is more appropriate for commercial kitchens because of the time and science involved. In cold-smoking, the fish is not cooked with heat but is instead cured in brine and then smoked over a period of a day or two.

Toasting and Grinding Spices, Nuts, and Seeds When Columbus went looking for Asia and bumped into the Americas, he was on a voyage financed by Spain with the understanding that he would find a better route to the spice markets of India—an illustration of how central spices have always been to cuisine. But spices, like other comestibles, are subject to loss of flavor if not properly prepared. Toasting whole spices, and, usually, grinding them, is the way to get maximum flavor from them. This is extremely easy to do: Gently warm the seeds or other whole spices in a dry skillet over medium heat. Once they become aromatic, they are toasted. When they have cooled a bit, grind them in a spice mill (or

a clean coffee grinder) or with a mortar and pestle. Toasting and grinding awakens the oils and aromatics within them. With spices like pepper and cumin, for example, which are staples of my cooking, you can prepare a batch of the toasted ground spice and keep it around for up to 2 weeks.

The same principles apply to toasting nuts: the heat maximizes their flavor. Grinding makes them the proper consistency for cooking in soups and stews.

Caramelizing One of the greatest magic acts in cooking is barely ever discussed in cookbooks and it's a mystery to me why. It is one of the single most important techniques to understanding how to create greater flavor in your soups, stews, roasts, and sauces. In my previous cookbook, *Norman's New World Cuisine,* I likened caramelizing to foreplay. It is the foundation for a final outcome that will be more greatly enhanced when it is properly and thoroughly employed. And what is it we mean by that? Naturally, the scientists have gotten involved and have even come up with a name for it. It's called the Maillard reaction. Louis Camille Maillard (1878–1936) was a French biochemist (of course, he was French!) who explained that the high temperatures change the sugar molecules in food. (This even includes the sugars that exist in meats.) A series of complex reactions begins when the inherent sugars dehydrate, forming more complicated molecules that taste more nuanced. That is why a charred steak has a more penetrating flavor and why an onion cooked to the point of caramelization is much more tantalizing than a raw one. Thank the French, once again, and enjoy a slowly cooked meal.

To caramelize onions (just one example of how to apply this method): Begin by adding 2 tablespoons of butter and 2 tablespoons of olive oil to a heavy saucepan over medium heat. Add 2 peeled and sliced red or white raw onions. Stir well and then leave them alone for a few minutes to allow the heat to build in the pan. When they are almost at the stage of sticking to the pan, stir well again. Now just stir intermittently for about 8 minutes. They will become very fragrant and sweet. I usually add a touch of sugar and some red wine or balsamic vinegar at this point for a little extra sweetness and depth.

Deglazing *Deglazing* is a term that means adding wine or another liquid to a pan to help loosen up any bits of food that have stuck there during the roasting, sautéing, and/or browning stages of preparing a dish. There is a lot of flavor in those caramelized bits and the addition of liquid to the hot pan helps lift them off the bottom and form the foundation of a sauce. When alcohol is used to deglaze, you must be very careful of the flames, which can shoot right up out of the pan.

Ice-Water Baths Safety is a big issue with me, and cleanliness and orderliness are the hallmarks of a good cook. Few things give me greater pleasure than to see four or five of my soups and sauces cooling in a big tub of icy water. Ice-water baths are a common sight in a professional kitchen. It's easy to set one up at home. When you have made a sauce, broth, or soup that you want to chill until it is needed, pour the hot liquid into a nonreactive container. Fill a large pot with icy-cold water, then slowly lower the vessel into the pan, taking care that it does not capsize. Cooling the liquid as quickly as possible is crucial in preventing any bacterial growth. Using an ice-water bath also allows you to avoid putting steaming-hot food directly into your refrigerator, thus raising the inside temperature (and that of all the ingredients in it). Furthermore, an ice-water bath is a way to better lock in the flavors you've worked to create.

Cooking Pans In preparing recipes from this book, you should assume that you'll almost always cook in a nonreactive pan. The reason is that many foods, especially those high in acid, react with the materials from which many pots and pans are made. I never use aluminum pans. Why? Certainly, there is the concern about the possible link between aluminum and Alzheimer's Disease, but there is also this: have you ever *tasted* an aluminum pan? Aluminum tastes more metallic than copper, stainless steel, or cast iron. While science argues about the potential evils of aluminum, I simply find that the flavor of foods

is much better when they are not exposed to aluminum. Pans that will not react with foods are copper, stainless steel, nonstick, and such brands as All-Clad and Calphalon.

carnival and street foods

Why do carnival fare and street foods play such a major role in the cuisines of Latin America and the Caribbean? It has a lot to do with pre- and post-Lenten gusto: many of the countries in the New World are predominantly Catholic, and their populations frequently bookend the Easter ritual with *carnivales*. In this chapter, we will wander the streets and parties of Brazil and Jamaica, Trinidad and Venezuela, and see what the populations of Spanish, African, and Indian descent have concocted in the way of street and carnival food. Whether it's *acarajé* (fritters) in the Afro-Brazilian state of Bahía, *empanadas con huevos* (egg-filled *empanadas*) in Colombia's Cartageña de Indias district, or golden-browned flying fish in Barbados, the plazas and streets of the New World are filled with tantalizing aromas—most of which are the products of expert frying.

My good friend Luis Zalamea, a true Renaissance man, now retired from a distinguished career as a diplomat, is a walking encyclopedia of Latin and Caribbean history and culture. He tells me that it is somewhat ironic that frying is so integral to New World cuisine, because the region's great indigenous cultures—the Aztecs, Mayans, Mochicas, Incas, and Chibchas—did not number frying among their cooking methods. They simply never refined animal and vegetable oils in large enough quantities to develop a style of cooking with them. The Andalusians of Spain, however, had learned from the Moors the art of using the purest olive oil and a delicate kiss of flour to fry food so light that it seems the work of magic. An observer can watch an Andalusian cook at work all day long and still not understand how she produces such succulent lightly fried food. For one thing, the cooks literally fry by ear: they know, from just slight changes in the crackling sound of the boiling oil when they have achieved the exact right juiciness inside and crispness outside. When the Spanish and Portuguese arrived in the New World, they brought that art with them.

African slaves too made their stamp on New World street foods. They introduced *dendé* (palm oil), as well as chiles. And in Mexico the inhabitants learned to pre-fry many tortilla-based *antojitos* (literally, "little bites"), like tacos, enchiladas, and quesadillas, thus sealing in flavor and texture before baking, braising, or stewing the foods.

(As for the diet-conscious who suffer from Fear of Frying, fear not: I use the lightest vegetable oils, such as canola or grapeseed, which contain only 6 percent saturated fat, compared to palm oil's whopping 79 percent. And, whenever possible, I bake, not fry.)

bacalao fritters
(Salt Cod Fritters)

MAKES ABOUT 40 FRITTERS

Bacalao is the Spanish word for salt cod. I first had these fritters as a teenager, when my mother used to make them for my sisters and me. I don't know who taught her the recipe—being the fair daughter of Scotch-Irish stock, it was not likely that she learned it at *her* mother's stove. I can't think of a much simpler introduction to salt cod than this recipe.

You'll find *bacalao* in better seafood markets, often in little wooden boxes, as well as in some Latin, Italian, and other ethnic markets. Its aroma is admittedly powerful, but once you soak out the preservative salt and then poach the cod, the fish's natural sweet, lean qualities reveal themselves.

Bacalao fritters are very good with Chipotle-Lime *Crema* (page 289).

1 pound salt cod, soaked in 3 or 4 changes of water for a minimum of 24 hours and drained
1 recipe Simple Court Bouillon (page 273) or enough water to cover
3 cups mashed Idaho potatoes (about 1 1/2 pounds potatoes)
1 tablespoon minced garlic
3 jalapeños, stemmed, seeded, and minced
1 Scotch bonnet chile, stemmed, seeded, and minced
1 1/2 teaspoons freshly ground black pepper
3 tablespoons minced Italian parsley
1 teaspoon minced fresh thyme
Kosher salt to taste
1/2 cup all-purpose flour
2 extra-large eggs
1 tablespoon water
2 cups bread crumbs
Canola or peanut oil for deep-frying

In a saucepan, cook the cod in the bouillon for 20 minutes. Drain; discard the bouillon.

Crumble the fish into a bowl. Stir in the potatoes, garlic, jalapeño, Scotch bonnet, black pepper, and half of the herbs. Season with salt; keep in mind that the *bacalao* can affect the salt level dramatically. Mix well, and chill for 30 minutes, or until cold.

Roll the cod mix into balls about 1 inch in diameter.

Put the flour in a small bowl. In another small bowl, beat the eggs with the water. Put the bread crumbs in another bowl and add the remaining chopped herbs. Roll the cod balls in the flour, dip them in the beaten eggs, and then roll them in the bread crumbs. (You can do this up to 12 hours before you are ready to serve the fritters; cover and refrigerate. You can also freeze the balls on a baking sheet until firm, then transfer to a freezer container, for later use.)

In a deep-fryer or deep pot, heat the canola oil to 350 degrees. Cook the fritters, in batches, for 2 1/2 to 3 minutes, until crisp and golden. Remove and drain on paper towels, then serve.

black bean and shrimp fritters

MAKES 30 TO 36 FRITTERS

One of the treats of the Florida Keys is stopping at tiki huts and roadside stands and enjoying crunchy-on-the-outside, pillowy-on-the-inside conch fritters, which you dip in spicy cocktail sauce. My version of those fritters uses the more widely available shrimp, plus another Keys mainstay: black beans.

Serve these with Jalapeño-Cumin-Lime *Crema* (page 289) for a deliciously rich pairing.

1 extra-large egg
¹/₃ cup milk
1 cup sifted all-purpose flour
1 tablespoon plus 1 scant teaspoon baking
    powder
¹/₂ teaspoon kosher salt
³/₄ cup minced red onion
¹/₂ jalapeño, stemmed, seeded, and minced
¹/₂ red bell pepper, stemmed, seeded, and
    minced
1 cup cooked black beans (see page 202)
3 tablespoons beer, at room temperature
³/₄ cup minced cilantro
¹/₂ teaspoon toasted and ground cumin seeds
    (see page 9)
1 tablespoon Tabasco
1 ¹/₂ cups (about 9 ounces) peeled and
    chopped shrimp
Canola or peanut oil for deep-frying
Lemon and lime wedges for garnish

Beat the egg in a large bowl. Add the milk, then add the flour, baking powder, salt, onion, jalapeño, bell pepper, black beans, beer, cumin, and Tabasco and mix thoroughly. Fold in the shrimp. Cover and refrigerate until ready to use, or up to 1 day.

In a deep-fryer or deep pot, heat the oil to 350 degrees.

With one tablespoon, scoop up the batter, and with another, carefully scrape the batter into the hot oil. Cook the fritters for 3 to 5 minutes, turning them over from time to time until golden. Remove and drain on paper towels. Serve hot.

acarajé with crabmeat stuffing
(Black-Eyed Pea Fritters)

MAKES 30 TO 36 FRITTERS

Slaves from Africa brought their religion, music, and cooking to the New World. They were particularly expert in frying foods, *acarajé* (pronounced *ah-car-a-ZHAY*) being a prime example.

My friend the great newspaperman Johnny Apple has written that these classic fritters are found in abundance in the colonial Pelourinho district of the Brazilian state of Bahía. Wearing distinctive white turbans, puffy skirts, and frilly tunics, the women of Bahía, Baianas, walk the streets selling *acarajé*. Pelourinho's "very name is a reminder of harsher days" in Brazil, Johnny writes. *"Pelourinho* means 'flogging post' in Portuguese." Happily, there's nothing harsh about *acarajé*. These are often served with a somewhat complex Brazilian sauce called *vatapá;* I stuff them with an equally delicious yet much easier crab salad.

1 pound dried black-eyed peas, rinsed and
    soaked overnight in water to cover
1 red onion, roughly chopped
1 Scotch bonnet chile, stemmed, seeded, and
    minced
1 ounce dried shrimp (optional but authentic),
    finely chopped
1 tablespoon kosher salt, or more to taste
2 teaspoons freshly ground black pepper, or
    more to taste
Canola or peanut oil for deep-frying
8 ounces cleaned crabmeat
2 1/2 tablespoons mayonnaise

Reach into the container of peas and rub them between the palms of your hands to loosen their skins; allow the peas to settle. Some of the skins will float to the top. Skim them off, then reach in and remove any remaining skins. Drain the peas.

Transfer the peas to a food processor, add the onion, and process until the texture resembles oatmeal. Combine the mixture with the Scotch bonnet, dried shrimp, salt, and pepper in a medium bowl.

In a deep-fryer or deep pot, heat the oil to 350 degrees.

Using two tablespoons, mold the pea mixture into egg-shaped fritters about 1 inch long and carefully drop them, a few at a time, into the hot oil. Cook until golden, about 1 minute, using a slotted spoon to turn them occasionally so they cook evenly. Remove and drain on paper towels. Keep the first batches warm in a low oven while you cook the remaining fritters.

When all the fritters have been fried, toss the crabmeat with the mayonnaise. Slice open each fritter and make a little "sandwich" by filling it with about 1 teaspoon of the crab mixture.

note: You can flavor the crab mixture with a little mustard and minced scallions.

doubles
(Chickpea-Stuffed Pastries)

MAKES 40 TO 45 PASTRIES

Doubles, so called because of the way the pastry is folded over itself, turnover-like, are served on the island of Trinidad as an appetizer and sold in the street as well. The country's strong East Indian culinary influences reveal themselves in the snack: it is made from *roti*, an Indian flatbread, and the filling is of curried chickpeas, known in Trinidad as *channa*. Golden Pineapple Chutney (page 265) would not only complement the *channa's* slight dryness, but also contrast sweetly with the heat in the curry.

FOR THE FILLING

1 pound chickpeas, rinsed and soaked
    overnight in water to cover
2 chipotle chiles
1/2 cup hot water
3 tablespoons pure olive oil
5 cloves garlic, minced
2 medium Spanish onions, finely chopped
3 tablespoons *garam masala* (a spice mix
    available in Indian markets and many
    grocery stores)
1 teaspoon toasted and ground cumin seeds
    (see page 9)
2 1/2 cups Chicken Stock (page 267)
Kosher salt and freshly ground black pepper to
    taste

FOR THE *ROTI*

6 cups bread flour
2 tablespoons baking powder
1 1/2 teaspoons salt

1 pound unsalted butter, diced
1 cup cold water

Canola or peanut oil for cooking the *roti*

Drain the chickpeas. Place in a pot, cover with fresh water, and bring to a boil. Reduce the heat and simmer, covered, until soft. (This can take anywhere from 1 hour to 2 hours, depending on how old the chickpeas are.) Drain.

Meanwhile, toast the chiles in a small skillet over medium heat, then soak them in the hot water until softened. Drain; reserve the liquid. Stem, seed, and finely chop the chiles.

to make the *roti*,
sift the flour, baking powder, and salt into the bowl of an electric mixer. Add the butter. Using the paddle attachment, with the mixer at its lowest speed, incorporate the butter until the mixture resembles coarse crumbs, about 1 minute.

Switch to the dough hook and, still on low speed, drizzle in the water until the dough comes together, then knead on medium speed for 1 minute. Wrap the dough in plastic wrap and chill for 1 hour. (You can make the dough by hand, using a pastry cutter, or even a fork or potato masher to incorporate the butter.)

to make the filling,

heat the oil in a large skillet. Add the garlic and onions and cook over medium heat for 5 minutes. Add the *garam masala* and cumin and stir for 1 minute. Add the chickpeas, chiles, the reserved soaking water, and the chicken stock.

Simmer, uncovered, for 30 to 40 minutes, or until almost no liquid remains and the filling is stew-like. Season to taste. Keep warm.

to shape the *roti,*

dust your work surface generously with flour. Pull off pieces of dough and roll into balls 1 1/2 inches in diameter. Roll each one out to a thickness of 1/6 inch and a diameter of 4 to 5 inches. Stack between sheets of parchment.

Place a large nonstick skillet over medium-high heat and add just enough oil to lightly coat the bottom of the pan. Cook the *roti,* one or two at a time, depending on the skillet size, for 45 to 60 seconds on each side, until the dough bubbles and blisters. Wrap the *roti* around the filling, using about 1 1/2 tablespoons per *roti,* and serve immediately.

jamaican patties
(Curried-Beef-and-Squash-Stuffed Pastries)

MAKES 12 PASTRIES

This snack is rumored to have originated in Haiti, though now it is practically the national Jamaican street food. I've added *calabaza*, a squash found throughout the Caribbean and Latin America, to the traditional meat filling for sweetness and to lighten the dish a bit.

FOR THE DOUGH

2 cups all-purpose flour

2 teaspoons curry powder

1 ¹/₂ teaspoons kosher salt

¹/₄ cup vegetable shortening

4 tablespoons unsalted butter, diced

¹/₂ cup ice water

FOR THE FILLING

1 cup fresh orange juice

1 cup peeled and diced *calabaza* (you can substitute acorn squash)

2 tablespoons canola oil

¹/₄ small Spanish onion, diced

2 scallions, green and white parts, chopped

4 cloves garlic, minced

1 Scotch bonnet chile, stemmed, seeded, and minced

2 teaspoons Madras curry powder

8 ounces ground beef

1 ¹/₂ teaspoons minced fresh thyme

¹/₂ teaspoon freshly ground black pepper, or more to taste

¹/₄ cup bread crumbs

Kosher salt to taste

1 egg

Pinch of kosher salt

for the dough

Combine the flour, curry, and salt in a medium bowl. With your hands, work in the shortening and butter until the mixture resembles coarse crumbs. Add the water, mixing until a dough forms. Shape into a disk, wrap tightly in plastic wrap, and refrigerate for at least an hour (the dough can chill for up to 12 hours).

for the filling

Combine the orange juice and *calabaza* in a saucepan and simmer until the squash is tender but not mushy, 10 to 15 minutes. Drain, reserving the orange juice, and set aside to cool.

Heat a medium skillet over medium heat, and add the canola oil. When it is hot, add the onion, scallions, garlic, and Scotch bonnet and sauté for about 3 minutes, stirring occasionally. Add the curry powder and stir for another minute, then stir in the ground beef. Cook, stirring, until the meat is browned. Add the thyme, black pepper, reserved orange juice, and the bread crumbs. Season with salt, turn the heat to low, and cook for 3 to 5 minutes, stirring frequently, until the liquid has been absorbed and the mixture forms a dense paste. Remove from the heat and allow to cool completely.

Fold the squash into the beef mixture and adjust the seasoning to taste. Now you are ready to assemble the patties.

Dust your work surface with flour. Remove the chilled dough from the refrigerator and divide it in half. Roll each half out to a thickness of $^1/_4$ inch, and cut out 6 circles about 4 inches in diameter from each half.

Break the egg into a small bowl, add the salt, and whisk lightly. Spoon a tablespoon or so of the filling on to one half of each dough round. Using your fingers, dab the edges of each round with egg, and fold over to cover the filling. Seal the edges and crimp them using the back of a fork. Put the turnovers on a baking sheet lined with parchment and refrigerate for 15 minutes or so. Reserve the egg wash.

Preheat the oven to 400 degrees.

Brush the turnovers generously with the egg wash. Bake for 30 minutes until golden.

note: You can also fry the turnovers in canola oil heated to 375 degrees, in batches, for 3 to 4 minutes; omit the final brushing with egg wash if frying.

salt and pepper

The instructions in nearly every recipe in the world state the obvious: "Salt and pepper to taste." And we do. These two ingredients are the edible ebony and ivory, and no other food couple has the ability to play the piano of your palate like these two keys. Cream and sugar are a romantic-comedy duo; garlic and butter conjure up a steamy bedroom scene. Salt and pepper, however, are the alpha and the omega. Pepper perfumes the meat, while salt draws it back to its primordial home.

Salt and pepper may occupy the cupboard with dozens of other more exotic members of the alchemical cast, but they are the only spices that rate center stage on almost every dining room table. Have you ever seen any other spice set out on a tablecloth? If you have, you certainly may have wondered, "Why's the cumin out?" "What's the turmeric supposed to go with?" But while you may take salt and pepper for granted, you would never question their presence. They color every taste. They are the spine, the illumination, the narrator of every dish, the judge and jury of every flavor. So do it . . . to taste.

Now, let's get practical: When it comes to salt, I use kosher salt 99 percent of the time. Occasionally, I will use *fleur de sel*—a special sea salt—for a finishing salt on a rich dish, such as foie gras.

When it comes to pepper, the best black peppercorns, the berries of the *Piper nigrum* plant family, come from the Indian Malabar coast and include the varieties known as Tellicherry from the north and Alleppey from the south. Pepper's pungency comes from the volatile oil within it, called *piperine*. The spice increases the flow of saliva and that stimulates the appetite.

For tips on how to use salt and how to toast and grind pepper, see pages 7 and 9.

malanga fritters

The Tupi Indians, who lived along the coast of Brazil when the Portuguese first came ashore, taught the Europeans how to adapt to life in the New World, including how to incorporate *malanga* into their diet. *Malanga* is a cousin to the Polynesian tuber known as *taro*. (In Puerto Rico, the tuber is called *yautía*.) And, like *taro, malanga* has it fans and foes. These fritters, however, can win over almost anyone, especially when you serve them with a citrus honey *crema*.

FOR THE *CREMA*

¹/₄ cup sour cream

1 ¹/₂ tablespoons mashed Roasted Garlic (page 262)

1 tablespoon honey

1 ¹/₂ teaspoons fresh lime juice

1 ¹/₂ teaspoons fresh orange juice

1 teaspoon grated orange zest

1 tablespoon minced cilantro

Kosher salt and freshly ground black pepper to taste

FOR THE FRITTERS

1 pound *malanga*, peeled and cut into large dice

1 tablespoon pure olive oil

1 ¹/₂ teaspoons minced garlic

2 tablespoons all-purpose flour

2 tablespoons chopped Italian parsley

1 ¹/₂ teaspoons grated orange zest

1 egg, beaten

1 ¹/₂ teaspoons kosher salt

¹/₂ teaspoon freshly ground black pepper

Canola or peanut oil for deep-frying

for the *crema*

Mix all the ingredients in a bowl until smooth. Set aside to let the flavors marry while you prepare the fritters.

In a large saucepan, cover the *malanga* with water, bring to a simmer, and simmer, uncovered, until very soft, about 35 minutes. Drain, reserving ²/₃ cup of the cooking water.

Transfer the *malanga* to a bowl and mash until relatively smooth (a few small lumps are okay). Stir in the reserved ²/₃ cup water and set aside.

In a small skillet, heat the olive oil over medium heat. Add the garlic and sauté until it begins to turn translucent, about 1 minute. Mix the garlic into the *malanga,* and allow to cool to room temperature.

Stir the flour, parsley, orange zest, beaten egg, salt, and pepper into the *malanga* until well incorporated. Chill for 15 minutes.

In a deep-fryer or deep saucepan, heat the canola oil to 350 degrees. Carefully drop a few heaping tablespoons of the dough at a time into the hot oil and fry for 2 to 3 minutes, until the fritters are golden. Drain on paper towels. Serve with a dollop of citrus honey *crema*.

papas rellenas

(Crispy Stuffed Mashed Potato Balls)

MAKES 40 TO 44 *PAPAS*

These can be made with leftover turkey *picadillo* or Pork *Carnitas* (page 147). They also freeze well, making them a nice impulse *bocadito* (snack) on a weekend, served with a glass of wine or a cocktail. I like to squeeze lemon juice over the *papas rellenas,* and I mix up a little Jalapeño-Cumin-Lime *Crema* (page 289) for a dipping sauce.

3 cups mashed Idaho potatoes (about
     1 1/2 pounds potatoes)

3 cups mashed boiled yuca (about 1 1/2 pounds
     yuca)

5 extra-large eggs

1/4 cup chopped fresh thyme

2 teaspoons kosher salt, plus more to taste

1 1/2 teaspoons freshly ground black pepper,
     plus more to taste

1 teaspoon cayenne pepper

3 cups or 1/2 recipe *Picadillo de Pavo* (page 143)
     or any leftover stewed meat or fish

1 cup all-purpose flour

3 tablespoons water

3 cups fine bread crumbs

Canola or peanut oil for deep-frying

Combine the mashed potatoes and yuca in a large bowl. Lightly beat 2 of the eggs, and add to the potato mixture, along with the thyme, salt, black pepper, and cayenne. Cover and refrigerate for 30 minutes.

Form the potato mixture into balls about 1 1/2 inches in diameter. Using your thumb or forefinger, make a little well large enough to hold 1/2 tablespoon of filling in each ball. Add the filling and pinch the dough to seal. Pat the seam gently, then roll the ball to make it smooth and round.

Bring out three shallow bowls. Put the flour in one and season with salt and pepper. In another, beat the remaining 3 eggs with the water. Put the bread crumbs in the third bowl. Roll each ball in the flour, then in the eggs, and then in the bread crumbs to coat.

In a deep-fryer or deep pot, heat the oil to 375 degrees. Drop the *papas rellenas* into the oil, in batches, and cook until golden brown, approximately 3 minutes. Remove and drain on paper towels, then serve.

pork and *boniato croquetas*
(Pork and Sweet Potato Croquettes)

MAKES 20 TO 22 *CROQUETAS*

Croquetas, made from a variety of tubers, are found all over the Caribbean and Latin America. You'll see them served with a plethora of fillings, but in Cuba, where there are not vast expanses of cattle-grazing and farm land, pork is the meat of choice. Here *boniato,* a kind of sweet potato, create a perfect gustatory marriage with the savory richness of the pork.

4 eggs

3 cups *Boniato* Mash (page 205), allowed to cool

1 teaspoon kosher salt, plus more to taste

1/2 teaspoon freshly ground black pepper, plus more to taste

1/2 teaspoon cayenne pepper

2 tablespoons chopped cilantro

2 cups Pork *Carnitas* (page 147)

1/2 cup all-purpose flour

2 tablespoons water

1 1/2 cups fine bread crumbs

1 or 2 egg yolks (optional)

Canola or peanut oil for deep-frying

In a large bowl, beat 2 of the eggs. Add the *boniato* mash, salt, pepper, cayenne, and cilantro. Stir in the *carnitas.* Cover and refrigerate for 30 minutes.

Bring out three shallow bowls. Put the flour in one and season with salt and pepper. In another, beat the remaining 2 eggs with the water. Put the bread crumbs in the third bowl.

Shape the *boniato*-pork mixture into 3-inch-long cylinders by rolling it between the palms of your hands. (One of the keys to making successful *croquetas* is that the mixture be firm enough to hold its shape; if your *croquetas* seem too loose, add 1 or 2 egg yolks to the mixture, then shape the *croquetas.*)

Roll each *croqueta* in the flour, then in the beaten eggs, and then in the bread crumbs to coat. Set aside on a plate.

In a deep-fryer or deep pot, heat the oil to 375 degrees. Drop in the *croquetas,* in batches, and fry until golden brown, about 3 minutes. Drain on paper towels and serve.

potato tacos with avocado salsa

MAKES 8 TACOS

You can experiment with so many tastes in this savory, rustic dish, depending on the leftovers in your refrigerator. Bits of cooked ham, venison, or sausage, various squashes, even sautéed mushrooms can be added to the potato mixture.

FOR THE SALSA (MAKES 2 CUPS)

1 large, ripe avocado, seeded, peeled, and diced
1 large tomato, peeled, seeded, and diced
1 Scotch bonnet chile, stemmed, seeded, and minced
2 tablespoons chopped cilantro
1 tablespoon minced Spanish onion
Juice of 1 lime
1 tablespoon extra virgin olive oil
Kosher salt to taste

FOR THE FILLING

1 ¹/₂ pounds Red Bliss potatoes
2 tablespoons pure olive oil
4 tablespoons unsalted butter
1 medium Spanish onion, thinly sliced
1 tablespoon sugar
1 tablespoon red wine vinegar
1 jalapeño, stemmed, seeded, and minced
1 cup shredded green cabbage
Kosher salt and freshly ground black pepper to taste
1 tablespoon mashed Roasted Garlic (page 262)
1 cup grated Manchego cheese
1 poblano pepper, roasted (see page 7), peeled, seeded, and minced

FOR THE TACO SHELLS

Canola or peanut oil for shallow-frying
Eight 6-inch corn tortillas

for the salsa

In a bowl, combine all the ingredients. Cover and refrigerate.

for the filling

Preheat the oven to 375 degrees.

Put the potatoes in a roasting pan and bake for 1 hour, or until tender when pierced with a knife. Remove from the oven and cover with foil to keep warm.

Meanwhile, in a medium skillet, heat 1 tablespoon of the olive oil and 1 tablespoon of the butter over medium-high heat. Add the onion and cook for 1 minute. Add the sugar and vinegar and continue to cook for 8 to 10 minutes, until the onions begin to caramelize and are completely soft. Add the jalapeño and cook for 1 more minute. Remove from the heat and reserve.

Heat the remaining 1 tablespoon oil in a sauté pan over medium-high heat. Add the cabbage and cook until it wilts, about 2 minutes. Season with salt and pepper. Remove from the heat.

When the potatoes are cool enough to handle, peel and discard the skins. In a medium bowl, mash the potatoes with the roasted garlic and the remaining 3 tablespoons butter. Stir in the cheese, the caramelized onions, the poblano, and the cabbage. Season with salt and pepper. Cover with foil to keep warm, and set aside while you prepare the taco shells.

Pour about $1/8$ inch of canola oil into a sauté pan and heat over medium-high heat. When the oil is quite hot but not smoking, set a tortilla in the pan for a scant 5 seconds. Using tongs, flip the tortilla over and cook for another 5 seconds (this softens the tortilla just enough). Flip it again, fold it in half, and heat for just 7 seconds, or until crisp. Flip it again and heat for 7 seconds, then remove and drain on paper towels. Repeat with the remaining tortillas.

Fill each taco shell generously with the potato mixture. Serve with the avocado salsa on the side.

ELEMENTS OF NEW WORLD STYLE
tortillas

"The tortilla is at one and the same time a plate, a meal, and spoon or scoop. It can be eaten by itself or can accompany other foods. . . . [I]t is the perfect everyday food," writes José Coronel Urtecho in *A Text on Corn*. When I think of perfect foods, I often think of bread or doughs with a wide host of fillings or toppings: pizzas, pitas, bagels, burritos, and sandwiches fill the bill (and the belly) and are portable, to boot.

Before I became a cook, I had many odd jobs. One was in Kansas, spraying soft concrete out of heavy canvas hoses, building silos that were used to hold livestock feed. I was nineteen and working with a couple of buddies, just trying to make enough bucks to hitchhike up to Alaska and maybe get some work on the pipeline. I hated the nearly constant taste in my mouth of Kansas dust kicking up around us from the sun-baked earth, but there was a bright side. Most of the other workers were from Mexico, and sometimes they offered me one of their warm, tasty lunches of scrambled eggs, sweet onions, and spicy chorizo wrapped in a warm tortilla.

During the time of the Conquistadores, a Franciscan friar named Bernardino de Sahagún kept one of the most thorough accounts of Aztec life. In Raymond Sokolov's pivotal work, *Why We Eat What We Eat*, he notes that from the friar's observations, "We know that the Aztecs' diet was based on corn, tortillas, tamales, and plenty of chiles in many varieties. In other words, Sahagún provides evidence of a continuity from Aztec food to the demotic Mexican food of today."

Empanadas de "Perico"

MAKES 15 TO 20 EMPANADAS

On the streets of Caracas, the Venezuelan capital, *empanadas* are so familiar and so dear to the populace that they've earned a variety of nicknames. The *Domino* is filled with black beans and crumbled *queso blanco*. The *Reina Pepeada* ("The Polka-Dotted Queen") is stuffed with chicken salad and avocado mayonnaise. And these, *Huevos Pericos,* literally, "Parrot Eggs," derive their name from the colorful ingredients—cilantro, onions, tomato—that go into them. The dough here is different from classic *empanada* dough—in fact, it is the same dough used to make *arepas,* another Venezuelan favorite.

FOR THE FILLING

4 extra-large eggs
2 ¹/₂ tablespoons unsalted butter
2 cloves garlic, minced
¹/₂ medium Spanish onion, diced
¹/₂ large ripe tomato, peeled, seeded, and diced
¹/₂ cup crumbled *queso blanco*, plus about
    ¹/₄ cup for garnish
2 tablespoons chopped cilantro
Kosher salt and freshly ground black pepper to
    taste

FOR THE DOUGH

1 ¹/₂ cups milk
¹/₃ cup (5 ¹/₃ tablespoons) unsalted butter
1 ¹/₂ cup *arepa* flour (see Note)
1 ¹/₂ teaspoons kosher salt
1 tablespoon Annatto Oil (page 261) or pure
    olive oil

Canola or peanut oil for deep-frying
Lime wedges

for the filling

In a medium bowl beat the eggs; set aside.

Heat a large skillet over medium heat. Melt the butter, and sauté the garlic for 30 seconds. Raise the heat to medium-high, add the onions, and cook for 2 minutes, or until they begin to soften. Whisk in the tomatos, beaten eggs, and the ¹/₂ cup *queso blanco,* and cook, stirring continuously, until the eggs begin to scramble. Add the cilantro, season with salt and pepper, and cook until the tomato liquid is absorbed. Remove from the heat and set aside.

for the dough

Pour the milk into a pot, add the butter, and bring to a boil. Remove from the heat and let cool until just warm enough to handle.

Put the *arepa* flour, salt, and annatto oil in a medium bowl. Add a little of the warm milk and knead it in. Repeat this process until all the milk is incorporated and you have a smooth dough without any lumps. Cover it with a damp cloth so it does not dry out, and allow it to sit for 5 to 10 minutes.

Set a small bowl of water beside your work space. Divide the dough into rough balls about 1 inch in diameter. Keep them covered with the damp cloth as you work.

Lay a piece of plastic wrap on your work space and lightly coat it with canola oil. Shape a dough ball into a smooth sphere, then flatten it slightly. Lay it on the plastic wrap and cover with another sheet of lightly coated wrap (this will keep the dough from sticking to your hands). With your hands, flatten the dough ball into a disk about $1/4$ inch thick. If it seems to be drying out or cracking at the edges, wet your fingers and smooth the dough.

Remove the top sheet of plastic. Place 1 tablespoon of the filling in the center of the dough and sprinkle 1 teaspoon of the *queso blanco* atop it. Press lightly to spread the filling.

Using the plastic wrap, fold over the dough to form a half-moon–shaped *empanada*. Pinch the edges to seal—but don't crimp; the dough is too delicate to take it. Repeat this process until the *empanadas* are all made. Arrange them on a large tray and cover with a warm damp towel.

In a deep-fryer or deep pot, heat the canola oil to 325 degrees. Working in batches, one by one, drop the *empanadas* into the oil, taking care not to crowd them, and cook until golden-crisp. (You can keep the *empanadas* warm in a 250-degree oven for about 20 minutes.) Serve immediately, with lime wedges on the side.

note: *Arepa* flour is precooked finely ground white cornmeal, available in Latin American markets. It is also called *masarepa* and *harina de pan,* and *greparina.*

pipián-stuffed *empanadas*

(Potato-and-Pumpkin-Seed-Stuffed *Empanadas*)

MAKES ABOUT 40 *EMPANADAS*

Empanadas are fried pastries filled with almost anything you can imagine—they are an excellent way to use up your leftovers. Offered by street vendors in Mexico, Guatemala, Venezuela, Cuba, Argentina, Peru, Colombia, and Brazil (where they are called *empadas),* they are Latin America's answer to the sandwich.

Pipián—a thick *mole*-like sauce that contains pumpkin seeds, sesame seeds, or peanuts—is a culinary gift from the Incas. It was the Spaniards who christened the dish *pipián,* derived from their word for pumpkin seed, *pepita.*

FOR THE DOUGH

6 cups all-purpose flour
1 tablespoon baking powder
1 1/4 teaspoons kosher salt
1 1/2 cups vegetable shortening
1 1/2 cups ice water, or as needed

FOR THE FILLING (MAKES 4 CUPS)

1 1/2 pounds red potatoes, peeled and diced
1 tablespoon unsalted butter
1 tablespoon Annatto Oil (page 261) or pure
   olive oil
1/2 medium Spanish onion, diced
1 clove garlic, thinly sliced
1/2 red bell pepper, stemmed, seeded, and
   minced
1 large ripe tomato, peeled, seeded, and diced
2 teaspoons toasted and ground cumin seeds
   (see page 9)
Kosher salt and freshly ground black pepper to
   taste

1/2 cup Chicken Stock (page 267)
3 tablespoons Spanish sherry vinegar
1 hard-boiled egg, cut into medium dice
3/4 cup unsalted *pepitas* (hulled pumpkin
   seeds), toasted and finely ground
   (see page 9)
2 scallions, green and white parts, finely
   chopped
1 tablespoon mashed Roasted Garlic
   (page 262)

1 egg
1 tablespoon water
Canola or peanut oil for deep-frying

for the dough

In a medium bowl, mix the flour, baking powder, and salt. Using a pastry cutter or a fork, work the shortening into the flour until the mixture resembles coarse crumbs. Add the water and stir with a fork until the dough is firm enough to be formed into a ball. Wrap in plastic wrap and refrigerate for 45 minutes.

While the dough rests, prepare the filling: Cook the potatoes in boiling salted water for 10 to 15 minutes, until they are easily pierced with a knife. Drain and set aside.

Preheat the oven to 250 degrees.

Heat the butter and oil in a large ovenproof sauté pan. Add the onion, garlic, and bell pepper and, cook until soft, about 3 minutes. Add the tomato and season with the cumin and salt and pepper. Add the chicken stock and sherry vinegar and stir well. Add the potatoes, hard-boiled egg, and *pepitas* and mix thoroughly.

Transfer the pan to the oven and bake for 20 minutes (this reduces the moisture and concentrates the flavors).

Fold the scallions and roasted garlic into the filling. Season to taste. Let cool.

In a small bowl, whisk the egg with the water. Divide the dough into smaller portions. (Rewrap any that you are not using.)

One at a time, on a well-floured work surface, roll out each piece of dough to a $1/6$-inch thickness. Cut out rounds with a 4-inch round cutter (if you don't have a cutter, an empty can works well). Drop $1 1/2$ tablespoons of the filling atop each circle of dough. Brush the edges with the egg wash. Fold over the dough, sandwiching the filling, and pinch the edges to seal, then crimp the edges with the back of a fork; dip the fork in flour to prevent sticking. Set the *empanadas* aside on a floured baking sheet.

In a deep-fryer or deep pot, heat the canola oil to 350 degrees. Fry the *empanadas,* in batches, until golden brown, 3 to 4 minutes. Drain on paper towels and serve.

stamp and go

(Beer-Batter Seafood Fritters)

MAKES ABOUT 70 FRITTERS

The name of this dish comes from a famous Jamaican expression: When people are hurrying about, shopping and doing errands, and they want to grab a quick bite, what they want is to "stamp and go." These are usually made with codfish.

1 ¼ pounds crabmeat, cleaned of any shells and cartilage

¾ cup milk

1 medium red onion, minced

4 cloves garlic, minced

1 Scotch bonnet chile, stemmed, seeded, and minced

2 tablespoons Tabasco

2 tablespoons finely chopped chives

2 teaspoons finely chopped fresh thyme

2 tablespoons Spanish sherry vinegar

2 extra-large eggs, beaten

2 cups all-purpose flour

2 teaspoons kosher salt

1 teaspoon freshly ground black pepper

6 tablespoons beer, at room temperature

Canola or peanut oil for deep-frying

Lemon and lime wedges

In a bowl, break up the crabmeat. Add the milk, onion, garlic, Scotch bonnet, Tabasco, herbs, and sherry vinegar and mix thoroughly. Stir in the eggs. Add the flour, salt, and pepper. Stir until just incorporated. Stir in the beer.

In a deep-fryer or deep pot, heat the oil to 350 degrees. With one tablespoon, scoop up the batter, and with another, carefully push the batter into the hot oil. Repeat, adding only as many fritters as will fit in the pot without lowering the temperature of the oil. Cook, turning the fritters so that they brown evenly, for about 2 to 3 minutes. Remove and drain on paper towels. Repeat with the remaining batter.

Serve with lemon and lime wedges.

pastelillos de carne
(Meat-Stuffed Pastries)

MAKES 32 PASTRIES

Pastelillos are known as *empanadas* in other parts of the Caribbean. The stuffing varies from region to region. For this reason, we often use leftover meats from a dinner made the night before in the filling.

4 cups all-purpose flour
$^1/_2$ teaspoon kosher salt, plus a pinch
2 teaspoons baking powder
1 cup vegetable shortening
1 cup plus 1 tablespoon ice water,
   or more as needed

1 extra-large egg

2 cups chopped stewed meat

Canola or peanut oil for deep-frying
Lime wedges

Sift the flour, the $^1/_2$ teaspoon salt, and the baking powder into a medium bowl. Add the shortening, breaking it into small chunks and working it into the flour with your fingers or a pastry cutter until the mixture resembles coarse crumbs. Add 1 cup of the ice water, working it into the dough with a fork; you may need to add another tablespoon or so. Wrap the dough tightly in plastic wrap and let rest in the refrigerator for 30 minutes.

Divide the dough into 8 equal portions. On a well-floured work surface, one at a time, roll out each portion to a $^1/_8$-inch thickness. Using a 4-inch round cutter (if you don't have one, an empty can 4 inches in diameter works well), cut out 4 dough rounds from each portion, and transfer to a floured baking sheet.

In a small bowl, whisk the egg, the remaining tablespoon ice water, and the pinch of salt. Using your finger, lightly paint the edges of each pastry round with egg wash; then drop a tablespoon of the meat filling onto half of the round. Fold the pastry over in a half-moon and press the edges firmly together. Use the back of a fork to crimp the edges, if desired.

In a deep-fryer or deep pot, heat the oil to 375 degrees. Cook the *pastelillos,* in batches, for 3 to 4 minutes, or until golden brown. Drain on paper towels.

Serve with lime wedges.

tapas and little plates

On Easter Sunday last year, my wife, Janet, and I had about twenty friends and family for dinner. In addition to traditional American holiday fare, we served some of the tapas and little plates that you'll find in this chapter. By about 9:00 P.M., one guest had put on a tape of 1970s disco hits and everyone, from my college-age son and his friends to folks Janet's and my age and beyond, was getting down. Then we really got down—to the bottom of the swimming pool. Everyone jumped in, fully clothed, for a swim . . . and more dancing.

Was it the food that inspired our Easter parade? I certainly like to think so. For this chapter, I tracked down some of New World cuisine's most treasured flavors and packed them into small taster-size dishes that are perfect for less-than-formal entertaining. The common elements here are full, bright, and satisfying flavors that have developed in the hands of the native populations. These dishes aren't large, yet they satisfy hunger pangs immediately and skillfully.

The translation of the Spanish word *tapa* is "cover," or "lid." Naturally, this ancient appetizer comes with some history. It dates back to sixteenth-century Spain and King Philip II. The monarch would steal away from the palace at night, or so the story goes, and, disguised with a black cape and wide-brimmed hat, he'd make the rounds of the rough tavernas around the Plaza Mayor, mingling with the populace to get a sense of what they were saying about their king. One evening he was disgusted to spot a fly swimming in his glass of sherry. The next day a royal edict was issued: henceforth, tavern proprietors were to protect their patrons' glasses with a cover or lid. Most simply used a small dish to satisfy the decree; some took it a step further, proffering on each *tapa* a thirst-producing morsel: a roasted prawn, a bit of pickled octopus, a slice of cold potato omelet. In time, these modest little plates became more elaborate and abundant, and customers were so pleased with the ritual that they didn't even mind when the taverns started charging for the food.

Nowadays the ancient taverns frequented by the king are called tapas bars, each specializing in its own kind of appetizer, from mini-paellas and tripe stew to precious baby eels and rare edible barnacles. Spaniards are big eaters, and they'll visit three or four of these places before adjourning to a restaurant for a more serious sit-down dinner.

Tapas were brought to the New World by Spanish settlers, and most Latin American and Caribbean countries serve them in the Iberian fashion. A curious exception is Central America, where little plates are known as *bocas* ("mouthfuls"). In older bars, the tradition is to serve a different *boca* with each round of drinks, and one particular place in San José, Costa Rica, is proud of having once served thirty-four *bocas* in a seating without repeating a dish.

In the 1940s, when tiny and passionately democratic Costa Rica was known as the Switzerland of Latin America, its former president, Otilio Ulate, a plain-speaking ex-newspaperman, would make like King Philip, stepping out of the presidential palace to visit a local tapas spot. There, free of motorcades and bodyguards, he'd transact official business while enjoying his usual Scotch and an endless line of *bocas*.

black bean, tropical fruit, and *queso blanco* salsa

SERVES 4

My talented friend chef Douglas Rodriguez gave me the inspiration for this salsa one night at a fantastic party he threw. *Queso blanco,* a staple of Latin cuisine, is uniquely textured, simply yet assertively flavored, and quite pleasant to nibble. In this recipe, the cheese balances the acidity of the orange and mango. A no-brainer with chips, *queso blanco* salsa is a great accompaniment to grilled chicken breasts as well. You can prepare the dressing up to a day before you assemble the salsa. And the salsa is also a good day-after leftover—assuming there is any left over.

FOR THE SALSA (MAKES 4 CUPS)

1 cup cooked black beans (see page 202) or
    well-rinsed canned beans
$^1/_3$ cup finely diced red bell pepper
$^1/_4$ cup finely chopped scallions, white and light
    green parts only
1 Scotch bonnet chile, stemmed, seeded, and
    minced
$^3/_4$ cup crumbled *queso blanco*
$^3/_4$ cup diced mango
$^1/_2$ cup coarsely chopped orange sections
1 $^1/_2$ teaspoons Spanish sherry vinegar
Kosher salt and freshly ground black pepper to
    taste
1 tablespoon fresh orange juice
1 cup diced ripe avocado

FOR THE DRESSING

1 $^1/_2$ teaspoons minced shallot
1 clove garlic, minced
1 tablespoon coarsely chopped Italian parsley
$^1/_2$ teaspoon toasted and ground cumin seeds
    (see page 9)
$^1/_4$ teaspoon freshly ground black pepper
Kosher salt to taste
2 tablespoons Spanish sherry vinegar
$^1/_4$ cup extra virgin olive oil

for the salsa

In a large bowl, combine all the ingredients except the avocado in the order listed. *Very gently* fold in the avocado, to avoid smashing the delicate ingredients. Cover and refrigerate until chilled.

for the dressing

In a small bowl, combine all the ingredients and whisk them well. Cover and refrigerate.
To serve, gently fold the dressing into the salsa. Season to taste and serve.

recommended wine: A rich tropical fruit Chardonnay with good acidity.

black bean *muñeta* with chipotle-corn skillet bread
(Black Bean Puree on Corn Bread)

SERVES 4 TO 6

Don't let the word *muñeta* slow you down. A chunky puree of cooked black beans, it is easy to make, and its uses are wide-ranging. Here I feature it in a little plate with Chipotle-Corn Skillet Bread, but it also makes a perfect partner for grilled fish or meats. I also like the corn bread under a poached egg as a great alternative to toast, or on the more elaborate end, with the Tamarind Barbecued Duck (page 142).

FOR THE *MUÑETA* (MAKES 3 ¹/₂ CUPS)
1 ounce smoky bacon, diced
1 ¹/₂ teaspoons pure olive oil
1 tablespoon unsalted butter
3 cloves garlic, finely chopped
2 jalapeños, stemmed, seeded, and minced
¹/₂ medium red onion, diced
1 large stalk celery, diced
1 carrot, peeled and diced
1 ¹/₂ teaspoons toasted and ground cumin
     seeds (see page 9)
1 ¹/₂ teaspoons freshly ground black pepper,
     plus more to taste
1 bay leaf, broken in half
¹/₄ cup Spanish sherry vinegar
1 cup dried black beans, rinsed, soaked
     overnight in water to cover, and drained
2 smoked ham hocks
5 cups Chicken Stock (page 267)
Kosher salt to taste

FOR THE CORN BREAD
1 chipotle chile
2 tablespoons unsalted butter
2 ears corn, husked and kernels removed
     (about 1 ¹/₂ cups kernels)
1 clove garlic, minced
¹/₂ cup yellow cornmeal
¹/₂ cup all-purpose flour
¹/₂ teaspoon baking soda
1 teaspoon kosher salt
2 extra-large eggs
¹/₃ cup vegetable shortening, melted
1 cup plus 2 tablespoons buttermilk
1 cup grated Manchego cheese

Thinly sliced scallions for garnish

for the *muñeta*
Put the bacon and olive oil in a medium pot and cook over medium heat until the bacon is beginning to crisp. Add the butter. When the butter begins to foam, add the garlic and jalapeños and stir for about 30 seconds. Add the onion, celery, and carrot, stirring to coat, turn the heat to medium-high, and cook, stirring occasionally, until some nice caramelizing occurs, about 10 minutes.

Add the cumin, black pepper, and bay leaf and stir. Add the vinegar, drained beans, ham hocks, and chicken stock and bring to a boil. Skim off any impurities that rise to the surface. Reduce the heat to medium-low and cook, uncovered, until the beans are soft, 2 to 2 1/2 hours.

Take the pot off the heat and remove the ham hocks and bay leaf. Drain the beans, reserving the liquid. Puree the beans in a food processor until somewhat smooth.

Pour the reserved bean liquid into a small saucepan and reduce over medium-high heat to about 1/4 cup. Mix this reduction into the bean puree, transfer to a nonstick saucepan, and set aside.

meanwhile, make the corn bread

Toast the chipotle in a small skillet over medium heat, then soak it in warm water for about 20 minutes, until soft.

Preheat the oven to 375 degrees. In the meantime, prepare the corn mixture: In a medium skillet, melt 1 tablespoon of the butter. Add the garlic and corn and blister the kernels until they begin to "pop"; stir occasionally, but not too often, or the kernels won't caramelize, they'll sweat. Then sauté for about 3 minutes. Remove the skillet from the heat.

Drain the soaked chile. Remove the stem and seeds, and finely chop.

In a medium bowl, combine the cornmeal, flour, baking soda, and salt. In a blender, combine the eggs, shortening, and buttermilk and blend until smooth. Fold the wet ingredients into the dry. Stir in the corn and chipotle, then fold in the cheese, stirring just to incorporate; do not overmix.

Melt the remaining 1 tablespoon butter in an ovenproof 9-inch skillet over medium heat. Pour in the batter and leave over the heat for another minute. Place the skillet in the oven and bake for 25 minutes, or until the center of the bread springs back when touched.

To serve, gently reheat the *muñeta*. Cut the corn bread into wedges. Spoon a dollop of the *muñeta* onto each wedge of corn bread and garnish with scallions.

recommended wine or beer: An old Bual Madeira, or, going in the other direction, a crisp Pilsner beer.

camarones al ajillo
(Shrimp with Garlic, Citrus, and Butter)

SERVES 4

To say this dish is forward in its robust flavors is an understatement. I am unapologetic in my fervor for big, lusty flavors, and this dish is in my "Big, Lusty Pantheon." Cut back on the garlic if you must, but please don't tell me about it.

1/2 cup pure olive oil
12 large shrimp, peeled and deveined
4 tablespoons unsalted butter
1/2 cup very thinly sliced garlic
1 Scotch bonnet chile, stemmed, seeded, and minced
3/4 cup Chicken Stock (page 267)
1/3 cup fresh lime juice
2 tablespoons Spanish dry sherry
1/2 cup coarsely chopped cilantro
1/2 cup coarsely chopped Italian parsley
Kosher salt and freshly ground black pepper to taste
1 small ripe tomato, peeled, seeded, and chopped
Four 1/2-inch-thick slices soft white country bread
1/4 cup mashed Roasted Garlic (page 262)

Heat the olive oil in a large skillet over medium-high heat. Add the shrimp and cook, flipping them once, for 2 to 4 minutes. With a slotted spoon, transfer the shrimp to a warm bowl.

Turn the heat down to low and melt the butter. Stir in the garlic and Scotch bonnet and sauté until fragrant for 40 to 60 seconds. Turn the heat back up to medium-high, add the chicken stock, lime juice, sherry, herbs, and salt and pepper, and stir well. Cook for 5 to 6 minutes to reduce the liquid until thick enough to blend the flavors and to coat the back of a spoon. Gently stir in the chopped tomato and cook for another 2 minutes. Add the shrimp and turn off the heat.

Toast the bread. Spread 1 tablespoon of the roasted garlic on each piece. Place each toast in the middle of a soup bowl and top with 3 shrimp. Ladle the sauce into the bowls and serve immediately.

recommended wine: A dry Pinot Grigio from Friuli or a Sauvignon Blanc from Graves in Bordeaux.

cachapas with queso fundido
(Corn Cakes with Melted Cheese and Hot Sauce)

SERVES 4

Here the down-to-earth pleasures of melted cheese and meaty sausages team with the rich Venezuelan corn cake called *cachapa*. Given a little kick with the *Sauce au Chien,* this little plate is a perfect fusion of Mexican and Venezuelan cuisines.

8 ounces chorizo, casings removed
12 ounces pepper Jack cheese, grated
$^1/_2$ recipe *Cachapas* (page 221), freshly prepared
     and kept in the oven, loosely covered with
     foil
1 recipe *Sauce au Chien* (page 287)

Break up the chorizo in a skillet and cook over medium heat. When cool, crumble more finely.

Preheat the oven to 300 degrees.

Combine the chorizo and cheese in a small heatproof saucepan or baking dish. Heat in the oven until the cheese has melted. Remove from the oven, pat with a paper towel to soak up the excess oil, and stir well.

Spread a generous tablespoon of the chorizo mixture over each pancake, and spoon on the sauce—or let your guests help themselves at the table. Serve immediately.

recommended wine: A Tokay Pinot Gris from Alsace.

llapingachos

(Golden Potato Cakes with Goat Cheese and Smoked Ham)

SERVES 12

For centuries, Ecuadorian Indians have been making *llapingachos* (pronounced yah-pihn-GAH-chos). Typically, these yellow potato cakes are made with cream cheese, but I substitute goat cheese and add smoked ham for a more complex flavor. Think of these *llapingachos* as New World eggs Benedict, minus the hollandaise sauce.

2 pounds red potatoes, peeled, cooked in boiling salted water until easily pierced with a knife, and drained
1/4 cup crumbled goat cheese, at room temperature
2 tablespoons unsalted butter
4 ounces smoked ham, cut into small dice
Kosher salt and freshly ground black pepper to taste

FOR THE SALSA

1 tablespoon unsalted butter
2 cloves garlic, thinly sliced
1 medium red onion, chopped
2 medium ripe tomatoes, peeled, seeded, and diced
1 tablespoon red wine vinegar
Kosher salt and freshly ground black pepper to taste

FOR THE POTATO CAKES

1/2 cup all-purpose flour
14 extra-large eggs
2 tablespoons water
1 1/2 cup bread crumbs
Canola or peanut oil for panfrying
1 1/2 teaspoons white distilled vinegar

Ancho-Cumin Oil (page 261) (optional)

Put the potatoes in a bowl and mash with the goat cheese and butter. Stir in the ham and season with salt and pepper. Cover and refrigerate until chilled.

for the salsa

Melt the butter in a medium saucepan over medium-high heat. Add the garlic and red onion and sauté for 5 minutes. Add the tomatoes and red wine vinegar, season with salt and pepper, and cook for about 5 minutes more, until the mixture thickens. Cover to keep warm and set aside.

for the potato cakes

Set the oven to Warm.

Bring out three shallow bowls. Put the flour in one and season with salt and pepper. In another, beat 2 of the eggs and the water with a fork. Put the bread crumbs in a third bowl.

Divide the potato mixture into 12 portions and shape into 1/2-inch-thick patties. Dredge each patty in the flour, then the egg wash, and finally the bread crumbs. Put on a plate.

Set a nonstick skillet over medium-high heat and pour in enough canola oil to coat the bottom of the pan. In batches, cook the cakes, turning once, until golden brown and crisp on each side. As you finish them, set them on a plate covered with paper towels in the oven.

Bring a deep skillet of water to a low boil. Add the white vinegar (the vinegar helps keep the whites intact around the yolks). Poach the eggs. With a slotted spoon, transfer the eggs to a warm plate to drain completely.

Place the potato cakes on a platter. Top with the tomato salsa and then the poached eggs. Season with salt and pepper, and, if you have it, drizzle with the oil. Serve.

recommended wine: A vintage Champagne or a dry fino sherry from Jerez in Spain.

masa-crusted chicken with piquillo peppers, avocado butter, and greens

SERVES 6

You are going to fall in love with this gorgeous lit-tle dish. Furthermore, I'm sure you will want to use the Avocado Butter and the Grapefruit-Honey Vinaigrette in other dishes you make.

FOR THE AVOCADO BUTTER (MAKES 1 CUP)

1 ripe avocado, seeded, peeled, and roughly
    chopped
Juice of 2 limes
$^1/_4$ teaspoon cayenne pepper
$^1/_2$ cup sour cream
Kosher salt and freshly ground black pepper
    to taste

FOR THE VINAIGRETTE

3 tablespoons Roasted Garlic Oil (page 262)
    or pure olive oil
1 tablespoon fresh pink grapefruit juice
1 $^1/_2$ teaspoons Spanish sherry vinegar
1 teaspoon honey
Kosher salt and freshly ground black pepper
    to taste

FOR THE CHICKEN

1 $^1/_2$ cups all-purpose flour
3 $^1/_2$ tablespoons *Escabeche* spice rub
    (page 266)
2 extra-large eggs
$^1/_4$ cup sour cream, plus more to finish the dish
$^1/_2$ cup *masa harina* (available in many grocery
    stores and in Latin American markets)
3 boneless, skinless chicken breasts, sliced
    lengthwise into 3 strips each
1 cup canola or peanut oil
4 cups mixed greens, washed and patted dry
2 $^1/_2$ ounces jarred piquillo peppers, cut into
    $^1/_2$-inch-thick slices (or substitute jarred
    roasted red peppers, cut into $^1/_2$-inch-thick
    slices)

for the avocado butter

In a food processor, puree the avocado with the lime juice, cayenne, sour cream, and salt and pepper until smooth. Cover and re-frigerate.

for the vinaigrette

Whisk together the garlic oil, grapefruit juice, vinegar, honey, and salt and pepper in a bowl. Set aside while you finish preparing the dish.

for the chicken

Bring out three bowls. Put 1 cup of the flour in one and season with 1 tablespoon of the spice rub. In the second, beat the eggs and sour cream until smooth. Season with 1 $1/2$ tablespoons of the spice rub. In the third bowl, combine the *masa harina* with the remaining $1/2$ cup flour and 1 tablespoon spice rub.

Coat the chicken strips in the flour, shaking off any excess, then dip them into the egg-and-sour-cream mixture. Finally, coat them in the *masa harina* mixture. In a large skillet, heat the oil to 325 degrees, and cook the chicken strips, in batches, turning once or twice, until golden brown. Drain them on paper towels.

To assemble the dish, toss the greens with just enough dressing to coat. Arrange the pepper slices around the greens on six salad plates. Cut each chicken strip crosswise in half and place them atop the peppers. Place the dressed salad greens in the center of the plates. Drop $1/2$ tablespoon of avocado butter, followed by $1/2$ teaspoon sour cream, on top of each piece of chicken. Drizzle a little of the remaining vinaigrette over each plate and serve.

recommended wine: A white wine from Crozes-Hermitage or a young Napa Valley Sauvignon Blanc.

mojo chicken nachos

SERVES 4

You don't see nachos in many books on Mexican cookery. The fact is, they are a relatively new invention. According to my research, the first nachos were served in the Mexican border town of Piedras Negras. It was there in 1943 that the chef of the old Victory Club, one Ignacio ("Nacho") Anaya, created the dish, which he offered to some ladies who were in town on a shopping trip. (Apparently, Piedras Negras was quite the cosmopolitan center.)

I may be the first to give nachos a Cuban twist, but I am supported in this move by a centuries-old cultural and culinary bridge between Mexico and Cuba called the Yucatán Peninsula.

$^1/_2$ cup Classic Sour Orange *Mojo* (page 283)
2 whole boneless chicken breasts, skin-on
    (or 2 $^1/_2$ cups leftover chicken cut into
    bite-sized pieces)

FOR THE PICKLED JALAPEÑOS (OR
    SUBSTITUTE STORE-BOUGHT DICED
    PICKLED JALAPEÑOS TO TASTE)
2 jalapeños, stemmed, seeded, and sliced
    into skinny strips
2 cloves garlic, sliced
$^1/_2$ cup white wine vinegar
$^1/_4$ cup water

6 ounces lightly salted tortilla chips
$^1/_2$ cup cooked black beans (see page 202)
    or well-rinsed canned beans
$^1/_2$ cup crumbled cooked chorizo
2 tablespoons minced roasted poblano
    peppers (see page 7)
1 $^1/_2$ cups grated pepper Jack cheese
1 cup grated *queso blanco*
$^1/_2$ cup Avocado–Pumpkin Seed Salsa
    (page 276) or diced avocado dressed
    in lime juice
1 tablespoon minced cilantro
1 small ripe tomato, peeled, seeded, and
    chopped
$^1/_4$ cup sour cream

Reserve 2 tablespoons of the *mojo* to drizzle over the nachos. Pour the rest of the *mojo* over the chicken in a large resealable bag. Refrigerate for 1 to 2 hours.

While the chicken marinates, prepare the pickled jalapeños if you are making them: In a small bowl, combine the jalapeños and garlic. Bring the vinegar and water to a boil in a small saucepan and pour over the jalapeños. Set aside for 1 hour.

Preheat the oven to 350 degrees.

Transfer the chicken to a roasting pan; discard the marinade. Roast for 20 to 30 minutes, or until the juices run clear when pierced. Remove from the oven and raise the oven temperature to 425 degrees.

While the chicken is still warm, shred the meat with your fingers.

Spread the tortilla chips in an ovenproof casserole dish or serving platter. Scatter the chicken, black beans, chorizo, poblano, and the cheeses over the chips. Place the dish in the oven for about 10 minutes, until heated through and the cheese is completely melted.

Drizzle the reserved 2 tablespoons *mojo* over the nachos and top with the avocado salsa, cilantro, tomato, sour cream, and pickled jalapeños.

recommended beer: An English ale or Negro Modelo beer.

coconut-almond snapper fingers

SERVES 6

Coconut-crusted shrimp has long been a mainstay in food shacks around the Caribbean. Here I've created coconut-crusted snapper. Either way, it is a delicious party food.

1 cup unblanched whole almonds
2 cups freshly grated coconut (or substitute
    unsweetened dried coconut flakes, available
    at health food markets)
1 1/4 cups sifted all-purpose flour
Kosher salt and freshly ground black pepper to
    taste
1 1/2 cups unsweetened coconut milk
1/4 teaspoon cayenne pepper
2 teaspoons Tabasco
1 1/2 pounds snapper fillets, cut into 3- to
    4-inch-long "fingers"
Canola or peanut oil for deep-frying

Preheat the oven to 350 degrees.

Spread the almonds on a baking sheet and toast for 12 minutes. Remove from the oven. If using fresh coconut, reduce the heat to 225 degrees.

Spread the fresh coconut on another baking sheet and bake for 15 minutes or until dry but not toasted.

In a food processor, finely chop the toasted almonds. Combine them with the grated coconut in a shallow bowl and mix well. Put the flour in another bowl and season with salt and pepper. Pour the coconut milk into a third bowl, add the cayenne and Tabasco, and mix well.

Season the snapper fingers with a bit of salt and pepper. Dip them in the coconut milk, coating them completely, then dredge them thoroughly in the flour. Shake off the excess, then submerge them again in the coconut milk. Finally, toss the fingers in the dried coconut mixture, coating them fully. As you work, set the coated fingers on a large plate (and rinse your fingers from time to time, as they'll get sticky with the ingredients).

Heat the oil in a large deep skillet or deep-fryer to 350 degrees. In batches, gently slide in the fish fingers and fry until golden brown on both sides, 2 to 3 minutes. Drain on paper towels and serve.

recommended drink: An *añejo*-style rum, chilled or on the rocks.

mussels *callao*
(Chilled Mussels Topped with Salsa)

SERVES 6

Callao refers to a style of cooking native to the port area of Lima, the coastal city that's the capital of Peru. This dish consists of plump mussels, simply steamed and then chilled, served topped with a gorgeous *salsita*.

1 cup Simple Court Bouillon (page 273) or water

3 dozen mussels, scrubbed and debearded

¹/₂ cup corn kernels, cooked

2 medium ripe tomatoes, peeled, seeded, and chopped

¹/₃ cup peeled, seeded, and minced cucumber

¹/₂ small red onion, minced

1 *ají amarillo* chile, stemmed, seeded, and minced (you can substitute a Scotch bonnet chile)

2 cloves garlic, minced

2 tablespoons extra virgin olive oil

1 ¹/₂ tablespoons fresh lemon juice

2 tablespoons chopped cilantro

Kosher salt and freshly ground black pepper to taste

In a deep skillet, bring the court bouillon to a boil. Add the mussels, cover, and cook until they have opened, 2 to 4 minutes. Discard any that do not open. Drain. Transfer the mussels to a bowl and refrigerate until cold.

Remove the top half of each mussel shell. Detach the meat from the lower shell, leaving the meat in the shell. Arrange the mussels on a platter.

In a small bowl, combine the corn, tomatoes, cucumber, red onion, chile, and garlic. Stir in the oil, lemon juice, and cilantro. Season with salt and pepper. Let stand for 5 minutes,

Drop a spoonful of salsa onto each mussel. Serve immediately.

recommended wine: A Tocai Friulano from the Collio region in northern Italy; the wine has a clean finish with enough acidity to make a suitable match for this dish.

fresh corn tamales

MAKES ABOUT 24 SMALL TAMALES

While tamales are most commonly associated with Mexican cuisine, they are found throughout Latin America. Here's a Peruvian version I like a lot. I use ground *chile molido* (mixed chiles) in this recipe, but in Peru they'd use their native *ají amarillo*.

Tamales are one of the great all-time vessels for leftovers. If you have pork roast, steak, or any braised meat left from the night before, you've already completed one step of this dish.

FOR THE DOUGH

1 ¹/₂ cups corn kernels (from 2 to 3 ears)
10 tablespoons unsalted butter
2 cloves garlic, minced
1 medium Spanish onion, diced
2 tablespoons pure ground *chile molido* or other pure chile powder
2 tablespoons lard or vegetable shortening
2 cups *masa harina* (available in many grocery stores and in Latin American markets)
1 teaspoon baking powder
1 ¹/₂ teaspoons kosher salt
¹/₂ cup cold Chicken Stock (page 267)

FOR THE FILLING

¹/₄ cup peanuts
2 chipotle chiles
1 tablespoon unsalted butter
1 clove garlic, minced
¹/₂ cup minced red bell pepper
1 cup shredded cooked pork
¹/₂ cup Pork Stock (page 270) or Chicken Stock (page 267)

¹/₂ cup pitted and chopped Niçoise olives
2 tablespoons chopped cilantro
Kosher salt and freshly ground black pepper to taste
Juice of 1 lime

Roughly 30 large fresh corn husks, thoroughly washed and patted dry (see Note)

for the dough

Puree the corn kernels in a food processor; leave them in the processor.

Melt 2 tablespoons of the butter in a sauté pan over medium heat. Add the garlic and cook for about 45 seconds. Add the onion and sauté for 1 minute or so, then add the *chile molido*. Continue to cook until the onions are soft, about 3 minutes. Transfer to the food processor with the corn and process until almost smooth.

Add another 2 tablespoons of butter to the sauté pan and melt over medium heat. Sauté the corn puree, stirring constantly, until thick and shiny, about 2 minutes. Remove from the heat. Let cool.

Using an electric mixer fitted with a paddle attachment, beat the remaining 6 tablespoons butter and the lard until creamy. Scraping down the bowl as necessary, alternately add the corn puree and the *masa* in 2 or 3 additions and beat until the dough is light and fluffy. Beat in the baking powder and salt. Transfer to a bowl and chill for an hour.

for the filling

Preheat the oven to 400 degrees.

Toast the peanuts on a baking sheet for about 10 to 12 minutes. Let cool.

Meanwhile, toast the chipotles in a small skillet over medium heat. Then soak them in hot water until softened, about 20 minutes; drain. Remove the stems and seeds from the chiles, and mince them.

Once the peanuts are cool, coarsely grind them in a food processor.

In a sauté pan, melt the butter over medium heat. Add the garlic and sauté for about 45 seconds, then add the red bell pepper and the chipotles and sauté for about 2 minutes. Add the pork and stock and bring to a simmer. Add the olives, cilantro, and peanuts and heat through. Season with salt and pepper, and remove from the heat. Add the lime juice, and set aside.

to finish the dough

Return the chilled *masa* to the mixer. Using the paddle attachment, beat the dough until it is soft again. Slowly add the chicken stock, beating until the dough is light and fluffy. Wrap the dough in plastic wrap and let rest at room temperature for 30 minutes, then refrigerate for 30 minutes.

to assemble the tamales

Pull apart a few corn husks so that you have strings for tying up the ends (you can also use butcher's string for this). Lay a corn husk flat on your work surface. Spread about 2 tablespoons of the *masa* dough down the center of the husk. Spoon a tablespoon of the pork mixture on top of the *masa,* and top that with about 2 tablespoons more *masa,* spreading it over the pork mixture, so it is sandwiched in the dough.

Fold the top of the husk over the *tamal,* then fold the sides of the husk over, and, finally, fold the bottom over, enclosing the dough completely. Secure the *tamal* by tying one or two corn husk strings around it, just as you would a ribbon on a package. Repeat the process until all the tamales are made.

Fill a deep steamer pot with an inch or so of water; there should be 1 inch between the water and the bottom of the steamer insert. Set the tamales on the steamer rack, place it in the pot, and cover tightly. (You can stack the tamales, but allow them more time to cook.) Steam over medium-high heat for about 1 hour, replenishing the water as necessary. You'll know the tamales are done when the husks pull easily away from them. Let them rest for 5 minutes before serving. Open and enjoy.

note: Dried corn husks are available at some grocery stores and at ethnic and gourmet food markets; you can substitute banana leaves, which are usually available frozen.

recommended wine: A mineral-layered wine such as a German Kabinett Riesling, or, in a different direction, try a sangria.

tamales

I love to pack a little basket of food before getting on a plane. My wife, Janet, and I call them our "sky picnics." In Mexico City, on our way to the airport, we once bought a few dozen tamales from a small Indian woman. They were heavenly, just plain, out of the paper bag. Our fellow travelers, poor things, were chewing on factory-made pretzels.

In the New World's sacred and lay cults of maize, tamales play a key role (their name derives from the Aztecs' Náhuatl word *tamalli*). These wondrous bundles are found from Chicago to Patagonia, in all shapes and sizes, filled with seasoned chicken, beef, or pork, olives, raisins, and chile peppers, varying from country to country, depending on the local taste for heat. (Despite the Old West expression "hot tamales," many tamales are not at all spicy, but rather corn-sweet in their dough and fairly mild in their stuffings. If you want to add hot sauce, well, that's another story.) Sometimes only a dab of lard is used as the filling; more and more, modern chefs are incorporating fillings that include foie gras, smoked salmon, and truffles.

Masa harina (literally, "dough flour") is the common denominator in making most tamales. The flour comes from dried *masa,* which is to say it is made with sun- or fire-dried corn kernels that have been cooked in lime-infused water, then soaked overnight. The next day the wet corn is ground into doughy *masa*.

Once they are filled, tamales are typically wrapped in corn husks, but you also see them wrapped in banana or avocado leaves, depending on what is available locally. Then they are tied up and usually steamed, though some cooks bake them. You never eat the wrapper, but you'll find yourself scraping it with the side of a spoon so as not to leave behind one morsel.

Tamale sizes vary. In Colombia, tiny Popayan *tamalitos* are stuffed with pipián; in Peru, tamales are less-than-delicate one-pounders, and one makes an entire meal. The aristocrat of the tamale family is Venezuela's hallaca. Its fine-grain cornmeal, savory stuffing, and medium build make it an ideal appetizer and a popular dish at Christmastime.

piononos

(Stuffed Savory Plantain Pinwheels)

MAKES 32 TO 34 *PIONONOS*

Piononos are a Puerto Rican specialty that probably came to the island by way of Argentina and Italy. Pope Pius IX, or "Pio Nono," as he was both affectionately and not so affectionately known, was a glutton who loved a cake with cream inside, somewhat like a jelly roll; thus the Vatican cooks renamed the cake for him. Italian immigrants brought *piononos* to Argentina in the 1900s, and there different renditions were created, some sweet, some savory. Here I use pork, and I bake the *piononos* instead of the more traditional method of deep-frying, to reduce some of the fat.

2 tablespoons pure olive oil

1 tablespoon unsalted butter

1 teaspoon minced, seeded Scotch bonnet chile

2 cloves garlic, minced

1 scallion, green and white parts, minced

$^1/_2$ medium Spanish onion, diced

1 red bell pepper, stemmed, seeded, and diced

1 poblano pepper, stemmed, seeded, and diced

$^1/_2$ cup chopped cilantro

12 ounces ground pork

2 teaspoons toasted and ground cumin seeds
     (see page 9)

Kosher salt and freshly ground black pepper to
     taste

8 large plantains—yellow but starting to turn
     black

$^1/_2$ cup canola or peanut oil

$^1/_2$ cup finely grated Manchego cheese

Heat the oil and butter in a large skillet over medium-low heat. Add the Scotch bonnet and garlic and stir for 15 seconds. Add the scallion, onion, bell pepper, poblano, and cilantro. Sauté over medium-high heat, for 4 minutes, or until the vegetables are soft and aromatic. Stir in the pork and cumin and cook, stirring frequently, until the pork is cooked through, about 5 minutes. Season with salt and pepper, and set aside.

Peel the plantains and slice them lengthwise into $^1/_2$-inch-thick strips. In a 12-inch nonstick skillet, heat the oil over medium-high heat until it is hot but not smoking. Sauté the plantains in batches of 3, without crowding, until golden brown, 1 to 2 minutes on each side; be sure not to get them too dark, or they'll turn brittle. Transfer the plantain slices to paper towels to drain.

Preheat the oven to 400 degrees.

When the plantain strips are cool enough to handle, one at a time, spread each strip with a thin layer of pork filling. Roll it up—it will look like pinwheel—and secure with a toothpick. Place the *piononos* on a parchment-lined baking sheet and top with the grated cheese.

Place the *piononos* in the oven for 10 minutes, or until heated through. Transfer to plates and serve.

recommended wine or beer: An assertive white wine from Spain or a microbrewed Pilsner beer.

snapper *escabeche*–stuffed tacos
(Tacos Stuffed with Seared and Marinated Snapper)

MAKES 10 TACOS

There are many kinds of snapper. I like the delicate yellowtail variety, which has a nice texture. Yellowtail is a somewhat thin snapper compared to other varieties, such as American red or mutton; if you have thicker fillets, the cooking period will be slightly longer. As always when selecting fish, let freshness be your guide.

1 to 1 ¹/₂ pounds skinless snapper fillets
4 teaspoons *Escabeche* Spice Rub (page 266)
2 tablespoons canola or peanut oil

FOR THE MARINADE
4 cloves garlic, thinly sliced
³/₄ cup thinly sliced red onion
¹/₂ cup torn cilantro leaves
6 tablespoons gold tequila
¹/₄ cup Spanish sherry vinegar
¹/₄ cup fresh lime juice
¹/₄ cup fresh orange juice
¹/₄ cup virgin olive oil

FOR THE DRESSING AND SALSA
1 tablespoon Spanish sherry vinegar
¹/₃ cup pure olive oil
1 tablespoon fresh orange juice
³/₄ teaspoon kosher salt
1 ¹/₄ teaspoons freshly ground black pepper
4 handfuls mixed lettuces, washed and dried
¹/₂ cup diced papaya
¹/₂ cup diced pineapple
¹/₂ cup diced mango
1 cup diced avocado
¹/₄ cup minced red onion

Canola or peanut oil for shallow-frying
10 blue corn or regular corn taco shells

Lay the fish fillets on a platter and rub them on one side with the spice rub.

In a nonstick sauté pan or a well-seasoned cast-iron skillet, heat the canola oil until smoking hot. Sear the fish fillets for about 40 seconds per side, shaking the pan constantly so the fish does not stick. Transfer the fillets to a plate and allow them to cool.

For the marinade: Mix together the garlic, onion, cilantro, tequila, vinegar, lime and orange juices, and olive oil in a large shallow bowl.

Slide the seared fish into the marinade. Refrigerate, covered—the marinating time will vary depending on the thickness of the fish. Check it periodically; it will generally take from between 1 and 3 hours. It is ready when the fish is opaque throughout.

Remove the fish fillets from the marinade, gently brushing off any excess liquid. Slice the fillets into "fingers" 1 ¹/₄ to 1 ¹/₂ inches thick.

Shortly before serving, make the dressing and salsa: In a small bowl, whisk together the vinegar, olive oil, orange juice, salt, and pepper. Put the lettuces in another bowl and pour on just enough dressing to coat. In a third bowl, combine the papaya, pineapple, mango, avocado, and onion, and pour on the rest of the dressing. Set aside.

to make the taco shells

Pour about $^1/_8$ inch of canola oil into a sauté pan and heat over medium-high heat. When the oil is quite hot but not smoking, set a tortilla in the pan for a scant 5 seconds. Using tongs, flip the tortilla over and cook for another 5 seconds (this softens the tortilla just enough). Flip it again, fold it in half, and heat for just 7 seconds, or until crisp. Flip it again and heat for 7 seconds, then remove and drain on paper towels. Repeat with the remaining tortillas.

Fill the taco shells with the fish, lettuces, and salsa. Serve immediately.

recommended drink: Libardo's Pisco Sour (page 300) would be just perfect.

tacu-tacu

(Bean and Rice Cakes with Smoked Salmon)

SERVES 8 (MAKES 16 TO 18 CAKES)

The name of this humorous-sounding dish comes from a translation of a Quechua word that means "when things are mixed up." *Tacu-tacu* is indeed that; despite its Indian name, it is African in origin, brought to Peru by slaves. Even its preparation has layers of meaning. The way they see it in Peru, the bottom layer is the *cama,* or "bed," followed by the *sabana*—the "bedsheet"—often a pounded piece of pork or beef. Topping this delightful dish is a fried egg, the *cabeza,* or "head," which rests on a *cojin* ("pillow") of plantain.

Lately, many chefs in Peru have been creating new variations on this specialty. My version combines the rusticity of the basic *tacu-tacu* with a rice and bean bed and, instead of the plantain and fried egg, garnishes of smoked salmon, minced red onion, and sour cream.

Canary Beans are pale yellow, medium-sized beans, native to Peru. They can be found in Latin and specialty markets.

4 cloves garlic, minced
1 Scotch bonnet chile, stemmed, seeded, and minced
1 tablespoon Annatto Oil (page 261)
8 ounces dried canary beans, rinsed, soaked overnight in water to cover, and drained
2 cups cooked rice
1/4 cup Roasted Garlic Oil (page 262) or pure olive oil
1 large red onion, diced
1 large ripe tomato, diced
1 tablespoon toasted and ground cumin seeds (see page 9)

Kosher salt and freshly ground black pepper to taste
2 extra-large eggs, beaten
3 tablespoons chopped cilantro

FOR THE GARNISH
16 to 18 thin slices smoked salmon
1/2 small red onion, minced
1/2 cup sour cream

With a mortar and pestle, make a paste of the garlic, Scotch bonnet, and annatto oil. Reserve.

Put the beans in a large pot and add water to cover by 2 inches. Bring to a boil, reduce the heat, and simmer until the beans are tender, about 1 1/2 hours. Drain and set aside to cool.

Mash the beans with a fork to make a coarse puree. Add the rice to the beans and mash to combine.

Preheat the oven to 400 degrees.

In a large nonstick skillet, heat 1 1/2 tablespoons of the roasted garlic oil over medium-high heat. Add the onion and chile paste and cook for 3 minutes. Add the tomato, cumin, and salt and pepper and cook, stirring, for 3 more minutes. Stir into the beans and rice. Stir in the beaten eggs and cilantro. Season with salt and pepper.

In another large nonstick skillet, heat 1 1/2 tablespoons of the garlic oil. When it is hot but not smoking, scoop the bean mixture, 1/4 cup per cake, into the pan; add only as many as will fit without overcrowding. When the cakes are dark golden brown and crispy on the bottom, turn them over with a spatula and cook until browned on the second side. Transfer to a baking sheet lined with parchment paper. Repeat with the rest of the mixture, using more oil as needed. Bake the cakes for 15 minutes to heat them through. Transfer to plates and garnish with smoked salmon, minced red onion, and dollops of sour cream.

recommended wine: A light, refreshing, fruity, herbal white wine, such as Vidal Blanc, or an easier-to-find Sancerre from the Loire.

soups and stews

It seems like a long time ago, but I used to be somewhat shy about going into new restaurants and trying unfamiliar foods. When I moved to Key West in 1973, I happened upon a little spot on lower Duval Street called El Cacique. The portrait of a fierce-looking Indian hung over its door, and the people who frequented "The Chief" were the shopkeepers, cops, fishermen, and other such denizens of the funky island town.

I walked past the restaurant one day just as the door opened, and the aroma of Cuban cooking wafted my way. The smells of cumin, garlic, pork, beans, and citrus were so heavenly as to allow me to overcome my shyness and take a seat at the counter. A pretty waitress asked me in Spanish what I was having. When I asked her what smelled so good, she smiled, switched to English, and said, "Maybe you smell the *caldo gallego.*" She brought me a steaming bowl full of the *caldo* and a side order of toasted Cuban bread. White beans dominated the bowl, but the flavors of beef, pork, chicken stock, potatoes, and garlic also competed for my attention. As I ate, I forgot the world outside the door of the restaurant, and as I finished sopping up the last of my *caldo* with the bread, the Cuban waitress sized me up and said, "I guess you will be back."

The hearty peasant soups of Spain—*caldo gallego* from Galicia, *favada Asturiana* from Asturias, *caldereta* from Catalonia, *cocido* from Castile—were created in cold, harsh, windy climates as a way to nourish the inhabitants in the winter months. These soups and stews were meals in themselves. The same can be said of the fish and seafood soups and stews indigenous to the north coast of

Spain, on the stormy Cantabrian Sea, which were created both by fishermen aboard their vessels and by their wives at home. In contrast, what could be more appropriate in the hot, dry southern climate of Andalusia than *gazpacho,* the cold soup of Moorish origin.

Their soups and stews traveled with the Spaniards and the Portuguese to the New World, where the immigrants encountered the same range of climates and terrain they'd known at home. In the harsh, barren snow-capped highlands of the Andes, a Spanish-Indian *mestizo* branch of soups developed: *cocidos* in Venezuela and Peru; *ajiaco* and *cuchuco* in Colombia; *chupes* in Peru and Chile.

The New World's equatorial belt developed its own versions of many of the Old World soups and stews, with a pragmatic and intelligent reliance on regional ingredients, such as tubers and fish. One Caribbean housewife explained the appeal of soups: "To revive the spirit and regain the strength lost in strenuous domestic chores," she said, "they are the fastest way."

fish chowder

SERVES 10 TO 12

This chowder is hearty enough to be the main course at lunch or dinner. As with many soups, it actually improves if prepared a day ahead of time, which makes it an ideal party dish.

I like to offer it with a shot of dry sherry at the table, as the liquor really rounds out the flavors. Because the chowder is a touch spicy, serve it with warm bread and butter.

2 ounces smoky bacon, diced

$^1/_4$ cup pure olive oil

4 cloves garlic, sliced

1 Scotch bonnet chile, stemmed, seeded, and minced

1 medium Spanish onion, diced

4 stalks celery, diced

1 carrot, peeled and diced

1 small fennel bulb, cored and diced

1 yellow bell pepper, stemmed, seeded, and cut into medium dice

1 tablespoon crushed red pepper

4 cups crushed, peeled plum tomatoes

2 cups homemade or prepared tomato sauce

10 cups Blue Crab Stock (page 272)

3 bay leaves, broken in half

2 tablespoons chopped fresh thyme

2 tablespoons chopped fresh basil

2 $^1/_4$ pounds fish fillets, such as snapper, grouper, sole, and/or cod, cut into bite-sized pieces

2 $^1/_4$ pounds red potatoes, scrubbed, cut into bite-sized pieces, boiled until tender, and drained

Tabasco (optional)

In the largest soup pot or Dutch oven you have, cook the bacon in the olive oil over medium-low heat until beginning to crisp. Add the garlic and Scotch bonnet and cook for 30 seconds. Turn up the heat to medium-high, add the onion, celery, carrot, fennel, and yellow bell pepper, and stir to coat. Cook, stirring occasionally, to caramelize the vegetables, 8 to 12 minutes.

Stir in the crushed red pepper, then add the tomatoes, tomato sauce, stock, bay leaves, and herbs. Bring to a simmer, then reduce the heat and add the fish and potatoes. Cook for 10 minutes more, or until the fish is just cooked through.

Add Tabasco to taste, if desired, and serve.

recommended wine: An Alsatian Pinot Blanc with good intensity or an off-dry Riesling from Washington State.

black bean soup
with roasted squash

SERVES 6 (MAKES 12 CUPS)

I've served this classic simple soup for decades. With the addition of the West Indian pumpkin known as *calabaza* and a coriander-lime *crema*, it becomes a little more complex and satisfying. Use the time the beans take to cook to prepare the *calabaza* and *crema*.

6 ounces smoky bacon, diced

2 tablespoons pure olive oil

1 Scotch bonnet chile, stemmed, seeded, and minced

3 cloves garlic, thinly sliced

1 large Spanish onion, diced

1 red bell pepper, stemmed, seeded, and diced

3 stalks celery, diced

2 tablespoons toasted and ground cumin seeds (see page 9)

2 bay leaves, broken in half

1 cup Spanish dry sherry

2 cups black beans, rinsed, soaked overnight in water to cover, and drained

1 smoked ham hock

3 quarts Chicken Stock (page 267)

Kosher salt and freshly ground black pepper to taste

FOR THE *CALABAZA*

2 pounds *calabaza*, peeled, seeded, and cut into bite-sized pieces (you can substitute acorn or another winter squash)

2 tablespoons unsalted butter, melted

2 tablespoons sugar

1 teaspoon kosher salt

1/2 teaspoon freshly ground black pepper

FOR THE *CREMA*

1 cup sour cream

1 1/2 teaspoons fresh lime juice

1/4 teaspoon kosher salt

1/2 teaspoon toasted and ground coriander seeds (see page 9)

to prepare the beans,

cook the bacon in the olive oil in a large soup pot over medium heat until beginning to crisp. Stir in the Scotch bonnet and garlic. Turn up the heat to medium-high, add the onion, bell pepper, and celery, and stir to coat. Let the vegetables caramelize, stirring occasionally, for about 10 minutes.

Add the cumin, bay leaves, and sherry, bring to a simmer, and simmer until the liquid is reduced by half, 4 to 5 minutes. Add the beans, ham hock, and stock and bring to a simmer. Skim the impurities off the top, reduce the heat to medium-low, and simmer until the beans are tender but not mushy, 1 to 1 1/2 hours.

In the meantime, prepare the *calabaza*: Pre-heat the oven to 350 degrees.

Combine the *calabaza,* butter, sugar, salt, and pepper in a roasting pan or heavy oven-proof skillet and give them a toss. Roast for 30 to 40 minutes, until the squash is tender when poked with a knife. Set aside in a warm place.

For the *crema:* Whisk together all the ingredients in a bowl. Chill until ready to serve.

Remove the bay leaves from the beans. Scoop 2 $^1/_2$ cups of the beans and their broth into a blender, and puree. Pour back into the pot—this will give the soup more body—stir well, and simmer for another 30 minutes.

Season the soup with salt and pepper. Fold in the *calabaza* and cook for 5 more minutes.

Ladle the soup into bowls and finish with a spoonful of *crema* in each.

recommended wine: A spicy Côtes du Rhône or a fino sherry.

barley *cuchuco* with pork back ribs

SERVES 12 (MAKES 20 CUPS)

Barley *cuchuco* is barley that has been coarsely ground, and *cuchuco* is the name the Chibcha Indians in the highlands of Colombia have given to this hearty, peasant soup, made with barley or wheat. In Colombia, cooks use pork spine to supply the soup with some meat and a whole lot of flavor. I substitute the more readily available pork spareribs.

I use Colombian garnishes: diced tomatoes, avocados, chopped cilantro, and/or minced chiles.

2 pounds spareribs, membranes removed and
    cut into 2- to 3-inch pieces (ask your
    butcher to do this)
Kosher salt and freshly ground black pepper
2 tablespoons pure olive oil
1 tablespoon unsalted butter
6 cloves garlic, thinly sliced
1 large Spanish onion, diced
2 large carrots, peeled and diced
2 bay leaves, broken in half
3 ½ quarts Pork Stock (page 270) or Chicken
    Stock (page 267)
4 ounces coarse-ground barley
2 cups shucked fava beans
8 ounces new potatoes, scrubbed and cut into
    bite-sized pieces
1 pound small yellow potatoes, scrubbed and
    cut into bite-sized pieces
8 ounces cabbage, sliced
2 cups green peas, cooked in boiling salted
    water until tender
½ cup cilantro leaves, torn, for garnish
    (optional; see headnote)

Season the meat with salt and pepper; set aside.

In a large pot, heat the olive oil and butter over medium-high heat. Add the garlic, onion, and carrots, season with salt and pepper, and cook for 5 minutes. Push the vegetables aside and brown the meat. Add the bay leaf, 10 cups of the stock, the pork, and barley and bring to a low boil, then lower the heat and simmer for 1 hour, or until the meat is tender. Skim; stir so the *cuchuco* doesn't stick to the bottom.

Meanwhile, for the fava beans, bring a pot of water to a boil and blanch the beans for 1 minute. Drain and run cold water over them to cool. Using your fingernail, break the outer skin of the beans, and squeeze the beans out between your forefinger and thumb. Cook the beans in boiling salted water until tender, 4 to 5 minutes. Drain and set aside.

Remove the pork from the pot and cut it into small pieces (or remove it from the bones, if you prefer). Return to the pot. Add the remaining 4 cups stock, the potatoes, and cabbage. Season with salt and pepper and simmer, uncovered, over medium heat for 20 to 30 minutes, until the potatoes are tender.

Cover and cook over low heat for 7 minutes. Add the peas and fava beans, give the soup a stir, cover, and cook for another 4 minutes.

Ladle into bowls and garnish with the cilantro, if desired.

recommended wine: A red from Cahors in the southwest of France.

caldo gallego
(White Bean Soup with Mixed Meats and Vegetables)

SERVES 8 (MAKES 20 CUPS)

Caldos, as soups like this one are called, are served all over the Caribbean, but their roots are in Spain and Portugal. The word *caldo* derives from the Latin root word for "cauldron." This particular *caldo,* common in Puerto Rico, came from Spain's northwestern province of Galicia, hence the name *gallego.* But the soup is also filled with multicultural influences from the cuisines of Portugal, West Africa, the Caribbean's Taíno Indians, and South America.

3 tablespoons pure olive oil

8 ounces chorizo or other spicy sausage, pricked in a few places with a fork

2 tablespoons unsalted butter

6 cloves garlic, thinly sliced

1 Scotch bonnet chile, stemmed, seeded, and minced

2 poblano peppers, stemmed, seeded, and minced

1 large red onion, diced

One 12- to 14-ounce bag dried white beans, rinsed, soaked overnight in water to cover, and drained

3 quarts Chicken Stock (page 267)

2 smoked ham hocks or 1 ham bone

2 bay leaves, broken in half

Kosher salt and freshly ground black pepper to taste

1 rutabaga (about 1 pound), peeled and cut into bite-sized pieces

About 1 pound red potatoes, scrubbed and cut into bite-sized pieces

2 cups packed spinach or *callaloo*, stems removed, thoroughly washed, and shredded

Heat the olive oil in a large heavy soup pot over medium heat. When the oil is warm but not hot, add the chorizo and cook until it is nicely browned. Transfer it to paper towels to drain and cool for a few minutes, then refrigerate while you cook the rest of the soup ingredients.

Melt the butter in the same pot over medium heat. Add the garlic, chiles, and red onion and cook for 7 to 8 minutes, stirring occasionally. Add the drained beans, stock, ham hocks, and bay leaves, turn up the heat, and bring to just under a boil, skimming the impurities from the top as necessary. Lower the heat and cook, uncovered, for 1 to 1 1/2 hours, until the beans are almost tender. Stir the soup occasionally, taking care not to let the beans stick to the bottom.

Season the soup with salt and pepper. Add the rutabaga and simmer, uncovered, for 10 minutes. Add the potato and cook for about 20 minutes more, until the root vegetables are just tender. Add the spinach and cook for 5 minutes.

Cut the chorizo into 1/2-inch rounds, and add it to the soup. Remove the ham hocks and bay leaves and discard. Season to taste and serve.

recommended wine: Sangria or a Pinot Grigio, or, if you can get one, a Spanish white from the Costa Brava.

chupe de camarones
(Shrimp Soup with Bass, Potatoes, Corn, and Rice)

SERVES 6 (MAKES 8 CUPS)

If you've traveled to New Orleans, you may have encountered the local tradition of eating shrimp and crawfish by sucking on the crustaceans in order to get to the most flavorful bits (i.e., the best fatty parts). In Peru they do this too, and they even have a word for it: *chupe* (pronounced *shoo-pay*), which gives this dish its name. In the most rustic presentations of *chupe de camarones,* you may be served the shrimp or crab still in their shells, along with pieces of corn on the cob. In my version of this recipe, I've made the ingredients a little easier to eat.

In Peru, this *chupe* would be served with an herb called *huacatay,* or "black mint." You can find it in the United States in specialty markets in jars, but I don't really like the taste, so I've omitted it. And while the traditional version of the soup doesn't include bass, I couldn't resist putting some in.

1 pound sea bass fillets, cut into $1/4$-inch-thick medallions

Kosher salt and freshly ground black pepper to taste

$1/4$ cup all-purpose flour

1 tablespoon unsalted butter

$1/4$ cup pure olive oil

2 cloves garlic, sliced

1 Scotch bonnet chile, stemmed, seeded, and minced

1 large Spanish onion, finely chopped

2 large ripe tomatoes, peeled, seeded, and chopped

$1 1/2$ pounds new potatoes, scrubbed and cut into $1/2$-inch-thick rounds

8 cups Chicken Stock (page 267)

$1/2$ cup long-grain white rice

1 pound shrimp, peeled, deveined, and cut into bite-sized pieces

1 cup corn kernels

1 cup heavy cream

$1/4$ cup chopped fresh basil

$1 1/2$ tablespoons white wine vinegar

6 extra-large eggs

Season the sea bass with salt and pepper and dredge it in the flour; shake off the excess. In a large nonstick skillet, heat the butter and 2 tablespoons of the oil. Sear the fish over medium-high heat, turning once, until golden on both sides. Drain on paper towels; reserve.

In a large soup pot, heat the remaining 2 tablespoons oil over medium-high heat. Add the garlic and Scotch bonnet and sauté for about 45 seconds, then add the onion and sauté until soft, about 3 minutes. Add the tomatoes, season with salt and pepper, and sauté for another 3 minutes.

Add the potatoes, chicken stock, and rice and bring to a simmer, then reduce the heat to medium and cook until the rice is tender, about 10 to 15 minutes.

Add the browned sea bass, the shrimp, and corn kernels and simmer for another 3 to 4 minutes until the shrimp are cooked. Stir in the cream and basil and season with salt and pepper. Bring the soup just to a simmer, then turn off the heat.

In a small skillet, bring about 4 inches of water to a simmer, and add the vinegar. Gently drop in the eggs 2 at a time and poach for about 2 minutes, until firm enough to lift out with a slotted spoon.

Gently drop a poached egg into the center of each soup bowl. Ladle about a cup of soup into each, and serve.

recommended wine: A white from Cassis in Provence.

sopa de mariscos
(Seafood Soup)

SERVES 8 (MAKES ABOUT 12 CUPS)

With coastlines on both the Pacific and the Caribbean, plus a large system of rivers and lakes, Nicaragua has earned a reputation for excellent seafood dishes such as this fish-and-crab soup. It is customary to see *sopa de mariscos* garnished with split whole crabs and rounds of corn on the cob, making for a rather rustic presentation. The cheese added at the end is optional, but I think it lends just the right note of earthiness in this ode to the sea.

The recipe calls for 10 ears of corn, because you need 10 corn cobs to give the broth its flavor, but you will have some corn kernels left over for another dish.

8 ounces smoky bacon, cut into small dice
2 tablespoons pure olive oil
3 tablespoons unsalted butter
8 cloves garlic, sliced
1 medium Spanish onion, roughly chopped
1 large carrot, peeled and roughly chopped
2 large stalks celery, roughly chopped
8 live blue crabs, cut in half (ask your fishmonger to do this)
$^3/_4$ cup bourbon
8 cups water
2 bay leaves, broken in half
8 cups Chicken Stock (page 267)
10 ears corn, husked and kernels removed; reserve the cobs
4 cups heavy cream
1 pound yuca, peeled and cut lengthwise in half and then into 1-inch half-moons
1 $^1/_2$ teaspoons freshly ground black pepper, or more to taste
1 $^1/_2$ teaspoons kosher salt, or more to taste
12 ounces white cabbage, halved lengthwise and cut into thin wedges
10 ounces fish fillets, such as wahoo or snapper, cut into 1 $^1/_2$-inch-thick medallions
$^1/_3$ cup diced or crumbled *queso blanco*, for garnish (optional)

handy to cover the pot in case that happens). Add the water and bay leaves, cover, and steam the crabs for 8 minutes. Uncover and reduce the liquid to about 1 $1/2$ cups, skimming off impurities as they rise to the top.

Add the chicken stock and corncobs and bring to a simmer, then reduce the heat to medium-low and cook for 30 minutes. Strain the broth; reserve the 8 largest crab halves.

Pour the broth back into the pot, add the cream, yuca, salt, and pepper, and bring to a simmer. Simmer for 15 minutes. Add the cabbage and cook for another 15 minutes. Add 2 cups of the corn kernels (reserve the rest for another dish) and the fish and cook for 10 minutes more. Add the reserved crab pieces, bring the soup to a simmer, and remove from the heat. Adjust the seasoning.

Ladle into bowls, garnish with the *queso blanco,* if desired, and serve.

recommended wine: A Viognier from California or southern France.

In a soup pot, cook the bacon in the olive oil over medium heat until beginning to crisp. Melt the butter, add the garlic, and cook for 30 seconds. Turn the heat up to medium-high, add the onion, carrot, and celery, and stir to coat. Cook for 5 minutes. Add the crabs, then pour in the bourbon and deglaze the pot, stirring to burn off the alcohol and cooking until there is almost no liquid left in the pot (be careful: the whiskey may flame; have a lid

lentil soup

SERVES 6 (MAKES 10 CUPS)

Latin America inherited Spain's nearly fanatical reverence for hearty soups and stews. This lentil soup is very simple but utterly delicious.

2 tablespoons olive oil

4 ounces smoky bacon, diced

1 medium Spanish onion, diced

3 cloves garlic, thinly sliced

1 medium carrot, peeled and diced

1 large ripe tomato, peeled, seeded, and diced

12 ounces lentils, rinsed, soaked for 2 hours in water to cover, and drained

7 cups Pork Stock (page 270), Beef Stock (page 268), or Chicken Stock (page 267)

Kosher salt and freshly ground black pepper to taste

Heat the oil in a medium soup pot. Add the bacon and cook over medium heat until beginning to color. Add the onion, garlic, and carrot and cook for 5 minutes. Add the tomato and cook for another 2 minutes.

Add the lentils and stock and season with salt and pepper. Bring to a boil, then turn the heat to low and simmer, covered, for 45 to 55 minutes, or until the lentils are tender. Serve.

recommended wine: A dry oloroso sherry from Jerez in Spain to match the earthiness of the lentils.

sopa de pavo
(Turkey Soup)

SERVES 10 (MAKES 16 CUPS)

Nearly half the meat in this soup comes from the neck of the turkey, an unsung poultry part that, given its size, packs more than its share of flavor. I sometimes garnish this with Basic White Rice (page 196) or the cheese-topped cornmeal pancakes called *Arepas* (page 220).

2 1/2 pounds turkey legs and/or thighs, rinsed and patted dry

2 pounds turkey neck, rinsed and patted dry

Kosher salt and freshly ground black pepper

3 tablespoons pure olive oil

4 tablespoons unsalted butter

6 cloves garlic, sliced

1 large Spanish onion, diced

5 large stalks celery, diced

3 large carrots, peeled and diced

1 small fennel bulb, cored and diced

1 cup dry white wine

3 quarts Chicken Stock (page 267)

3 sprigs thyme, plus 2 tablespoons chopped thyme

2 bay leaves, broken in half

1 1/2 cups green peas, blanched in boiling salted water until tender

Season the turkey pieces all over with salt and pepper. Heat the olive oil in a large soup pot or Dutch oven over medium-high heat. When it is quite hot, add the turkey pieces, in batches, and brown them on all sides, about 10 minutes. Transfer them to a platter.

Add the butter, then add the garlic, onion, celery, carrots, and fennel and stir to coat. Season with salt and pepper and cook until the vegetables are caramelized, 10 to 15 minutes, being careful not to scorch the bottom of the pot. Transfer the vegetables to a bowl and reserve.

Add the wine to the pot and deglaze it, scraping the bottom with a wooden spoon. Return the turkey to the pot and pour in the stock. Bring to a simmer, then lower the heat and skim any impurities that have risen to the top. Add the thyme sprigs and bay leaves, season with salt and pepper, cover, and simmer for 1 1/2 to 2 hours, or until the turkey is tender. The necks will probably take longer, so remove the legs and/or thighs when they are done and transfer to a platter to cool; cook the necks for another 20 to 30 minutes, then transfer to the platter.

Strain the broth through a fine-mesh strainer into a clean pot. Add the chopped thyme, stir, and keep warm over medium-low heat.

When the turkey is cool enough to handle, take it off the bones, pulling it apart with your fingers, then cut it into bite-sized pieces. Put the meat back in the broth, along with the reserved vegetables and the peas, and season with additional salt and pepper if necessary. Bring back to a simmer. Serve.

recommended wine: Either a Chassagne-Montrachet or a Sonoma Coast Chardonnay.

tortilla soup with sugarcane-marinated chicken

SERVES 8 (MAKES ABOUT 14 CUPS)

This dish combines Caribbean-flavored chicken with one of the classic soups of Mexico. Simple, nourishing, and restorative, it can be made well in advance—in fact, the chicken must marinate overnight—but the soup should be *assembled* at the table so that the guests fully experience its magical textures. Serve the soup in shallow bowls, so that the tortilla chips keep their crispness.

One 3- to 4-pound chicken, cut into serving
    pieces
Kosher salt and freshly ground black pepper to
    taste
$^1/_2$ recipe Sugarcane Marinade (page 281)
$^1/_2$ cup Roasted Garlic Oil (page 262) or pure
    olive oil
6 cloves garlic, thinly sliced
2 jalapeño or serrano chiles, stemmed, seeded,
    and minced
9 cups Chicken Stock (page 267)
4 to 5 corn tortillas, cut into very thin strips
2 avocados, pitted, peeled, and (at the last
    moment) diced
2 poblano peppers, roasted (see page 7),
    stemmed, seeded, and diced
40 grape tomatoes, quartered, or 20 cherry
    tomatoes, each cut into 6 to 8 wedges
$^1/_4$ cup chopped cilantro sprigs
8 lime wedges (optional)
Sour cream for garnish

Season the chicken pieces with salt and pepper. Place them in a large resealable plastic bag and pour in 1 $^1/_2$ cups of the marinade. Seal the bag and shake to coat the chicken well. Refrigerate overnight to marinate.

The next day, preheat the oven to 350 degrees.

Take the chicken out of the marinade and place it in a roasting pan. Cook for 25 to 35 minutes, until the juices run clear when you pierce the thigh. Let cool slightly.

When the chicken is just cool enough to handle, remove the meat from the bones, and shred it with your fingers (you should get 3 to 4 cups). Season with salt and pepper, transfer to a saucepan, and toss with the remaining $^3/_4$ cup marinade. Cook, stirring occasionally to prevent sticking, until the liquid reduces to the consistency of a stew, 10 to 20 minutes. Set aside.

Pour 2 tablespoons of the garlic oil into a heavy pot over very low heat, add the garlic, and slowly sauté for about 10 minutes, making sure the garlic doesn't brown. Add the jalapeños and cook for 30 seconds. Pour in the chicken stock and bring to a simmer. Season with salt and pepper, turn off the heat, and cover to keep warm.

Heat $^1/_4$ cup of the garlic oil in a large heavy skillet until hot. Scatter in the tortilla strips and cook until crisp. Using a slotted spoon, transfer them to paper towels to drain. Season with salt and pepper and reserve.

In a bowl, toss the avocados, poblanos, tomatoes, and cilantro with the remaining 2 tablespoons oil. Season with salt and pepper.

Spoon the chicken into eight soup bowls, then sprinkle the avocado salad around it. Ladle the broth over the chicken and avocado mixture. Garnish with the corn tortilla strips and squeeze a lime wedge, if desired, into each bowl. Serve with sour cream on the side.

recommended wine: A dry fine sherry or a light Chardonnay from California.

ajiaco de pollo

(Chicken, Potato, and Vegetable Stew)

SERVES 10 (MAKES 16 CUPS)

I fell in love with my first *ajiaco* years ago in Key West. It was chock-full of meats and tubers and, at the time, I didn't realize there were other versions of this hearty soup, which is a cousin to chowder. A pretty Colombian woman later taught me this lighter version, made with chicken and three types of potatoes. The most important of those is the *papa criolla,* or yellow potato. Bright yellow, almost the color of an egg yolk, and packing a very high starch level, it gives the soup its vibrant color and creamy consistency. Also crucial to the *ajiaco* is its panoply of garnishes: avocado, sour cream, capers, and corn on the cob, sliced into rounds, so that you can eat it with your hands. In Colombia they sprinkle the soup with an herb called *guasca,* which grows wild in certain regions of the Andes. Fear not: I won't insist that you scour the continent in search of *guasca;* I've substituted oregano and cilantro.

3 tablespoons pure olive oil

4 boneless chicken breasts, skin-on

Kosher salt and freshly ground black pepper to taste

5 cloves garlic, minced

1 large Spanish onion, diced

1 large ripe tomato, peeled, seeded, and roughly chopped

1 1/2 pounds Yellow Finn or Yukon Gold potatoes, peeled and very thinly sliced

1 1/2 pounds white potatoes, peeled and very thinly sliced

10 cups Chicken Stock (page 267)

3 cups roughly chopped cleaned spinach leaves

3 ears corn, husked and cut into 1 1/2-inch rounds *or* kernels cut off the cobs

2 tablespoons minced oregano

FOR THE GARNISH

1/4 cup chopped cilantro

3 scallions, white and green parts, minced

1/4 cup minced capers

1 avocado, pitted, peeled, and diced

2 teaspoons fresh lime juice

1/4 cup heavy cream

Preheat the oven to 375 degrees.

Heat the olive oil in a large soup pot over medium-high heat. When it is very hot, season the chicken breasts with salt and pepper and sear, skin side down first, until golden on each side. Transfer the breasts to a baking pan (set the pot aside) and roast in the oven for 15 to 20 minutes, until cooked through. Transfer to a platter and cover, to keep warm.

Meanwhile, set the pot over medium heat, add the garlic, and sauté for about 30 seconds. Add the onion and cook for 5 minutes, then add the tomato and cook 3 more minutes. Add the potatoes and chicken stock, bring to a simmer, and cook until the potatoes are tender, 20 to 30 minutes.

Add the spinach, corn, and oregano to the soup, season with salt and pepper, and turn the heat to low. Cook gently for another 10 minutes while you set up your garnishes.

Bring out four small bowls. In one, combine the cilantro and minced scallions. Put the capers in another. In the third, toss the avocado with the lime juice. And in the fourth, whip the cream to soft peaks. Set aside.

Dice the chicken into $1/2$-inch cubes.

Pour the simmering soup into shallow soup bowls and garnish with the chicken, avocado, scallion-cilantro mixture, capers, and a drizzle of the whipped cream. Serve.

recommended wine: A rich, buttery Chardonnay from California or Chile.

carbonada en zapallo
(Veal Stew Served in a Pumpkin)

SERVES 8 TO 10

This recipe is an excellent example of the creativity and ingenuity common to cultures with a love of good food and a desire not to waste any of it. The meaty stew is served inside a hollowed-out pumpkin. Sometimes you will see this dish made with pasta rather than the potatoes used here.

Not only is it easier to make the veal stew a day in advance but doing so gives the flavors more time to marry.

1/2 cup all-purpose flour
Kosher salt and freshly ground black pepper to taste
2 pounds boneless veal for stew, cut into 1-inch cubes
1/2 cup Roasted Garlic Oil (page 262) or pure olive oil
1 1/2 cups dry white wine
2 cups Chicken Stock (page 267)
3 tablespoons unsalted butter, plus more as needed
1 Scotch bonnet chile, stemmed, seeded, and minced
4 cloves garlic, thinly sliced
1 large red onion, finely chopped
1 small fennel bulb, cored and finely chopped
1 red bell pepper, stemmed, seeded, and diced
1 large ripe tomato, peeled, seeded, and chopped small
3 tablespoons tomato paste
1 cup dry Madeira
1 pound red potatoes, peeled and cut into 1-inch cubes

1 pound sweet potatoes or *boniato*, peeled and cut into 1-inch cubes
2 zucchini, trimmed, cut lengthwise into 1-inch-thick strips, and halved
2 large pears or apples, peeled, cored, and sliced
3 large peaches, peeled, pitted, and sliced
Two 5- to 6-pound pumpkins (you can substitute winter squash, such as Hubbard, *kabocha*, butternut, or acorn; if using smaller squash, use 4, 1/2 per serving, and adjust the cooking time accordingly)
2 ears corn, husked and cut into 1-inch rounds

In a small bowl, season the flour with salt and pepper. Toss the veal in it, then put the meat into a colander and shake off the excess. Transfer to a plate.

Heat 1/4 cup of the garlic oil in a heavy skillet over high heat and sauté the veal, in batches if necessary, until nicely browned all over. Using a slotted spoon, transfer the veal to a bowl. Add the wine to the pan to deglaze it, scraping with a wooden spoon to release the browned bits of veal from the bottom. Add the chicken stock and bring to a boil, then set aside.

In a large heavy ovenproof pot, heat the remaining 1/4 cup oil and the 3 tablespoons butter over medium heat. Add the Scotch bonnet and garlic and cook for about 30 seconds. Add the onion, fennel, and bell pepper, season with salt and pepper, and cook until somewhat soft.

Add the tomato and tomato paste and cook

for about 3 minutes. Add the Madeira to deglaze the pot, then add the veal and the reserved chicken broth. Stir well. Add the potatoes, sweet potatoes, and zucchini and bring to a low simmer, then reduce the heat. Cover the stew with a round of parchment paper with a slit cut in the center and cook for 1 hour and 15 minutes. It is *very important* to keep the stew at a low simmer; look for slow steady bubbles. (Covering the pot with the parchment paper rather than a tight lid makes it less likely to burn.) The simmered veal should be almost fork-tender. Taste for seasoning.

Add the pears and peaches, cover again with the parchment paper, and cook for about 15 more minutes. Remove from the heat and allow to cool. Cover the pot and refrigerate, preferably overnight.

Preheat the oven to 350 degrees.

Meanwhile, clean the outside of the pumpkins. Cut them in half and scrape out the seeds and stringy fibers from each. Slice a very thin slice off the bottom of each so they will not wobble when you pour the soup into them. Lightly butter, salt, and pepper their insides.

Place them on a baking sheet, cut sides up, and bake until tender, about 1 1/2 hours. (Smaller squash can be cooked upside down, but not bigger squash—they might cave in!) Remove and set aside.

Meanwhile, bring a pot of lightly salted water to a boil. Blanch the corn rounds for 1 minute. Drain and keep warm.

Set the pot of stew over very low heat and slowly heat until hot, stirring from time to time.

Taste the stew and season, if needed, with salt and pepper. Transfer it to the cooked pumpkins. Top with the corn rounds. Carefully bring the filled pumpkins to the table, preparing yourself for the appreciative gasps of your guests, and serve.

recommended wine: A muscular white wine with good acidity, such as a Viognier from California or a French Marsanne; conversely, a Zinfandel from Sonoma would also work well.

cocido

(Stew of Pork, Potatoes, Cabbage, Squash, and Noodles)

SERVES 12 (MAKES 20 CUPS)

I once read that in Spain there are forty-nine provinces and forty-nine *cocidos* and that every one of them eventually made the journey to the New World. (In Brazil you find a close cousin called a *cozido*.) *Cocido* means "stew," and as is the case with so many stews, the cook has a lot of latitude when it comes to the ingredients that go into a *cocido*. This recipe includes egg noodles, which are certainly a late innovation.

2 tablespoons pure olive oil

2 tablespoons unsalted butter

⅓ cup thinly sliced garlic

2 large Spanish onions, chopped

2 large carrots, peeled and chopped

1 pound boneless pork, cut into 1-inch cubes

Kosher salt and freshly ground black pepper
    to taste

2 bay leaves, broken in half

¾ cup roughly chopped Italian parsley

2 medium ripe tomatoes, peeled, seeded,
    and chopped

⅔ cup dry white wine

1 ½ cups chickpeas, cooked and drained,
    1 cup of cooking liquid reserved

3 quarts Chicken Stock (page 267)

1 pork bone from the leg or shoulder or fresh
    ham hock (also known as pig's knuckle)

3 cups shredded green cabbage

1 pound new potatoes, peeled and cut into
    1-inch cubes

2 cups 1-inch cubes *calabaza* (or winter squash)

8 ounces medium egg noodles

Heat the oil and butter in a large soup pot over medium heat. Add the garlic, onions, and carrots and cook for 5 minutes. Stir, then push the vegetables to one side, raise the heat, and add the pork. Cook, turning the meat, until it loses its redness. Season with salt and pepper. Add the bay leaves, parsley, and tomatoes. Cook for a few minutes, then add the wine and bring to a boil. Add the stock, the 1 cup reserved chickpea liquid, and the pork bone and return to a simmer.

Add the cabbage, potatoes, and *calabaza* and bring just to a boil. Lower the heat and simmer for about 40 minutes, until the meat and vegetables are tender. About 5 minutes before the stew is done, add the noodles. When they are cooked, add the chickpeas and heat through. Season with salt and pepper.

Serve the *cocido* in large soup plates.

recommended wine: A straightforward Albariño from Rias Baixas in Spain or a Portuguese Vinho Verde.

guiso

(Corn and Clam Stew)

SERVES 8 TO 10 (MAKES 16 CUPS)

This could be called soup and probably would be in North America. In Latin America, however, they know it as a stew, so I include it in this section of the chapter. What is the difference? A few drops of liquid separate them physically, but their restorative natures make them kin.

Broken tortilla chips make a nice topping to this light yet very savory soup. The corn in the chips reinforces the corn in the stew very nicely.

2 tablespoons pure olive oil

4 ounces smoky bacon, diced

8 ounces chorizo or other spicy sausage, pierced in a few places with a fork

4 large cloves garlic, thinly sliced

1 Scotch bonnet chile, stemmed, seeded, and minced

1 medium Spanish onion, diced

1 red bell pepper, stemmed, seeded, and diced

1/2 cup Spanish dry sherry

3 ripe plum tomatoes, peeled, seeded, and diced

8 cups Chicken Stock (page 267)

1 tablespoon chopped fresh thyme

1/2 *boniato* or sweet potato (about 3/4 pound), peeled and cut into 1/2-inch dice

1 cup peeled *calabaza* (or winter squash) cut into 1/2-inch dice

Kosher salt and freshly ground black pepper to taste

4 cups corn kernels (from about 4 ears)

24 small clams, scrubbed

In a large saucepan, combine the oil and bacon over medium-high heat and cook until the bacon is about halfway done. Reduce the heat to low, add the chorizo, and cook until beginning to brown. Remove the chorizo from the pan and refrigerate it to firm it up.

Add the garlic and Scotch bonnet to the pan, stir, and let them flavor the oil for about 20 seconds. Turn up the heat, add the onion and red bell pepper, and let them caramelize, 10 to 12 minutes. Reduce the heat to medium-low, add the sherry, and cook for 1 1/2 minutes, or until most of the liquid has evaporated. Add the tomatoes, chicken stock, thyme, *boniato*, and *calabaza* and simmer until the vegetables are tender, about 20 minutes. Season with salt and pepper.

Turn the heat up to medium-high and add the corn, clams, and salt and pepper to taste. Cook, covered, until the clams have opened, about 3 to 5 minutes; discard any that do not open.

Slice the chorizo into 24 pieces, add to the soup, and allow to heat through. Serve.

recommended wine: Champagne or a sparkling wine from Spain or California.

pork *estofado*
(Pork Stew with Cumin and Sour Orange)

SERVES 4

Like many people, I love a great pork stew. Here the magical tandem of cumin and sour orange works its power. A simple squeeze of lime or a drizzle of Chipotle Vinegar (page 264) brings a welcome contrast to any pork dish. For a starch, serve Basic White Rice (page 196) or Corn-Turmeric Rice (page 196).

This dish makes great leftovers, so you might want to double the recipe.

2 tablespoons canola oil

1 tablespoon unsalted butter

3 1/2 pounds boneless pork shoulder, cut into
    1 1/2- to 2-inch pieces

6 cloves garlic, sliced

1 medium Spanish onion, roughly chopped

1 yellow bell pepper, stemmed, seeded, and
    roughly chopped

1 red bell pepper, stemmed, seeded, and
    roughly chopped

2 medium ripe tomatoes, peeled and roughly
    chopped

4 teaspoons toasted and ground cumin seeds
    (see page 9)

2 bay leaves, broken in half

Kosher salt and freshly ground black pepper to
    taste

3/4 cup fresh sour orange juice (or 3/8 cup each
    lime juice and regular orange juice)

2 cups water

Add the oil and butter to a soup pot and heat over medium-high heat until quite hot. Brown the pork pieces, a few at a time, so you don't crowd them. Transfer them to a bowl.

Add the garlic and onion to the pot and cook for 5 minutes. Add the peppers and cook for about 2 minutes. Add the pork, tomatoes, cumin, bay leaves, and salt and pepper to taste. Cook for 2 minutes, then add the sour orange juice and water. Bring to a boil, then turn the heat down and simmer, covered, for 30 minutes.

Take off the lid and cook for about 45 minutes more, or until the meat is tender. Serve.

recommended wine: Grenache-based wine from southern France or northern Spain.

tuli machi

(Coconut and Plantain Stew with Seafood)

SERVES 6 (MAKES 9 CUPS)

The original inhabitants of Panama were the Tuli Indians; the name Panama, which means "abundance of fish," comes from the Tuli language. Attesting to that bounty is *tuli machi*.

1 large very ripe (*maduro*) plantain (its skin should be almost black), peeled and cut into ½-inch-thick slices

Kosher salt and freshly ground black pepper to taste

3 tablespoons canola oil

2 tablespoons olive oil

6 cloves garlic, minced

1 Scotch bonnet chile, stemmed, seeded, and minced

3 shallots, minced

1 cup unsweetened coconut milk

4 cups Chicken Stock (page 267)

1 pound whitefish fillets, such as sea bass, grouper, or cod, cut into ½-inch-thick medallions

¼ cup all-purpose flour

2 tablespoons unsalted butter

6 cups chopped kale or collard greens

2 cups corn kernels (from about 3 ears)

1 cup crabmeat, cleaned of shells and cartilage

8 ounces shrimp, peeled, deveined, and cut into bite-sized pieces

Juice of 2 lemons

Season the plantain slices with salt and pepper. In a nonstick sauté pan, heat 2 tablespoons of the canola oil over medium-high heat. When it is quite hot, sear the plantain slices on both sides until golden brown. Drain on paper towels, then mash them in a bowl.

In a large soup pot, heat the olive oil over medium heat. Add the garlic, Scotch bonnet, and shallots, and sauté briefly. Add the mashed plantains; when the fruit just begins to stick, pour in the coconut milk and stir well until creamy and smooth. Add the chicken stock and bring to a boil. Turn the heat down and simmer for 10 minutes.

Meanwhile, season the fish fillets with salt and pepper and dust with the flour, shaking off any excess. In a large sauté pan, heat the butter and the remaining 1 tablespoon canola oil until hot. Sear the fish fillets on both sides until golden brown and crisp. Transfer to a plate and reserve.

Add the kale to the simmering soup. When the kale is tender, add the corn kernels, crabmeat, shrimp, seared fish fillets, and lemon juice. Stir carefully, so as not to break up the fillets, and cook for 5 minutes and serve.

recommended wine: A Mosel Riesling or perhaps a dry Chenin Blanc.

west indian pumpkin soup *colombo*
(Curried Pumpkin Soup)

SERVES 6 (MAKES 10 CUPS)

The capital of Sri Lanka is Colombo, and this dish got its name from the indentured Sri Lankan field workers who brought it with them to their new homes on Trinidad and Tobago. The major spice in this stew is curry, another transplant from the subcontinent.

FOR THE PUMPKIN

2 pounds West Indian (*calabaza*) pumpkin, peeled and cut into 1-inch cubes (you can substitute any other winter squash)
1 pound sweet potatoes, peeled and cut into 1-inch cubes
5 tablespoons unsalted butter, melted
$^1/_3$ cup sugar
1 teaspoon kosher salt
1 teaspoon freshly ground black pepper

FOR THE STEW

$^1/_4$ cup pure olive oil
1 large Spanish onion, roughly chopped
$^1/_2$ Scotch bonnet chile, stemmed, seeded, and minced
3 cloves garlic, minced
2 tablespoons peeled and minced ginger
2 teaspoons grated orange zest
$^1/_4$ cup Madras curry powder
1 teaspoon grated nutmeg
1 cinnamon stick
2 bay leaves, broken in half
2 tablespoons chopped fresh thyme
6 cups Chicken Stock (page 267)
$^1/_4$ cup heavy cream
$^1/_4$ cup unsweetened coconut milk
Kosher salt and freshly ground black pepper to taste

FOR THE GARNISH

2 Granny Smith apples
1 cup *pepitas* (hulled pumpkin seeds), lightly toasted (see page 9)

for the pumpkin

Preheat the oven to 350 degrees.

Toss the pumpkin and sweet potatoes with the melted butter, sugar, salt, and pepper. Put the squash in a roasting pan lined with parchment paper or aluminum foil and roast, uncovered, for 1 hour and 15 minutes, stirring occasionally. Remove and set aside.

for the stew

Heat the oil in a large pot. Add the onion and sauté for 3 minutes, or until translucent and soft. Add the Scotch bonnet, garlic, and ginger and sauté for another minute. Stir in the orange zest, curry powder, nutmeg, cinnamon stick, bay leaves, and thyme. Cook, stirring constantly, for another minute.

When the curry becomes fragrant and the mixture begins to resemble a paste, add the roasted pumpkin and sweet potatoes, including any pan juices, and stir to coat well. Add the chicken stock and bring to a boil, then turn down the heat and simmer gently, stirring occasionally, for 30 minutes.

Remove the pot from the heat and let cool for a few minutes. Remove the bay leaves and cinnamon stick. In a blender, puree the soup in batches, then return it to the pot. Stir in the cream and coconut milk. Reheat gently over low heat; do not boil.

Meanwhile, peel and core the apples and cut into small dice.

Ladle the soup into bowls, garnish with the apples and *pepitas,* and serve.

recommended wine: A big, bold white Rhône with a high percentage of Roussanne.

salads and ceviches

I first tasted conch salad in Key West in the mid-seventies, when I was engaged in the hectic and sometimes insane business of opening a brand-new restaurant. It was my first shot at being head chef, and my days were a mixture of terror and joy.

On one fateful summer day, a large shadow obscured the tropical light that spilled through the kitchen screen door. (It was like when you are skin diving in the ocean and a big fish swims behind you.) Then came the voice. It was a booming bass, singsong even, with Bahamian inflections: "Hey. Hey. I'm Frank, the Conch Salad Man. I'll sell you the world's best conch salad and you can sell it to your customers."

He pushed open the screen door and came into the kitchen, holding a big white pickle bucket brimming with conch salad. With a paper cup, he scooped up some for me to try. I tipped back a mixture of finely diced conch, tomatoes, red onions, Scotch bonnets, bell peppers, celery, citrus juices, and herbs. The flavors of the sea were in there too. I really looked at him now.

His saltwater-stained heavy black glasses were held on with fishing line. His hands were thick and meaty, scarred and callused from heavy labor. He wore canvas shoes, military-style pants, and a white T-shirt. A long gold chain around his neck drew attention to a nasty scar that ringed his collarbone.

When he scooped out more salad for each of the cooks and waiters working in my kitchen that day, I realized that he didn't know I was the chef. I thought, *"I can just make my own damn conch salad."* (And I did.) Yet, as I came to know Frank over the next few months, I understood that this possibility would have never occurred to him: he had 1,000 percent confidence that once a person had tasted his conch salad, none other would do.

Controversies over the provenance of certain dishes are part of the spice of life of any cuisine. For example, a spirited discussion revolves around the origin of conch salad's Latin cousin *ceviche*. This seafood salad, made of raw fish or shellfish marinated in citrus juices and laced with raw onion and hot peppers, is one of the many gifts ancient Peru bestowed upon New World cuisine. The most romantic story holds that *ceviche* was invented so that an Incan emperor, high up in his Andean citadel in Cusco, could enjoy fresh fish. The fish, caught on the Peruvian coast, was first marinated in the tart juices of the native *tumbo* to preserve and flavor it, then carried by relays of *chasquis,* or runners, up to the hungry emperor.

Another story attributes the invention of *ceviche* to Peruvian fishermen, who would bring with them in their boats pots of *tumbo* juice infused with chile peppers. At the end of each day's work, they would cure some of their catch in the pot to feed themselves during their long stretches at sea. Or maybe it was Polynesian voyagers, traveling across the ocean to pre-Columbian Peru on wind-driven reed rafts, who introduced the notion of eating marinated raw fish; the custom was common in their Pacific island homes.

Peruvian food scholar Juan José Vega, who has studied the influence on Peruvian cuisine of the Moorish slave cooks who arrived with the Spanish nobility in the sixteenth century, offers yet another theory. In his version, the slaves introduced to Peru a dish called *sei-vech,* made of fish or meat marinated in the juice of *ceuta* lemons, which they brought with them from North Africa and planted in the New World.

Regardless, a Peruvian *ceviche*—whether of Pacific bass, shrimp, or black clam, or a mixture of all—is a cool yet zesty noontime delicacy on a hot day at the beach. Washed down with an ice-cold beer, it is South America's number one cure for a hangover. Working with Peruvians and visiting their markets and restaurants has given me a very different understanding of the delicacy of a properly made *ceviche:* I used to think it could be made the night before it was eaten. Instead, you should think of it more like sushi. Sushi and sashimi are, after all, eaten raw—and eaten immediately.

Seafood salads are one important part of this chapter, yet salads per se are not traditionally a big part of the Latin and Caribbean table. My friend the great Mr. Zalamea explains why:

Spain was probably the strongest European influence on New World cooking, but it is where salads have been historically and gastronomically underestimated. In a way, they were replaced at the beginning of a meal by hearty *potajes* (freely translated as "hodge-podges") of dried fava beans, chickpeas, lentils, and so on, especially in northern Spain, with its cold and stormy weather. Other so-called salads featured cold seafood. These are probably two of the causes that led Alexandre Dumas *père* to label Spanish cookery as "barbarian" in a controversial nineteenth-century treatise on the subject. Even as recently as 1993, Carlos Arguiñamo, one of Spain's leading new chefs,

included just eight salads in his cookbook *A Menu for Each Day*, of which only two are actually based on vegetables. The rest are seafood in green costume.

The great irony is that Latin American and Caribbean markets offer an abundance of the fresh and vibrant produce that is so wonderful in a salad. I'll never forget a trip to Mexico City's El Mercado, led by chef Rick Bayless of Chicago's Frontera Grill and Topolobampo. With us were Thomas Keller, Matthew Kenney, Todd English, and the late, great Jean-Louis Palladin, to name a few. We were there to cook at the first International James Beard Foundation Dinner.

The best way to think of El Mercado is as a Yankee Stadium–sized arena packed to its farthest reaches with foodstuffs. We saw *moles*

arranged in multihued heaps; live chickens nervously awaiting their last ride; wooden tables piled ten feet in the air with dried smoked chipotles; row after row of stands filled with corn, chiles, tomatoes, carrots, squashes, onions, and fruits; and endless batches of tortillas and tacos, steaming and sold for pennies. It was cinematic; I thought of movies like *Cleopatra* and *Gladiator* as we marveled at the sheer scale of it. I can only wonder what scenes we *gringo* chefs evoked for the Mexican merchants.) What I took home with me that day were the makings of a memorable salad, which I prepared for our group. And what I made was an antecedent to *Salpicón de Huachinango* (page 98).

orange, hearts of palm, and fennel salad with pickled red onions

SERVES SIX 1-CUP SERVINGS

The refreshing qualities of this salad make it a good companion for rich foods. I serve it with our Brazilian Feast Day dish, *Feijoada* (page 188).

$^1/_2$ cup red wine vinegar

$^1/_4$ cup sugar

$^1/_2$ medium red onion, sliced paper-thin

1 small fennel bulb, cored and julienned

2 cups julienned hearts of palm (if you use
  canned or jarred hearts of palm, rinse well
  and pat dry before using)

5 oranges, peeled, segmented, seeded, and
  diced

$^1/_3$ cup pure olive oil

3 tablespoons Spanish sherry vinegar

2 tablespoons fresh lime juice

$^1/_4$ cup chopped Italian parsley

1 clove garlic, minced

$^1/_4$ teaspoon kosher salt

$^1/_2$ teaspoon freshly ground black pepper

Combine the red wine vinegar and sugar in a small bowl and stir until the sugar dissolves. Add the onion slices, toss, and set aside for the moment.

Combine the fennel, hearts of palm, and orange segments in a salad bowl.

Make the dressing by whisking together the olive oil, vinegar, lime juice, parsley, garlic, salt, and pepper. Drain the red onions, then toss the onions into the salad. Toss well with the dressing and serve.

recommended wine: A light Marsanne from France's Rhône Valley, one that neither possesses nor expresses too much oak.

ensalada nicaragüense
(Tomato and Beet Salad with Cabbage and Avocado)

SERVES 4

When I first had this salad, I immediately connected it with the classic American steakhouse salad. Both rely on unabashedly huge presentations of a few simple ingredients at the peak of freshness. The Nicaraguan rendition, however, is decidedly more exotic. Here beets contrast sweetly with the acidity of the dressing and the bite of the onions. They also bleed just a little, making the vinaigrette dazzling. Create a dinner with this as the first course, followed by a big Salvadoran Steak (page 165).

1 beet, scrubbed and patted dry

2 cups white cabbage shredded paper-thin

1 small white onion, sliced paper-thin

$^1/_4$ cup fresh lime juice, plus a squeeze or two

1 ripe avocado, pitted, peeled, and sliced into
   $^1/_4$-inch rounds

$^3/_4$ cup white wine vinegar

1 cup canola oil

2 cloves garlic, minced

3 tablespoons chopped cilantro

1 $^1/_2$ teaspoons brown sugar

Kosher salt and freshly ground black pepper to
   taste

2 large ripe tomatoes, sliced into $^1/_4$-inch
   rounds

6 to 8 slices peeled cucumber

Preheat the oven to 325 degrees.

Wrap the beet in foil. Roast until easily pierced with a fork, 25 to 40 minutes, depending on size. When cool, peel and slice into $^1/_4$-inch rounds.

In a medium bowl, combine the shredded cabbage and onion slices; set aside. Squeeze a little of the lime juice over the sliced avocado to prevent it from browning.

To make the vinaigrette, whisk together the $^1/_4$ cup lime juice, the vinegar, oil, garlic, cilantro, sugar, and salt and pepper to taste in a large bowl. Add the vinaigrette to the cabbage and onion, toss, and let them pickle for 15 minutes.

Arrange the beet, avocado, tomatoes, and cucumber slices on a large plate. Season with salt and pepper. Remove the pickled cabbage and onions from the dressing and arrange them atop the other vegetables. Drizzle the vinaigrette over the salad and serve.

recommended wine: The Venetian white wine Soave Classico. (Make sure it is a young vintage so you can experience the liveliness, richness, and long finish the wine has to offer.)

ceviche mixto

(Mixed *Ceviche* with Sweet Potato and Corn on the Cob)

SERVES 8

Peru abounds with *cevicherías*, evidence of Peruvians' devotion to what they hail as their national dish. In his tremendous book *The Art of Peruvian Cuisine*, Tony Custer says Peruvians "affectionately call the spicy marination juice of *ceviche* 'tiger's milk' and will drink a small glass to cure a hangover." In the Cocktails chapter of this book, I include my restaurant's recipe based on this notion, *Levantamuertos*—Raise the Dead.

One of my favorite places in Miami serves the classic *ceviche mixto* with sweet potatoes that smell as if they've been cooked in the smoky embers of a campfire. If you can engineer a way to do that at home, I salute you!

FOR THE VEGETABLES
Kosher salt
1 red onion, halved and sliced into paper-thin
    half-moons
$^1/_4$ cup sugar
1 sweet potato
1 star anise
1 lime, halved
2 ears corn, husked and cut into 1 $^1/_2$-inch-thick
    rounds

FOR THE *CEVICHE*
12 ounces sea bass fillets
12 ounces shrimp, peeled and deveined
12 ounces squid, cleaned
$^1/_4$ cup fresh lime juice
$^1/_4$ cup chopped cilantro
$^1/_4$ cup chopped Italian parsley

1 Scotch bonnet chile, stemmed, seeded, and
    minced
1 teaspoon Worcestershire sauce
Tabasco to taste (optional)
Kosher salt to taste

for the vegetables
Lightly salt the sliced onion and set aside in a colander for about 15 minutes. When they begin to sweat, rinse them under cold water, then immerse them in cold water and refrigerate.

Add 2 tablespoons of sugar to a small pot, fill it with water, and add the sweet potato. Bring to a boil and cook until the potato is tender, about 35 minutes. Drain and refrigerate the sweet potato.

When it is cool enough to handle, peel the sweet potato, halve it lengthwise, and slice into half-moons. Reserve.

Add the remaining 2 tablespoons sugar to a large pot and fill it with water. Add the star anise. Squeeze in the lime juice, and add the lime halves. Bring to a boil, add the corn, and cook for 2 minutes; drain. Discard the star anise and limes. Set aside while you make the *ceviche*.

for the *ceviche*

Cut the sea bass into $1/4$-inch-thick slices. Rinse well under cold water, cover, and chill.

Slice the shrimp into $1/4$-inch pieces. Rinse well under cold water and set aside. Slice the squid into $1/4$-inch-wide rings, then slice each squid ring into pieces. Rinse well under cold water.

Bring a large pot of water to a boil. Fill a large bowl with ice water. Put the shrimp and squid in a strainer and immerse them in the boiling water for about 10 seconds, then immediately immerse them in the ice-water bath. Chill for about 10 minutes, then drain.

Meanwhile, make the pickling juice: In a small bowl, whisk together the lime juice, herbs, Scotch bonnet, Worcestershire, and optional Tabasco.

Combine the chilled sea bass, shrimp, and squid in a medium bowl and toss well with the pickling juice. Cover and marinate in the refrigerator for 30 minutes.

Season the *ceviche* with salt. Arrange the *ceviche* in the middle of a serving platter, and arrange the sweet potato slices and corn rounds around the perimeter. Scatter the onion over all. Serve immediately.

recommended wine: A young Sauvignon Blanc from Chile or a dry, clean, layered Riesling from Austria.

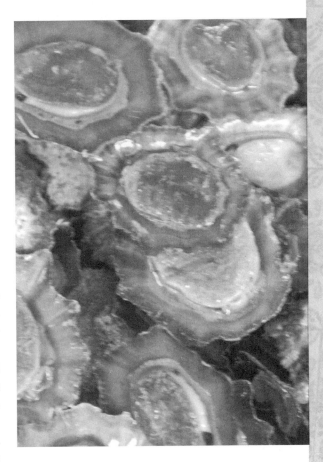

grouper *ceviche* with three fruit juices

SERVES 6

Tumbo, a fruit native to Peru in the same *Passiflora* family as *maracuyá,* or passion fruit, was probably employed in the making of the first *ceviches*. It is not as acidic as lime or lemon but it is sufficiently tart to marinate fish. Today Peruvians still use the fruit to make the dish, but because it is unlikely you'll find *tumbo* in any grocery store north of Lima, I've used grapefruit and lime juice here; I add passion fruit juice at the very end to make sure its distinctive taste stays clear.

12 ounces grouper fillets

1 cup fresh grapefruit juice

$^1/_2$ cup fresh lime juice

$^1/_2$ Scotch bonnet chile, stemmed, seeded, and minced

Kosher salt

1 small ripe tomato, peeled, seeded, and chopped

$^1/_2$ small red onion, minced

3 tablespoons finely diced black olives

2 scallions, white parts only, chopped

$^1/_4$ cup extra virgin olive oil

1 tablespoon chopped cilantro

$^1/_3$ cup passion fruit juice

Freshly ground black pepper to taste

Cut the grouper into $^1/_6$-inch-thick bite-sized pieces. In a bowl, combine the grapefruit juice, lime juice, and Scotch bonnet. Add the fish and marinate, covered, for about 10 minutes in the refrigerator.

Drain the fish in a strainer, pressing firmly to release as much moisture from the grouper as possible. While the fish is still in the strainer, salt it evenly.

Transfer the fish to a bowl, add the remaining ingredients, and stir well. Serve.

recommended wine: For a dry wine with some initial fruit offerings, such as an Arneis from Piedmont, or, for more fruit, a big-style Soave from Veneto.

sea bass *ceviche* with jicama and avocado slaw

SERVES 4

This recipe demonstrates the new thinking on *ceviches* in Peru. The idea nowadays is to greatly reduce the length of the marinating period. In a sense, you are making a dressing rather than a marinade. So now you don't have to plan to make this the day before you want it—you can stop at your fishmonger on the way home and have *ceviche* on the table that night. Here I serve the sea bass in a bowl over ice, with bowls containing the chilled salad components. It is more or less a Japanese approach, and I like to use chopsticks to eat this *ceviche*.

If you can get *cancha* (Latin American corn nuts) and toast them, they make a fantastic addition to this dish. I like to drizzle coconut milk onto the citrus juices after serving the ceviche. Or I garnish the plates with tiny dots of soy sauce and sesame oil.

12 ounces skinless sea bass fillets

FOR THE MARINADE/DRESSING

1 cup fresh grapefruit juice
1/2 cup fresh lime juice
1/2 small red onion, thinly sliced
2 tablespoons coarsely chopped cilantro
1 jalapeño, stemmed, seeded, and minced
Kosher salt to taste

FOR THE SALAD

2 tablespoons extra virgin olive oil
2 tablespoons minced red onion
2 tablespoons chopped cilantro

1/4 teaspoon toasted and ground cumin seeds (see page 9)
Kosher salt and freshly ground black pepper
1 cup julienned peeled jicama
1 avocado, pitted, peeled, cut into 1/4-inch dice

Thinly slice the fillets and then cut them into 3/4-inch squares. Cover and refrigerate while you prepare the rest of the recipe. Put four small serving bowls in the refrigerator to chill.

for the marinade/dressing

Combine all the ingredients in a bowl. Set the bowl inside a larger one filled with ice while you prepare the salad.

for the salad

In a small bowl, whisk together the olive oil, onion, cilantro, cumin, and salt and pepper. In a larger bowl, toss the vinaigrette with the avocado and jicama. Refrigerate.

to finish the dish,

add the sea bass to the marinade/dressing and gently mix. Let stand for about 10 minutes. Spoon the *ceviche,* with its liquid, into the four chilled bowls. Serve with the salad, and encourage your guests to top their *ceviche* with salad.

recommended wine: A California Chardonnay with muscle and acidity, preferably from the Russian River Valley.

shrimp *ceviche rojo*

(Shrimp *Ceviche* in a Spicy Tomato Marinade)

SERVES 10

Ecuadorians worship *ceviches,* and they adore shrimp, making this recipe a natural.

2 pounds shrimp, peeled, deveined and cut into small bite-sized pieces

2 jalapeños, halved, stemmed, and seeded

1 red bell pepper, halved, stemmed, and seeded

Canola oil for roasting

2 large ripe tomatoes, cored, halved and seeded

$^1/_2$ large Spanish onion

One 6-ounce jar piquillo peppers, drained (you can substitute jarred roasted red peppers or pimientos)

$^1/_3$ cup fresh lime juice

$^1/_4$ cup fresh orange juice

2 tablespoons Spanish sherry vinegar

1 tablespoon sugar

1 $^1/_4$ teaspoons kosher salt, or more to taste

1 tablespoon chopped cilantro

Tabasco to taste

Bring a large pot of water to a boil. Set a bowl of ice water within reach. Put the shrimp in a strainer and gently lower it into the boiling water for 15 seconds, then immerse in the ice-water bath for 10 seconds. Remove and allow to drain well. Cover and refrigerate.

Preheat the oven to 500 degrees. Line a baking sheet with parchment paper.

Rub the jalapeños and bell pepper with canola oil. Arrange them, along with the tomatoes and onion, cut side down, on the baking sheet and roast until charred, about 30 minutes. Set aside to cool.

Slip the skins off the tomatoes, jalapeños, and red pepper. Place them, along with the onion, in a blender, and add the piquillo peppers, lime and orange juices, vinegar, sugar, and salt. Blend until smooth. Taste and season with the cilantro, Tabasco, and salt if needed. Pour over the shrimp and toss. Chill until ready to serve.

Serve the *ceviche* in small bowls garnished with scallions and corn nuts if you like.

recommended wine: The French aperitif Lillet Blonde, with a couple drops of lime juice added, or try a white sangria.

conch salad with pickled onions, sweet peppers, and watermelon

SERVES 4

Many have never had the treat of fresh conch. I often tell people to substitute fresh clams (and, in fact, you can substitute almost any kind of fresh fish—this recipe is really very adaptable). But with the wonders of overnight delivery, you can now easily have fresh conch (see Source Guide, page 310). Conch freezes well too, so why not buy a few pounds?

8 ounces conch, cleaned and cut into very thin julienne
Kosher salt and freshly ground black pepper to taste
Juice of 2 limes
Juice of 2 lemons
1 teaspoon sugar
$^1/_4$ teaspoon minced seeded Scotch bonnet chile
1 clove garlic, minced
12 thin slices watermelon
$^1/_2$ recipe Pickled Red Onions (page 211)
$^1/_2$ red bell pepper, stemmed, seeded, and julienned
$^1/_2$ yellow bell pepper, stemmed, seeded, and julienned
1 $^1/_2$ teaspoons extra virgin olive oil
2 tablespoons coarsely chopped cilantro

Lay the conch between two pieces of plastic wrap and pound with a mallet until tender and very thin. Season with salt and pepper.

Combine the citrus juices, sugar, Scotch bonnet, and garlic in a bowl. Add the conch, mixing well. Cover and refrigerate for about 20 minutes.

On a platter, fan out the watermelon slices, leaving room in the middle for the *ceviche*. Remove the conch from the marinade and arrange in the center of the platter, allowing it to spill over the melon.

Remove the pickled onion from its pickling juices and toss in a bowl with the bell peppers, olive oil, and chopped cilantro. Season with salt and pepper. Serve on the side for the guests to take as they desire, or, garnish the top of the whole salad with the onions.

recommended wine: A rosé from Provence or, perhaps, for more roundness, a dry Chenin Blanc from the Loire.

chiles

The New World gave the rest of the globe one of the spices of life: chile peppers. The word *chile* comes from the Aztecs' Náhuatl word *chilli*. The Taino Indians called the peppers *ajíes*, and in the Incan Quechua tongue they are known as *uchu*. Although it is not yet widely known, January 1 marks the anniversary of the day in 1493 that Columbus tasted chiles for the first time, on the island of Hispaniola (now Haiti and the Dominican Republic). What he sampled was probably of the ancient genus *Capsicum*, as there is evidence that its peppers were harvested by the cave dwellers who peopled the Andes. These fierce little peppers, together with conventional black pepper and other spices, would revolutionize Europe's bland cuisines and spark world trade during the sixteenth and seventeenth centuries. Peppers of both types brought prices as high as that for gold, in part because of the fact that they were reputed to be aphrodisiacs (as were many of the products that came from the New World). Exported to Africa by European traders and explorers, chiles became an essential part of the native diet there and, ironically, were later re-introduced to the New World through the hands of African slave cooks.

The controversial *Capsicum* question is, did the chile pepper originate in the New World or in the Pacific, where it is also indigenous to the cuisine? Some botanists have suggested that prehistoric voyagers from the Pacific Rim may have traveled what were almost unfathomable distances across the ocean, bringing the plants to the shores of what is now South America. Jean Andrews lays out two hypotheses and believes the second in her book *Peppers:* "(a) pre-Columbian Amerindians sailed to Polynesia; (b) Polynesians sailed to pre-Columbian America and returned with peppers." The thinking goes that these brave sailors found oceanic currents that sped them along from their island homes to the shores of South America. Andrews notes that while "there are no natural departure routes to the Old World on the Atlantic side of America, . . . there are two on the Pacific [side]. One of these sets of prevailing winds and currents, known as the North Equatorial Current, leads across the Pacific from Mesoamerica to the Philippines. The second, called the South Equatorial Current, carries from Peru to Polynesia."

Today there are literally thousands of types of chiles. Indeed, they have become so popular that a gauge called the Scoville system was devised to measure the thermic units of capsaicin, the colorless, tasteless alkaloid that gives chile peppers their heat. The heat of the chiles is present mainly in their seeds and veins. A red or yellow bell pepper measures zero Scoville units, while a Caribbean Scotch bonnet or a Peruvian *rocoto* may register from 250,000 to 300,000 units. Chile peppers are becoming increasingly popular in the United States, where fan clubs have spread from the Southwest to the rest of the country. The secret of using chiles in cooking is to know each type well, handle it with care, and apply its sting in concert with other flavors.

Chiles are much hotter when they are fresh and take on entirely different characteristics and nuances when they are air-dried and/or dried by smoke. For example, the *ají amarillo*, a Peruvian pepper to which I refer in this book, is most often used in its dried state, when it is known as *cusqueño* (sometimes spelled *cuzqueño*). It is featured in a Peruvian dish (not in this book) called *cau cau*, which is made from the lining of a cow's stomach.

There are several excellent books on the subject of chile peppers: Jean Andrews's *Peppers*, of course, and chef Mark Miller's indispensable *The Great Chile Book*. Another wonderful tome is *The Art of Peruvian Cuisine*, by Tony Custer (see Bibliography, page 315). The book, printed in Spanish and English, is not easy to find, so if you come across a copy, I urge you to grab it. Custer writes engagingly on the chile pepper and provides plenty of evidence on the innovative work in its preparation and uses happening among the chefs of Peru. My hope is that with the expanding interest in Latin cuisines in America, we will increasingly find the famed *ají* chiles in our produce markets alongside the now-familiar jalapeños, habaneros, Scotch bonnets, and poblanos.

salpicón de huachinango
(Snapper Salad)

SERVES 6

Huachinango is an Indian word dating back to the pre-Columbian inhabitants of what is now Mexico. But for generations the word has been synonymous in Mexico, particularly along the Gulf Coast, with red snapper. *Salpicón* is the Spanish word for a variety of composed salads. Here I combine the two.

Kosher salt and freshly ground black pepper to taste

1 pound red snapper fillets (or other fresh white-fleshed fish)

2 tablespoons canola oil

2 tablespoons unsalted butter

3 cloves garlic, minced

1 jalapeño, stemmed, seeded, and minced

1/2 cup packed minced scallions (white part only)

3/4 cup Spanish dry sherry

1 small ripe tomato, peeled, seeded, and chopped

1 teaspoon toasted and ground cumin seeds (see page 9)

Pinch of ground *canela* or cinnamon

Pinch of ground cloves

2 teaspoons minced cilantro

1 lime, cut into wedges, for garnish

Salt and pepper the fish fillets. Heat a heavy skillet over medium-high heat. Add the canola oil and heat until hot. Sear the fish on both sides until golden brown. Transfer to a plate.

Wipe out the skillet with a paper towel. Turn down the heat to medium and add the butter. When the butter has melted, add the garlic and jalapeño and cook until fragrant, about 1 minute. Add the scallions and sauté until they begin to soften, about 1 minute. Pour in the sherry and stir, then add the chopped tomato and spices and cook until the tomato begins to soften, about 3 minutes. Add the fish fillets and continue cooking until the fish flakes when tested with a fork.

Remove the skillet from the heat, stir in the cilantro, and season with salt and pepper. Shred the fish into small pieces with the fork and mix well with the sauce.

You can serve *salpicón* warm, at room temperature, or chilled. Just before you do, squeeze the lime juice over the fish.

recommended wine or beer: A white wine with a little fat to coat the spices, such as Saint-Romain, or perhaps a Bourgogne Blanc; a Pinot Gris from Oregon would keep the spices softly alive. An ale, such as a Sierra Nevada Pale Ale, would also work nicely.

tiradito of scallops
(Marinated Scallops)

SERVES 4

A *tiradito* is a slightly more uptown version of *ceviche*. The only real difference is that the fish or seafood in a *tiradito* is always very thinly sliced; if it is a *tiradito* of a larger fish than the sea scallops here, the fish would be cut into long, wafer-thin slices.

2 tablespoons finely diced fennel

2 tablespoons finely diced red bell pepper

2 tablespoons finely diced peeled and seeded tomato

1 to 2 teaspoons finely minced, seeded *ají amarillo* or Scotch bonnet chile

2 teaspoons finely chopped mint

2 teaspoons finely chopped cilantro

1/4 cup pure olive oil

2 tablespoons fresh Key lime juice or regular lime juice

1/2 teaspoon Spanish sherry vinegar

1/2 teaspoon Sriracha sauce (available in gourmet and Asian specialty food markets)

Kosher salt and freshly ground black pepper to taste

8 sea scallops, very thinly sliced and chilled

A few drops of dark roasted sesame oil

A few drops of soy sauce

Mix all of the ingredients except the scallops, salt and pepper, sesame oil, and soy sauce in a bowl. Chill this mixture over an ice-water bath. Chill four small serving plates.

Just before you are ready to serve, season the dressing with salt and pepper. Arrange the scallops on the chilled plates. Spoon the dressing over them. Sprinkle a drop of sesame oil and soy sauce on each plate, and serve immediately.

recommended wine: A delicate Muscat from Alsace or a Gruner Veltliner from the Wachau region in Austria would harmonize nicely with the sweet heat from the Sriracha and the *ají*.

xuxu slaw
(Squash Slaw with Jicama, Fennel, and Bell Peppers)
SERVES 6 TO 8

There are check forgers with fewer aliases than this squash. Here we go: *chayote,* mirliton, *christophine, chocho, chuchu,* vegetable pear, custard marrow, *pepinella,* and, my choice, *xuxu* (pronounced *zhoo-zhoo*). That's what this squash goes by in Brazil. Most of the time.

It is native to Mexico but it has become familiar in the cuisines of such farflung lands as Indonesia, North Africa, and Australia. (That accounts for its many names.) It is 6 to 8 inches long with a faint green color and a rough pear shape. *Xuxu*'s flavor is akin to that of zucchini and yellow squash. You can peel *xuxu,* or not peel; it's up to you.

I remember first encountering it, under the name mirliton, when I was studying Cajun cooking in the early 1980s. We stuffed the squash with a filling of cooked onions, herbs, the mirliton flesh itself, and some Parmesan bread crumbs, and baked it. Later in my career I began using *xuxu* raw in slaws with Asian flavors, often combining mango and pineapple with the squash. Later still, I integrated it into Caribbean dishes, like this one.

3 *xuxu* (*chayote*), peeled, pitted, and julienned (you can substitute 3 zucchini)
1 small jicama, peeled and julienned
1 red bell pepper, stemmed, seeded, and julienned
1 yellow bell pepper, stemmed, seeded, and julienned
1/2 medium red onion, julienned
6 scallions, white and green parts, thinly sliced on the bias
1 Scotch bonnet chile, stemmed, seeded, and finely minced
1/2 cup unblanched whole almonds, toasted (see page 9) and roughly chopped
1/2 cup virgin olive oil
3 tablespoons fresh orange juice
1 teaspoon toasted and ground fennel seeds (see page 9)
1 1/2 teaspoons sugar
Kosher salt to taste
1/2 teaspoon freshly ground black pepper

Mix the *xuxu,* jicama, bell peppers, onion, and scallions together in a large bowl. Set aside.

In another bowl, whisk together the Scotch bonnet, almonds, olive oil, orange juice, ground fennel, sugar, salt, and pepper. Pour over the slaw. Allow to stand covered for at least 1 hour in the refrigerator so the flavors marry before serving.

recommended wine: A Greco di Tufo from Campagna with a toasty almond and vegetal appeal.

causa with potato, crabmeat, and avocado

(Peruvian Potato Salad)

SERVES 6 TO 8

If the true bond between Peru and the rest of the world is the potato (no country has given us more varieties of the often-underestimated tuber), the *causa* may be Peru's goodwill ambassador. Pronounced *cah-OO-za*, it is a potato-salad type dish, served cold with whatever the cook wants to feature. In Quechua, the language of the Peruvian Andes, *causa* means "complete meal," probably on account of the nourishing qualities of this dish. Not only is it delicious, its beautiful colors and contrasts make it especially appealing at any festive event. While it is often served in a layered presentation, here I've gone with a simpler construction.

12 ounces new potatoes, scrubbed

1 cup corn kernels

1 ¹/₂ teaspoons Creole mustard

2 tablespoons fresh lemon juice

1 tablespoon plus 2 teaspoons Spanish sherry vinegar

1 tablespoon extra virgin olive oil

1 ¹/₂ teaspoons Tabasco

2 tablespoons minced chives

¹/₂ teaspoon minced fresh thyme

¹/₂ cup finely chopped celery (inner stalks only)

1 cup crabmeat, cleaned of any shells and cartilage

1 ripe avocado, pitted, peeled, and diced

Kosher salt and freshly ground black pepper to taste

1 ripe tomato, peeled, seeded, and chopped

¹/₄ cup pitted and chopped Arbequina or Niçoise olives

In a small pot, cover the potatoes with water, bring to a simmer over medium heat, and cook until just tender when pierced with a knife, about 30 minutes (cooking time will vary depending on the size of the potatoes). Drain them, then chill; they'll slice better that way.

Blanch the corn kernels in boiling water for 1 minute; drain and set aside.

In a small bowl, whisk together the mustard, lemon juice, vinegar, olive oil, Tabasco, and herbs.

Peel the potatoes and dice them into ¹/₄-inch cubes. Combine them in a bowl with the corn, celery, and crabmeat. Toss with the dressing. Season to taste. Very gently fold in the diced avocado and chopped tomato.

Arrange the salad on a large platter. Top with the chopped olives, and surround with a variety of potato and corn chips. Or, if you'd like to serve the *causa* in individual portions, nestle the salad inside lettuce leaves on serving plates.

recommended wine: A white Rully or a white from the Auxey-Duresses, both from Burgundy, would appeal with the *causa*.

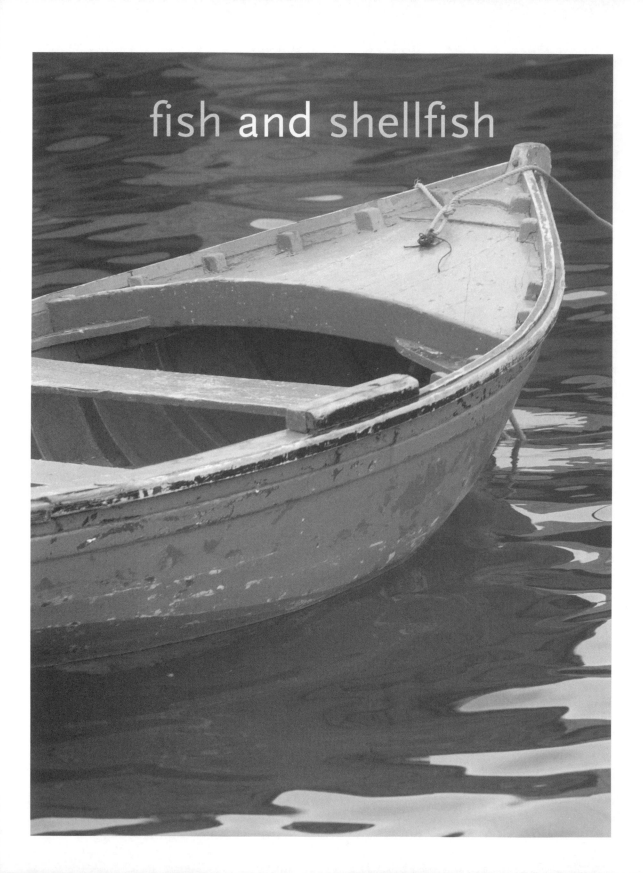

fish and shellfish

It is about water. It was about water in the beginning; it will be in the end. The ocean mothered us all. Water and darkness awaiting light. Night gives birth. An inkling of life over distant sea swells toward the brilliance. Dawn emerges from Africa, strikes light between worlds, over misting mountains of Haiti, beyond the Great Bahama Bank, touching the cane fields of Cuba, across the Tropic of Cancer to the sleeping island of Key West, farther to the Gold Coast of Florida.

—THOMAS SANCHEZ, *Mile Zero*

When I go back to Key West, one of my culinary loves, I can smell the ocean. I also smell the sea breeze here in Miami, but it competes with so many other scents that it gets muted, in the same way that light pollution in the city snuffs out starlight.

Many of the people I first hung out and worked with, in the early 1970s, were fishermen. In Key West, my then wife-to-be worked at a place called the Fisherman's Café. She was 19, selling baskets of sandwiches that the fishermen took to sea during their days and nights of shrimping and trolling for grouper, snapper, wahoo, and dolphin. In ancient times, a fish was considered "foreign" (i.e., not good, not fresh) if it came from even the opposite bank of the river. The idea was that freshness was God. That idea is crucially important to the recipes in this chapter. While the fish and dishes that I've selected here hail from faraway lands and waters, what is important is to make choices in the market according to freshness. In the end, what you want to taste is the primordial essence of the sea.

The fisherman's life may seem romantic, but it is not the life for me—I am not meant to float in that solitary silence. I was put here to face the flames. Yet, to head to the docks or walk the dunes or take a small boat out to sea, to be rocked in the heaving sigh of the waves, looking back at land distant but not so far away that I couldn't easily get back to my kitchen, or a glowing campfire and a little grill—that is the perfect life. When I smell water—lake, river, or ocean—I am home.

arroz con mariscos

(Seafood Stew with Rice and *Salsa Criolla*)

SERVES 6

The Humboldt Current meets El Niño off the coast of Peru, creating an oceanic ecosystem second to none in the world. This accounts for the superabundance of seafood in Peruvian cooking, and this stew is one of that country's classic vessels for the fruits of the sea.

Various flavorful pastes that give different dishes immense strength are a culinary tradition in Peru. Often these pastes are made with Peruvian *ají amarillo*. This stew uses such a paste, but because *ajís* are not yet widely available in North America, I've created a reasonable approximation here, substituting Scotch bonnet and yellow bell pepper. The *Salsa Criolla* that accompanies the dish acts much the way a squirt of vinegary hot sauce would.

1 yellow bell pepper, roasted (see page 7), peeled, stemmed, and seeded

1/2 Scotch bonnet chile, stemmed, seeded, and minced

7 cups Chicken Stock (page 267)

12 mussels, scrubbed and debearded

12 clams, scrubbed

A pinch of saffron threads

2 tablespoons all-purpose flour

Kosher salt and freshly ground black pepper to taste

8 ounces sea bass fillets, cut into 2-inch pieces

1/2 cup Annatto Oil (page 261) or pure olive oil

4 ounces cleaned calamari, cut into 1/4-inch rings

1 pound shrimp, peeled and deveined

One 12-ounce bottle dark beer, at room temperature

4 cloves garlic, minced

1 large red onion, cut into small dice

4 cups long-grain white rice

1 cup chopped cilantro

FOR THE *SALSA CRIOLLA*

1/2 medium Spanish onion, diced

2 limes, halved

2 cloves garlic, minced

1/2 Scotch bonnet chile, stemmed, seeded, and minced

3 tablespoons chopped cilantro

Kosher salt and freshly ground black pepper to taste

1 cup green peas, cooked in boiling salted water until tender

Mince the roasted pepper, then mash it into a paste with the back of a fork. Mix in the Scotch bonnet. Reserve the paste.

Simmer the stock in a large pot. Add the mussels and clams, cover the pot, and steam just until they open; check after a few minutes, and transfer them to a bowl as they open. Once they are all out of the pot (discard any that do not open), add the saffron, remove from the heat, and set aside to infuse.

In a small bowl, season the flour with salt and pepper. Lightly flour the sea bass; shake off the excess. Heat $^1/_4$ cup of the annatto oil in a sauté pan over medium-high heat. When it is quite hot, add the bass and sear, turning once, until golden and crisp on both sides. Transfer to a plate. Add the calamari to the pan and cook for 1 minute. Transfer to the plate with the sea bass. Add the shrimp to the pan, along with 2 tablespoons of the pepper paste and $^1/_4$ cup of the beer, and sauté until just cooked. Remove the shrimp with a slotted spoon and reserve with the rest of the seafood. Simmer the cooking liquid until reduced to a light syrup, and pour over the seafood. Set aside.

Add the remaining $^1/_4$ cup oil to a soup pot and heat over medium-high heat. When it is hot, add the garlic and onion. Cook until they start to caramelize, 8 to 10 minutes. Add the rice and stir to coat. Pour in the chicken stock, cover, and cook for 10 minutes.

Stir the rice with a fork, then add the seafood, the rest of the beer, and the cilantro and stir once more. Cover, turn the heat down to medium-low, and cook for 25 minutes.

While the rice cooks, make the salsa: Put the onion in a small bowl. Squeeze the juice of the limes over it; discard the rinds. Add the garlic, Scotch bonnet, and cilantro. Season with salt and pepper.

When the rice is done, stir in the peas. Serve with the salsa on the side.

recommended beer: A dark beer will complement this dish.

sea bass with creamy ragù of tomatoes, basil, potatoes, and onion

SERVES 4

I like to serve this rich dish in the wintry months. I have little copper dishes for cooking the ragù so that I can present the servings individually. Naturally you may find it hard to get nice ripe tomatoes at that time of year, so you can substitute high-quality canned tomatoes. You may wish to offer some lemon wedges as well.

Four 7-ounce portions sea bass or cod fillet, 1 $^1/_2$ inches thick
Kosher salt and freshly ground black pepper to taste
2 tablespoons fresh lemon juice
3 tablespoons unsalted butter, plus butter for the casserole(s)
1 tablespoon Roasted Garlic Oil (page 262) or canola oil
2 ounces smoky bacon, diced (optional)
4 cloves garlic, thinly sliced
1 large sweet onion, Vidalia if possible, finely chopped
4 large ripe tomatoes, peeled, seeded, and finely chopped (4 cups)
$^1/_4$ cup Spanish sherry vinegar
1 $^1/_2$ cups heavy cream
1 pound new potatoes, scrubbed, cooked in boiling salted water, peeled if desired, and sliced $^1/_8$ inch thick
1 red bell pepper, roasted (see page 7), peeled, stemmed, and diced
$^1/_4$ cup roughly chopped fresh basil
2 hard-boiled eggs, sliced

Preheat the oven to 350 degrees. Lightly butter a 3-inch-deep, 10- to 12-inch copper casserole or ovenproof dish.

Season the fish with salt and pepper and the lemon juice. Heat the butter and oil over medium-high heat in a large skillet and sear the fish, in batches, on both sides. Take care not to burn the butter; it should be only slightly browned when you are ready to remove the fish.

Transfer the fish to a plate and add the bacon, if using, to the pan; stir and cook for 1 to 2 minutes, until it starts to crisp. Add the garlic and onion and sauté over medium heat until somewhat soft. Add the tomatoes and vinegar, season to taste, and cook for 4 minutes longer, stirring. Remove from the heat.

Using a slotted spoon, transfer the tomato mixture into the prepared casseroles, leaving the liquid in the pan. Return the pan to the stove, add the heavy cream, and bring to a boil. Allow to boil for 2 minutes. Spoon this mixture evenly over the tomato ragù, pressing the mixture down with the back of the spoon. Arrange the potatoes in a layer on top. Season with salt and pepper, and cover the casserole with a lid or foil.

Bake the casserole for 5 minutes. Remove the casserole, place the seared bass on top, and re-cover. Return the casserole to the oven and bake for approximately 15 minutes, until the sauce bubbles throughout. Scatter the roasted red pepper and basil over the top, fan the hard-cooked eggs over the fish, and serve.

recommended wine: A creamy Chardonnay is the most likely choice, but a Marsanne Roussanne from the Languedoc or a white Grenache from Spain would also be excellent.

pastel de mariscos

(Chilean Seafood Pie with Corn Crust)

SERVES 6 TO 8

When this savory dish emerges from the hot oven, its corn-pudding–like topping reminds me of a cobbler. But this seafood pie is, of course, a savory dish, and one that is not difficult to prepare. I've added roasted poblano to the pie's sweet corn and *calabaza,* with its coat of sour cream. The chile gives the other ingredients the electric zap they need and keeps the dish lively. Some of you might like even more heat: feel free. You could also add pine nuts, currants, and/or peeled and chopped tomatoes to the seafood filling.

1 tablespoon unsalted butter, melted, plus 2 tablespoons

2 cups *calabaza* (or peeled acorn squash) cut into 1/2-inch dice

1 teaspoon toasted and ground cumin seeds (see page 9)

1 tablespoon sugar

Kosher salt and freshly ground black pepper to taste

2 cups corn kernels (from 3 to 4 ears)

1 poblano pepper, roasted (see page 7), peeled, stemmed, seeded, and minced

1/3 cup oil-cured black olives, pitted and coarsely chopped

10 ounces cooked chorizo, diced small or crumbled (or other favorite sausage)

12 ounces sea scallops

12 ounces snapper fillets, cut into 1-inch pieces

12 ounces sea bass fillets, cut into 1-inch pieces

2 tablespoons pure olive oil

4 cloves garlic, sliced

4 shallots, minced

1/4 cup chopped Italian parsley

1 1/2 cups dry white wine

1 cup sour cream

FOR THE CORN CRUST

3 1/2 tablespoons unsalted butter

2 cloves garlic, sliced

2 1/2 cups corn kernels (from 3 to 4 ears)

1 extra-large egg

1 extra-large egg yolk

1/4 cup milk

1/4 cup all-purpose flour

1/2 teaspoon baking powder

1 teaspoon kosher salt, plus more to taste

6 scallions, white and green parts, minced

1 jalapeño, stemmed, seeded, and minced

Freshly ground black pepper to taste

1/2 cup bread crumbs

Preheat the oven to 375 degrees.

In a medium bowl, toss together the melted butter, squash, cumin, and sugar. Season with salt and pepper; place in a shallow baking dish.

Roast for 25 to 35 minutes, until the squash is tender. Remove from the oven and add the corn, and toss. Put back in the oven for 10 minutes, then remove the baking dish from the oven and add the poblano, olives, and chorizo; reserve. Turn the oven down to 350 degrees.

Season the scallops and fish with salt and

pepper. Heat the pure olive oil and 1 tablespoon of the butter in a 12-inch ovenproof nonstick sauté pan over medium-high heat. Once the butter foams, sear the scallops on both sides for 1 to 1 $^1/_2$ minutes on the first side, and about 1 minute on the second, until golden. Transfer to a plate. Add the fish to the pan and sauté, gently shaking the pan so it doesn't stick, until browned all over. Using a slotted spoon, transfer the fish to a plate.

To make the sauce, add the remaining 1 tablespoon butter to a clean saucepan. When it melts, add the garlic and shallots and sauté for 1 minute. Stir in the parsley and wine and reduce the liquid to approximately $^1/_2$ cup. (As the seafood rests, some juices may accumulate in the plate; pour them into the reducing wine.) Whisk in the sour cream. Season with salt and pepper and remove from the heat.

Cut the scallops into bite-sized pieces. Toss together with the squash-corn-chorizo mixture and fish. Gently fold in the sauce and set aside while you make the crust.

for the crust

In a clean nonstick sauté pan, melt 2 tablespoons of the butter over medium-high heat. Sauté the garlic for 1 minute, then add the corn and cook for 3 to 4 minutes. Remove from the heat and let cool. Set the sauté pan aside.

Combine the corn in a blender with the egg, egg yolk, and milk and process until smooth. Set aside.

Sift together the flour, baking powder, and 1 teaspoon salt into a medium bowl. Pour in the egg mixture, folding the flour mixture into it with a spatula. Reserve.

In a small sauté pan, melt the remaining 1 $^1/_2$ tablespoons butter over medium heat. Sauté the scallions and jalapeño for 2 minutes, or until the scallions are bright green and starting to soft. Season with salt and pepper and reserve.

Wipe out the sauté pan. Dust the bottom with the bread crumbs. Spread the filling evenly over the bottom of the pan. Spread the corn batter over the filling and sprinkle the sautéed scallions and jalapeños over the top.

Bake for 50 minutes, or until the center of the pie springs back to the touch. Serve hot.

recommended wine: A Chardonnay from either Saint-Aubin in Burgundy or Carneros in California.

deviled lobster

SERVES 6

In cooking, the word "deviled" means heat. This dish gets its heat from West Indian curry, but I soothe the devil with orange juice and sherry. I use spiny lobsters, local to Florida and the Caribbean.

4 tablespoons unsalted butter

2 tablespoons pure olive oil or canola oil

1 Scotch bonnet chile, stemmed, seeded, and minced

4 scallions, green and white parts, minced

1 medium red onion, cut into small dice

1/2 fennel bulb, cored and cut into small dice

1 cup Spanish dry sherry

1 cup fresh orange juice

2 cups Chicken Stock (page 267)

3 ripe tomatoes, peeled, seeded, and chopped

Kosher salt and freshly ground black pepper

1/4 cup Spanish sherry vinegar

3 pounds cooked spiny lobster tail (or Maine lobster meat or shrimp), diced

5 hard-boiled eggs, whites diced, yolks crumbled

1 1/2 teaspoons minced fresh thyme

2 cups hot milk

2 tablespoons all-purpose flour

1 tablespoon Madras curry powder

1 tablespoon mashed Roasted Garlic (page 262)

1 tablespoon Creole mustard

2 dashes Tabasco

2 cups diced golden pineapple

1/3 cup unsweetened grated coconut, toasted (see page 9)

Heat 2 tablespoons of the butter and the oil in a large heavy saucepan. When the butter begins to melt, add the Scotch bonnet, scallions, onion, and fennel, stir, and cook for 2 minutes. Add the sherry and deglaze the pan, stirring. Add the orange juice and reduce the liquid by half. Add the stock and reduce by half.

Add the tomatoes, season with salt and pepper, and simmer for 2 minutes. Add the vinegar and cook for 5 minutes. Remove from the heat.

In a medium bowl, combine the lobster, eggs, and thyme; reserve. In a large saucepan, bring the milk to just under a boil; remove from the heat.

Meanwhile, in a large sauté pan, melt the remaining 2 tablespoons butter over low heat. Add the flour and cook, whisking constantly, for 2 to 3 minutes; the mixture should start turning amber. Remove from the heat and stir in the curry. Return to the heat, slowly whisk in the milk and cook, whisking constantly, until the sauce begins to thicken, about 2 minutes. Remove from the heat and whisk in the roasted garlic, mustard, and Tabasco.

Return the tomato sauce to the heat and simmer. Whisk in the deviled cream sauce and cook for 2 minutes. Add the lobster mixture and pineapple. Season with salt and pepper.

Spoon the mixture into individual serving bowls, garnish with the toasted coconut, and serve.

recommended wine: A Pinot Gris or one of the new Gewürztraminers from the Somontano region of northern Spain.

fish in foil with sweet onions, tomatoes, and *mojo verde*

SERVES 4

The magnificence of a beautifully presented cooked whole fish is experienced far too infrequently today. Most people prefer the convenience of fillets, but fish has so much more flavor when cooked whole. Wrapping the fish in foil is a simple, effective way to lock in the juices.

3 tablespoons pure olive oil

2 tablespoons unsalted butter

2 medium red onions, sliced

Kosher salt and freshly ground black pepper to taste

1 pound medium red potatoes, scrubbed and cut into ¹/₄-inch-thick slices

One 4-pound snapper, gutted, scaled, and pectoral gill cut out (but tail left on; ask your fishmonger to do this)

¹/₄ cup *Mojo Verde* (page 285), plus extra for serving if desired

1 pound ripe tomatoes, sliced

¹/₄ cup dry white wine

Lemon wedges for garnish

Preheat the oven to 400 degrees.

In a large sauté pan, heat 1 tablespoon of the olive oil and the butter over medium-high heat. When the butter foams, add the onions, stirring to coat, and season with salt and pepper. Cook for 8 to 12 minutes, stirring occasionally, until golden. Let cool.

Stack two pieces of aluminum foil that are large enough to wrap the fish in on top of one another. Fold up the sides of the foil so that it resembles a little boat. Pour the remaining 2 tablespoons olive oil into the boat and spread it over the bottom. Lay the potatoes in the boat in one layer, and season with salt and pepper.

With a sharp knife, make slashes in one side of the fish about 1 ¹/₂ inches apart, going almost to the bone, and season with salt and pepper. Repeat on the other side of the fish. Lay it on top of the potatoes. Spoon the *mojo verde* on top of the fish. Lay the tomatoes on top of it and spoon the rest of the *mojo* on them. Spoon on the caramelized onions. Pour the wine around the fish.

Fold the foil over to enclose the fish, crimping the edges to seal and set on a baking sheet.

Roast the fish for about 1 hour, or until cooked through (carefully open the foil to check: the fish should flake easily when tested with a fork); cooking times can vary significantly depending on the thickness and type of fish. (The baked fish can be kept warm, and still retain its moisture, for up to 30 minutes if kept wrapped.)

Serve with lemon wedges and, if you like, extra *mojo verde* on the side.

recommended wine: A wine with soft acidity and sweetness, such as a Vouvray or an American Pinot Blanc.

pescado frito
(Crispy Red Snapper)

SERVES 6

Whether fried at a humble stand on an isolated beach or prepared in a sophisticated kitchen, fresh native fish, like this snapper, is one of the Caribbean's best-loved treats.

$^1/_2$ European cucumber, peeled, cut lengthwise in half, seeded, and diced

Kosher salt

2 large ripe tomatoes, peeled, seeded, and diced

1 Scotch bonnet chile, stemmed, seeded, and minced

4 garlic cloves, minced

1 $^1/_2$ tablespoons minced cilantro

Freshly ground black pepper to taste

$^1/_2$ pound (2 sticks) unsalted butter

$^1/_4$ cup Spanish sherry vinegar

1 cup all-purpose flour

Six 1 $^1/_2$- to 2-pound red snapper (you can also use striped bass or tilefish) cleaned, scaled, and dorsal fins removed (ask your fishmonger to do this)

Canola oil for searing the fish

Preheat the oven to 425 degrees.

Put the cucumber dice in a bowl and sprinkle with salt, tossing it so it is evenly salted. Let sit for 10 minutes. (This will release some of the water.) Rinse off the salt, drain, and pat dry.

Combine the cucumber with the tomatoes, Scotch bonnet, garlic, and cilantro in a bowl. Season with salt and pepper, and stir.

In a medium pot, melt the butter over medium heat. Continue to heat it, stir occa-sionally, until it turns amber, about 10 minutes. Remove from the heat and pour off the liquid into a bowl; discard the brown solids in the bottom of the pot. Wipe out the pot and pour the butter back into it, then carefully pour in the vinegar; it may splatter. Add the tomato-cucumber-chile mixture and set aside.

Have ready two baking pans large enough to accommodate the fish comfortably. Make a series of three shallow incisions on both sides of each fillet, to allow the heat to better pene-trate the fillet. Put the flour on a large platter and season with salt and pepper. Lightly dredge each fish in it, tapping the fish gently to remove any excess.

Heat enough canola oil to cover the bottom of a large nonstick skillet over medium-high heat. When the pan is very hot, sear the fish on both sides until golden. (You'll have to do this in batches.)

Put the fish in the baking pans and roast them until completely cooked through, about 10 minutes, depending on the size.

Meanwhile, bring the sauce to a simmer. Place the fish on six plates, pour over the sauce, and serve.

recommended wine or beer: Macon Blanc, or, something more casual, a clean, crisp beer.

plantain-crusted soft-shell crabs with *sauce créole*

SERVES 4

Soft-shell crabs have become increasingly popular and so have plantains. Here we combine them for a somewhat nutty, banana-scented sweetness, partnered with the deep, spicy flavors of a classic *Sauce Créole*.

Sweet *Boniato* Mash (page 205) would meet the spiciness of the sauce perfectly. Place the mash in the center of your plates, arrange the crabs on top, and spoon the sauce on. Garnish with nothing more elaborate than lime wedges.

2 green plantains
Canola or peanut oil for deep-frying
Kosher salt and freshly ground black pepper to
    taste
$^1\!/_4$ cup cornmeal
2 tablespoons all-purpose flour
2 extra-large eggs
$^1\!/_3$ cup milk
1 cup all-purpose flour
8 soft-shell crabs, cleaned (have the fishmonger
    clean them, then cook them as soon as
    possible)
1 recipe *Sauce Créole* (page 288), heated
Lime wedges

With a sharp knife, cut off both ends of each plantain. Then make 3 or 4 lengthwise slits through the skin. Set the plantains in a bowl of hot water and let soak for 10 minutes. (This will make it easier to peel them.)

Remove the plantains from the water and peel them. Using a mandoline or other vegetable slicer or a sharp knife, slice the plantains lengthwise into very thin strips (about $^1\!/_{16}$ inch).

In a deep skillet, heat the oil to 375 degrees. Drop the plantain slices into the oil one at a time, so that they don't stick together, and cook for 2 minutes, or until crisp and golden. Transfer to a plate lined with paper towels. Season with salt and pepper.

When the plantains are cool, grind them in a food processor. Combine with the flour and cornmeal, and set aside.

In a shallow bowl, whisk together the egg and milk, and add a pinch of salt. In another bowl, season the flour with salt and pepper. Place the plantain mixture in a third shallow bowl. One at a time, dredge the crabs completely in the flour mixture and then coat them with the egg wash, then with the plantain crust.

Heat the oil in a large nonstick skillet over medium heat. Add the crabs and cook for 3 minutes on each side, until cooked through. Drain well on paper towels.

Divide the sauce among four plates. Arrange 2 crabs on each. Serve with lime wedges.

recommended wine: A California Chardonnay or a Soave Classico.

snapper *a la veracruzana*

SERVES 4

It makes perfect sense to name a beautiful preparation of snapper after a port. Veracruz is Mexico's main port on the Gulf Coast, and this dish is one of the most popular entrées I serve at the restaurant.

You could also serve this over the *Boniato* Mash (page 205) rather than with the bread.

FOR THE ONIONS

3 tablespoons canola oil
2 tablespoons unsalted butter
1 large red onion, halved and thinly sliced
$^1/_2$ large Spanish onion, thinly sliced
1 $^1/_2$ tablespoons sugar
$^1/_2$ cup Spanish sherry vinegar
Kosher salt and freshly ground black pepper
    to taste

FOR THE FISH

Four 6-ounce yellowtail snapper fillets
1 tablespoon kosher salt, or more to taste
$^1/_4$ teaspoon freshly ground black pepper, or
    more to taste
1 $^3/_4$ teaspoons toasted and ground cumin
    seeds (see page 9)
2 tablespoons pure olive oil
4 cloves garlic, minced
$^1/_4$ cup oil-cured black olives, pitted and
    coarsely chopped
$^1/_4$ cup capers, rinsed
1 large ripe tomato, peeled, seeded, and diced
$^1/_4$ cup Spanish dry sherry
$^1/_4$ cup Spanish sherry vinegar
1 tablespoon chopped fresh thyme
1 tablespoon finely chopped fresh sage
1 teaspoon minced fresh rosemary
$^1/_3$ cup Chicken Stock (page 267)
$^1/_4$ cup fresh lime juice
1 ripe but not *too* soft avocado, pitted, peeled,
    and diced
4 tablespoons unsalted butter, diced

4 slices *Medianoche* Bread (page 228) or *Pan
    Cubano* Bread (page 224), cut on the bias
    1 inch thick, toasted

for the onions

In a large sauté pan, heat the oil and butter over medium-high heat until quite hot. Add the onions and caramelize them, stirring occasionally, about 8 minutes. Add the sugar and cook for another 2 minutes. Add the vinegar and salt and pepper and simmer until almost no liquid remains. Reserve $^1/_2$ cup of the onions for the bread, and set the rest aside.

for the fish

Rub the fillets with the salt, pepper, and $^1/_4$ teaspoon of the cumin. In a large skillet, heat the olive oil. When it is quite hot, add the fillets and sear until golden brown on both sides. Transfer the fish to a plate.

Add the garlic to the pan and sauté for a minute. Add the onions (saving $^1/_2$ cup for the bread), the olives, capers, tomato, sherry, and sherry vinegar and stir constantly, for about 2 minutes, until some of the liquid evaporates.

Add the herbs, chicken stock, lime juice, the remaining 1 $^1/_2$ teaspoons cumin, and the avocado and continue cooking, until the sauce thickens and reduces a bit more, about 3 minutes. Turn the heat down to low and, stirring constantly, add the butter bit by bit. Adjust the seasonings as necessary (the capers and olives will provide a fair amount of salt).

Top with the toasted bread and the reserved caramelized onions.

recommended wine: Vernaccia from San Gimignano in Tuscany, or, for a red, a light Tempranillo from Rioja.

african *adobo*-rubbed tuna steaks

SERVES 4

Adobo means spice rub or marinade, and this particular recipe was introduced by African slaves brought to Bahía in Brazil in the seventeenth century. I think that it gives tuna a new and exciting dimension. There is spiciness in the dish, as would be expected from an *adobo*. To provide the American palate a little relief from the heat, the tuna is served on a bed of lightly pickled cucumbers.

FOR THE AVOCADO SALSA

2 ripe avocados, pitted, peeled, and cut into
$^1/_2$-inch cubes

3 scallions, white and green parts, thinly sliced
on the bias

2 jarred piquillo peppers, diced (or substitute
2 jarred roasted red peppers)

2 cloves garlic, minced

$^1/_3$ cup fresh orange juice

$^1/_4$ cup fresh lime juice

$^1/_2$ cup extra virgin olive oil

Kosher salt and freshly ground black pepper to
taste

FOR THE *ADOBO*

1 $^1/_2$ teaspoons toasted and ground coriander
seeds (see page 9)

1 teaspoon ground ginger

1 $^1/_2$ teaspoons crushed red pepper flakes

1 $^1/_2$ teaspoons ground turmeric

1 $^1/_2$ tablespoons dry mustard

1 $^1/_2$ teaspoons grated nutmeg

1 $^1/_2$ teaspoons ground allspice

1 $^1/_2$ teaspoons cayenne pepper

1 $^1/_2$ teaspoons freshly ground black pepper

1 $^1/_2$ tablespoons kosher salt

1 tablespoon paprika

1 $^1/_2$ tablespoons dried orange peel

1 tablespoon sugar

Four 6-ounce tuna steaks

$^1/_4$ cup peanut or canola oil

FOR THE CUCUMBERS

2 $^1/_2$ tablespoons sugar, or to taste

$^1/_2$ cup Champagne vinegar

1 European cucumber, peeled, halved lengthwise, seeded, and very thinly sliced

for the salsa

In a medium bowl, combine the diced avocados, scallions, peppers, and garlic. In another bowl, whisk together the orange and lime juices, olive oil, and salt and pepper. Pour over the avocado mixture and gently toss. Refrigerate for 15 minutes.

Meanwhile, for the cucumbers: Mix the sugar and vinegar in a bowl, stirring well. Add the cucumber and allow to marinate for about 15 minutes.

To serve, arrange the cucumber in neat slices across each plate. Slice the tuna and lay it over the cucumbers. Spoon the avocado salsa on top of or around the tuna. Spoon a little of the pickling juices around the cucumbers, and serve. (Sometimes I add a little grated orange zest for garnish as well.)

for the *adobo*
Mix all of the ingredients together in a bowl.

Rub each of the tuna steaks with 1 $^1/_2$ teaspoons of the oil and sprinkle generously with the *adobo*. (Reserve any extra adobo spice rub for another use.) In a nonstick skillet, heat the remaining 2 tablespoons oil until it begins to smoke. Sear the tuna on each side for only 1 minute—the tuna is served rare. Transfer to a plate and set aside.

recommended wine: A cold-pressed sake would be an unexpected but welcome accompaniment.

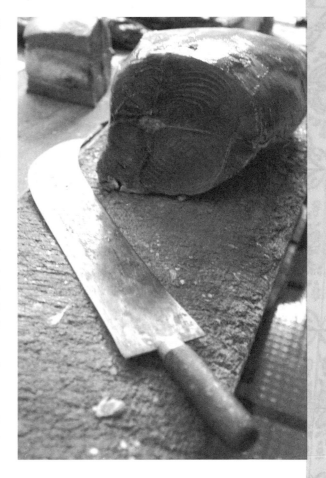

scallops and *papas chorreadas* with romaine

(Scallops with Potatoes in Cheese Sauce)

SERVES 4

The word *chorreadas* (or *chorreado*) describes the sensual way a thick sauce flows over a dish. Here the creamy sauce for the potatoes gets some sweetness from tomatoes and a tiny jolt of heat from the red pepper flakes in the pepper Jack cheese; in my interpretation, the sauce is served both under and over the potatoes. I like the non-traditional accompaniment of romaine leaves, which add a soft green hue.

The South American classic *papas chorreadas* is served both as a stand-alone dish and as an accompaniment to simple grilled steaks, chicken breasts, or pork chops. I propose that you follow this dish with Creole Mustard–Glazed Calves' Liver (page 168).

FOR THE SCALLOPS

2 tablespoons pure olive oil

1 1/2 pounds sea scallops

Kosher salt and freshly ground black pepper to taste

Papas Chorreadas with Romaine (page 207)

2 tablespoons extra virgin olive oil

Chopped herbs for garnish (optional)

for the scallops

Heat one or two large nonstick skillets over medium-high heat and add the oil. Season the scallops with salt and pepper. When the oil is quite hot, add the scallops and sear 1 to 1 1/2 minutes on the first side, 1 minute on the second side, until golden on the bottom. Turn them over and cook for about 20 seconds. Transfer them to a wire rack set over a baking sheet.

To serve, spoon the lettuce-in-cheese sauce onto four warm plates. Place the potato wedges atop it and drizzle the potatoes lightly with the extra virgin olive oil. Season the potatoes. Spoon the remaining warmed sauce over the potatoes. Garnish with chopped fresh herbs, if you like. Place the scallops on top and serve.

recommended wine: An Alsatian Pinot Blanc would be a nice match.

tuna *escabeche caliente*
(Seared Tuna Steaks with Spiced Butter)

SERVES 4

Escabeche is usually served cold. I've turned things around in two ways that allow me to serve a hot version. The fish is not spicy, but the *escabeche* spice butter I use to top the hot tuna steaks provides a nice contrast. I like to serve this dish on Peruvian Purple Potato Mash (page 206), with a mound of Fried Onions (page 210) on top.

I recommend trying this with other fish steaks too, such as salmon or another hearty fish. (Vary the cooking time accordingly.)

1 chipotle chile, stemmed and seeded
1 1/2 teaspoons coriander seeds
1 tablespoon black peppercorns
1/2 teaspoon whole cloves
3 bay leaves, broken in half
2 cups white wine vinegar
1 cup fresh orange juice
1/2 cup sliced fennel
1/2 small red onion, sliced
5 cloves garlic, halved
3 sprigs thyme
Four 6-ounce tuna steaks
8 tablespoons (1 stick) unsalted butter, softened
2 tablespoons plus 1/2 teaspoon *Escabeche* Spice Rub (page 266)
2 tablespoons canola oil

In a small saucepan, toast the chipotle, coriander, peppercorns, cloves, and bay leaves over medium heat until aromatic. Remove from the heat and add the vinegar, orange juice, fennel, onion, garlic, and thyme.

Strain off 3/4 cup of this marinade and reserve. When the remaining marinade is cool, pour it (without straining it) over the fish in a shallow bowl or a baking dish, making sure the tuna is completely immersed. Let sit for 30 minutes.

Meanwhile, make the spiced butter: Pour the reserved 3/4 cup marinade into a small saucepan and reduce it over medium heat to 1 tablespoon. Let cool to room temperature, then combine in a bowl with the butter. Add 1/2 teaspoon of the spice rub and mash together with a fork. It will take a little blending, but it will combine. Set aside. (This can be made in advance and refrigerated; bring back to room temperature just before serving.)

Take the tuna steaks out of the marinade and roll them in the remaining 2 tablespoons spice rub. In a large skillet heat the canola oil over medium-high heat. When the oil is quite hot, add the tuna and cook for about 3 minutes. Turn and cook for 2 minutes on the second side, then very briefly cook each side of the steaks. Remove the tuna and allow it to rest for just a moment.

You can serve the fish as whole steaks, or slice it. Put a dollop of butter on each fish. Serve the rest of the butter on the side and have your guests add it as they wish. Any extra butter can be saved for another use or frozen.

recommended wine: A Riesling Halbtrocken for contrast or an Oregon Pinot Noir.

the african influence

As we continue to learn of the ascent and ruin of the Mayan, Incan, and Aztec civilizations, we become more and more aware of periods in which the capabilities of mankind were illuminated. We also wonder what other lost civilizations our planet might have known. It is tempting to ponder what might have happened if dreams had not been so fatally deferred. We will never know, for instance, how the New World might have flourished had African immigrants been free to explore and settle it. Instead, what we know and must contend with forever is six hundred years of slavery and the seeds sowed in that infamy.

Yet if there ever was a glimmer of what might have happened had African princes and farmers, explorers and medicine men, and whole families sailed freely across the ocean and extended the fruits of their civilization to the New World, we glimpse it in Brazil, particularly in the state of Bahía. There African food is celebrated more richly and directly than probably anyplace else that practiced slavery. In Brazil there is a saying: "The blacker the cook, the better the food."

One of the most interesting observations posited by food and cultural historians is that slaves who were allowed to keep their drums in the New World almost always developed a more vibrant cuisine than those who were stripped of them. In Bahía, the slaves were allowed the instruments by their Portuguese masters, and historians deduce that playing them made a difference in the slaves' spirit, will, and ability to love, which they of course poured into their cooking and the rest of their existence. The Bantus, Yorubas, and Dahomeys, for example, worshipped seven *Orixás,* or deities, and the worship of those deities involved many rituals, among them drumming, group dancing, and chanting, and the offering of ceremonial foods. This feeding of the deities, as it were, involved transplanting crops and other African ingredients to the New World, as well as training cooks to prepare the holy recipes.

While the British and Dutch brutally forced their slaves to abandon their cultural heritages, the Portuguese, French, and Spanish tended to regard with a mixture of indifference and passive benevolence their slaves' African music, food, and cultural customs. Even today there remains a link between ancient African religions and cooking traditions. In Brazil's *candomble* and *macumba,* as well as in Haiti's voodoo and Cuba's *santería,* we see the relation between African-influenced religion and food in the New World.

Of course Africa's culinary-cultural reach stretches far beyond those epicenters. A wide swath of influence extends from New Orleans southeast through the West Indies and down the Atlantic coast of South America to Brazil. To protect their *Orixás* from the religious scrutiny of their European masters (who were hell-bent on converting their human "possessions") slaves cleverly camouflaged their gods as Catholic saints. To a Bahía slave, "Saint Barbara" was merely cover for Xango, the Virgin Mary doubled as Oxun, and "the Holy Ghost" was just another alias for Obatala. Because preparing and offering dishes to the gods and goddesses were an essential part of these Afro-American religions—which are still practiced by millions—they developed their own lofty, delicious, and subversive cuisines (which were, by the way, enjoyed by the oblivious plantation masters).

A list of ingredients brought to the New World from Africa would have to include dendé (palm oil); coconut meat and milk; black-eyed peas and various other beans; plantains and yuca; *manioc* and yams; sweet potatoes and *malanga;* and okra, *ackee,* and *callaloo.* Slaves also brought with them an impressive cast of chile peppers, some (perhaps all) of which had been originally exported to Africa from the Americas, then brought back to the Americas in the wondrous way that foods and cooking methods have always crisscrossed the earth.

Only anointed cooks were allowed to prepare these religious foods. I see a direct link of food knowledge and love between them and many of the great modern chefs born or trained in Bahía and Cartagena, or Havana and New Orleans. By including recipes for *acarajé* and *adobo,* Pepperpot and *Tacu-tacu, Sauce Créole* and *vatapá* in this book, I hope to do my part to keep the African influence alive and well.

vatapá

(Seafood Stew with Cilantro and Coconut)

SERVES 6

This complexly flavored Afro-Brazilian dish features a small riot of ingredients, among them both fresh and dried shrimp. You may have never had dried shrimp, but they are as intriguing in this stew as anchovies are in a good Caesar salad. *Vatapás* are a specialty of the Bahía, one of the most exotic spots on the planet, where the locals' love of surging flavors is celebrated in these stews. There are as many variations of this dish as there are kinds of gumbo. And, like gumbo, a *vatapá* can contain fish, chicken, or pork.

I like to serve this stew atop Basic White Rice (page 196) and garnish it with shredded cilantro, toasted unsweetened coconut, and lime wedges.

$^1/_4$ cup dried shrimp
$^1/_4$ cup unsalted peanuts, toasted (see page 9)
$^1/_4$ cup unsalted cashews, toasted (see page 9)
$^3/_4$ cup all-purpose flour
Kosher salt and freshly ground black pepper
    to taste
6 boneless chicken thighs and/or breasts,
    skin on
$^1/_4$ cup canola oil
2 tablespoons unsalted butter
3 cloves garlic, thinly sliced
$^1/_2$ Scotch bonnet chile, stemmed, seeded,
    and minced
1 large Spanish onion, diced
3 medium ripe tomatoes, peeled, seeded,
    and chopped
1 cup fresh orange juice
1 tablespoon peeled and minced ginger
1 bay leaf, broken in half
$^3/_4$ cup unsweetened coconut milk
$^3/_4$ cup Chicken Stock (page 267)
8 ounces skinless fish fillets, such as snapper,
    bass, or grouper, cut into bite-sized pieces
8 ounces shrimp, peeled, deveined, and cut
    into bite-sized pieces
3 tablespoons chopped cilantro

Preheat the oven to 375 degrees.

Soak the dried shrimp in warm water for about 10 minutes; drain.

Grind the toasted nuts and dried shrimp in a food processor until very finely chopped. Reserve.

In a bowl, season the flour with salt and pepper. Dredge the chicken pieces in it and shake off the excess.

In a large skillet, heat 2 tablespoons of the oil and 1 tablespoon of butter over medium-high heat until quite hot. Sear the chicken pieces until golden brown all over, then transfer them to a roasting pan and place in the oven (set the skillet aside). Thighs will take 30 to 35 minutes in the oven and breasts 15 to 20 minutes. When they are cooked, set aside, covered to keep warm.

Meanwhile, wipe the skillet clean. Set over medium heat, add the remaining 2 tablespoons oil and 1 tablespoon butter, and heat until hot. Stir in the garlic and Scotch bonnet and cook for 30 seconds. Add the onions and sauté until they start to caramelize, about 8 minutes.

Add the tomatoes, orange juice, ginger, and bay leaf, season with salt and pepper, and cook, stirring occasionally for about 2 minutes. Stir in the coconut milk, chicken stock, and the ground nuts and dried shrimp. Simmer for about 3 minutes. Add the fish, fresh shrimp, and the cilantro and simmer for another 3 minutes.

Divide the fish stew evenly among six bowls. Top with the roasted chicken.

recommended wine: An aromatic Muscat from Alsace.

birds

Sitting on a picnic bench at the tiny Haitian restaurant, I waited. I'd spent hours earlier in the morning walking and looking for beautiful little dishes that I love to use in presenting my tasting menus at the restaurant. But I'd had little luck, and a keen hunger was rising up in me. I was hot and wanted something with a little kick. An elderly white-haired Haitian gentleman seated nearby was served a platter of chicken and rice. I asked him what it was and though he spoke no English and I no Creole, he knew what I meant and, pointing to the brightly colored menu hand-painted on the wall of the sagging little building, indicated that the dish he was enjoying was *Poulet à la Créole* (page 136). I wasted no time in ordering the same.

Drifting from the cook's stove were the intoxicating aromas of the chicken melded with those of curry, coconut milk, bacon, garlic, saffron, tomatoes, and pineapple. The dish crossed through time, from markets in distant lands to the hands and memories of explorers and slaves, over impossible expanses of water, eventually reaching the tiny country of Haiti. I could hardly stand the wait, but wait I did. That Haiti, so tortured at the hands of history yet so spiritually steadfast, would produce this tantalizing dish seemed right to me: Haiti is a country for the patient.

Sitting there, I thought about how many centuries it took for domesticated fowl to reach the New World. The Aztecs had only five domesticated animals in their culinary repertory; ducks and turkeys were two of them. Of course, once poultry was introduced to the resourceful cooks of Latin America and the Caribbean, it became a delicious staple of their cuisine. The Spanish explorer Hernando Cortés feasted on turkey in the West Indies and so liked what he ate that he carried mating pairs of the birds back to Europe, where they became fashionable to eat—stuffed with truffles—in France in the 1800s.

The most common fowl served in the Caribbean, Mexico, Central America, and South America is the chicken. Because of the ways that chickens are mass-produced in the United States, I urge you to buy birds that were raised "free range." By now you can find them in almost any grocery store or market. With them, even the simplest preparation of chicken will be delicious.

jocon

(Chicken in Green Sauce)

SERVES 4 TO 6

After much research on the origin of the name of the famous chicken dish of Guatemala, I came up only with this: it appears to have originated in the town of Huehuetenango, where they like their *jocon* (pronounced *ho-CONE*) hot and spicy. But the ingredients vary depending on which region you are in, and my version of *jocon* leans toward Mexico, Guatemala's neighbor to the north. I use ground toasted tortillas and a sauce reminiscent of a *mole verde,* with sweet, smoky flavors. Plain white rice is the perfect foil to the intensely colored and flavored green sauce, and the vivid, pungent Pimiento Corn Relish (page 278) is an excellent accompaniment for the *Jocon.*

2 chipotle chiles
2 small corn tortillas, toasted and chopped
Two 3- to 4-pound fryer chickens, cut into 6 to 8 pieces each
Kosher salt and freshly ground black pepper to taste
$1/4$ cup canola oil
1 cup Chicken Stock (page 267)
6 to 8 ripe tomatillos, papery husks removed, rinsed, and cored
4 cloves garlic, sliced
1 cup chopped cilantro
1 cup chopped scallion greens
$1/2$ medium Spanish onion, diced
2 tablespoons toasted and ground pepitas (see page 9)

Preheat the oven to 350 degrees.

Toast the chipotles in a small skillet over medium heat, then soak them in a bowl of warm water until soft, about 20 minutes. Drain and remove the seeds and stems. Reserve.

In the same dry skillet over medium heat, toast the tortillas briefly on each side until fragrant. Chop them and set aside.

Meanwhile, season the chicken with salt and pepper. Heat the oil in a large ovenproof skillet over medium-high heat. When it is very hot, add the chicken, in batches, skin side down, and sear for about 2 minutes per side, until golden brown. Turn and brown on the other side.

Return all the chicken to the pan, transfer to the oven, and bake for 30 minutes.

Meanwhile, in a blender or food processor, puree the tortillas with the chicken stock, tomatillos, garlic, cilantro, scallion greens, onion, chipotles, and pumpkin seeds. Reserve.

Remove the skillet from the oven and place on the stove over medium heat. Add the pureed sauce to the skillet and simmer for 15 minutes, stirring occasionally. Season with salt and pepper, and serve.

recommended wine: A Mosel Riesling, as a contrast to the green sauce and spices.

arroz con pollo
(Chicken with Rice)

SERVES 6

I first had this dish in a neighborhood Cuban café on one of my first visits to Key West in the early 1970s. It wasn't long before I discovered that *arroz con pollo* strikes a chord with the people of Cuba the way chicken and dumplings might stir the memories of someone from the American South. Cooks often prepare this dish *a la chorrera,* or "with a spurt," achieved by adding a cup of beer to the recipes. (In bolder households, they use a cup of white rum.)

FOR THE MARINADE

3 cloves garlic, minced

2 tablespoons fresh chopped oregano

$^1/_3$ cup fresh sour orange juice (or half lime juice and half regular orange juice)

2 tablespoons Spanish sherry vinegar

$^1/_4$ cup virgin olive oil

2 teaspoons kosher salt

$^1/_4$ teaspoon freshly ground black pepper

One 3- to 4-pound fryer chicken, cut into 8 pieces

FOR THE RICE

4 $^1/_2$ cups Chicken Stock (page 267)

1 teaspoon annatto seeds, toasted and ground (see page 9) (optional)

A pinch of saffron threads

3 ounces smoky bacon, diced

2 tablespoons pure olive oil

2 cloves garlic, thinly sliced

1 large shallot, minced

1 poblano pepper, stemmed, seeded, and diced

2 tomatoes, peeled, seeded, and chopped

1 bay leaf, broken in half

$^1/_2$ teaspoon toasted and ground cumin seeds (see page 9)

1 tablespoon chopped cilantro

2 cups long-grain white rice

One 12-ounce bottle beer, at room temperature

Kosher salt and freshly ground black pepper to taste

GARNISH

$^1/_2$ cup green peas, cooked in boiling salted water until tender

4 jarred piquillo peppers, sliced into $^1/_4$-inch-wide ribbons (or substitute jarred roasted red peppers)

for the marinade

In a large shallow bowl, combine the garlic, oregano, sour orange juice, vinegar, oil, salt, and pepper. Set the chicken pieces in the mixture, turning to make sure they are thoroughly coated. Allow to marinate for 1 hour. Refrigerate.

for the rice

Bring the chicken stock to a simmer in a medium pot over medium heat. Add the saffron and annatto, if using, and remove from the heat.

In a casserole or skillet that is large enough to accommodate the chicken in one layer, cook the bacon in the olive oil over medium-high heat until it has rendered some of its fat. Add the chicken, skin side down and sear for about 2 minutes; then turn over and sear for another 2 minutes, or until the chicken is golden all over. Transfer the chicken to a plate.

Add the garlic, shallot, and poblano to the pot and sauté until the shallot is translucent, about 1 minute. Add the tomatoes, bay leaf, cumin, and cilantro and sauté for 1 minute. Add the rice and toast it for 30 seconds, stirring constantly so it doesn't stick, then add the beer for your spurt, *a la chorrera*. Return the chicken pieces to the pot, pour in the infused chicken stock, season with salt and pepper, and bring to a simmer. Turn the heat down to medium-low, cover, and cook for 20 minutes, or until the juices run clear when a chicken thigh is pierced.

Remove from the heat, top with the peas and pepper ribbons, cover, and let the flavors marry for 10 minutes. Serve.

recommended beer or wine: Widmer Hefe-Weizen is a seductive unfiltered wheat beer that would work well, as would a soft, fruity red wine, such as a Cru Beaujolais.

asopao de arroz con pollo

(Stewed Chicken and Rice with Tomatoes, Olives, Capers, and Peas)

SERVES 6

Asopao is a kissing cousin to *arroz con pollo*. Also in this family of dishes are *sancocho*, in the Dominican Republic, and the pan-Caribbean dish called *ajiaco*. Or think of *asopao* as Puerto Rican paella.

One of the touches that make this dish special is the *sofrito*—a concentrated, seasoned paste made from bell peppers, tomatoes, garlic, cilantro, and, in some cases, annatto, which adds color and flavor to the dish. *Sofrito* is widely used in Latin American countries, with slight variations from culture to culture. Some people like to add a little heat to their *sofrito*—as I've done here by using medium-spicy poblanos instead of bell peppers.

I like to accompany the *asopao* with Chipotle-Corn Skillet Bread (page 38) or *Roti* (page 229), and I usually have Ancho-Cumin Oil (page 261) or Chipotle Vinegar (page 264) on the table.

A pinch of saffron threads

6 cups Chicken Stock (page 267), warmed

2 tablespoons mashed Roasted Garlic (page 262)

2 tablespoons minced fresh oregano

1 tablespoon toasted and ground cumin seeds (see page 9)

1 teaspoon kosher salt

1 teaspoon freshly ground black pepper, plus more to taste

6 tablespoons Annatto Oil (page 261), or pure olive oil

One 3- to 4-pound fryer chicken, cut into 6 or 8 pieces

8 ounces cooked ham, diced

2 cloves garlic, minced

1 large red onion, diced

1 poblano pepper, stemmed, seeded, and minced

1 bay leaf, broken in half

2 cups long-grain white rice

1 1/4 cups freshly grated Parmesan cheese

3 large ripe tomatoes, peeled, seeded, and chopped

1 cup green peas, cooked in boiling salted water until tender

1 tablespoon small capers, rinsed and finely chopped

1 cup green olives stuffed with pimientos, sliced

2 pimientos, roasted, stemmed, seeded, peeled, and cut into strips

Steep the saffron in the warm chicken stock for at least 15 minutes.

Meanwhile, in a medium bowl, mix the roasted garlic, oregano, cumin, salt, pepper, and 2 tablespoons of the annatto oil together to make a paste. Put the chicken pieces in the bowl and rub them all over with the paste. Set aside.

In a very large nonstick casserole, heat 2 tablespoons of the annatto over medium-high heat. Add a few pieces at a time, skin side down, and sear, turning once, until golden brown; shake the pot periodically so they do not stick. Transfer the chicken to a large plate and set aside. Add the diced ham to the casserole and cook for 2 minutes. Using a slotted spoon, transfer the ham to a plate.

To make the *sofrito,* add 1 more tablespoon of the annatto oil to the pot and heat over medium heat. When it is hot, add the garlic, onion, and poblano and cook, stirring, until lightly caramelized, about 5 minutes.

Add the bay leaf and rice and stir well to coat. Pour in half of the saffron-infused stock and season with salt and pepper. Bring to a simmer, then reduce the heat to low and cook, covered, until the rice and vegetables have absorbed most of the stock. Add the remaining stock and the chicken and cook for 10 minutes.

Add the Parmesan, tomatoes, capers, olives, and the reserved ham, stirring to combine. Continue to cook over low heat for 20 to 30 minutes, or until the chicken is cooked through. Stir occasionally so that the rice doesn't stick to the bottom of the pot. Stir in the peas.

Transfer the *asopao* to a large serving dish, garnish with the pimiento strips, and serve.

recommended wine: A slightly chilled Barbera from Alba or Asti, or a light, cool Tempranillo red.

chicken *pelau*

(Chicken and Rice Stewed in Coconut Milk with Pigeon Peas, Currants, and Green Olives)

SERVES 4

East Indian immigrants have enriched the cooking of Trinidad with recipes like this *pelau*. The Puerto Rican *asopao* might be considered a simpler, soupier version of *pelau*, though no direct link is known. Keep in mind that you have to soak the pigeon peas overnight.

1 cup dried pigeon peas, rinsed, soaked
    overnight in water to cover, and drained

FOR THE MARINADE
6 cloves garlic, sliced
1 Scotch bonnet chile, stemmed, seeded, and
    minced
$^1/_2$ cup ketchup
2 tablespoons Worcestershire sauce
$^2/_3$ cup honey
3 tablespoons fresh lime juice
1 $^1/_2$ teaspoons salt
2 teaspoons freshly ground black pepper

4 chicken breasts
Kosher salt and freshly ground black pepper to
    taste
3 tablespoons canola oil
2 tablespoons unsalted butter
2 tablespoons pure olive oil
4 cloves garlic, thinly sliced
2 carrots, peeled and diced
1 poblano pepper, stemmed, seeded, and diced
1 red bell pepper, stemmed, seeded, and diced
1 large Spanish onion, diced
1 bay leaf, broken in half
$^1/_4$ cup chopped cilantro
2 $^1/_2$ tablespoons chopped fresh thyme
1 cup long-grain white rice
2 large tomatoes, peeled, seeded, and finely
    chopped
1 cup dried currants
1 cup unsweetened coconut milk
1 cup Chicken Stock (page 267)

GARNISH
1 cup green olives, pitted and chopped

Put the pigeon peas in a large saucepan, cover with fresh water, and simmer for 1 $^1/_2$ to 2 hours, until tender. Drain.

While the peas are cooking, make the marinade: Stir together the garlic, Scotch bonnet, ketchup, Worcestershire, honey, lime juice, salt, and pepper in a bowl. Season the chicken with salt and pepper. Put the breasts in a large resealable plastic bag and pour half of the marinade over them, reserving the other half for later. Seal the bag and refrigerate for 1 hour.

When the peas are cooked, remove the chicken from the marinade; discard the marinade. Heat the canola oil in a large nonstick sauté pan over medium-high heat. When the oil is very hot, add the chicken, skin side down, and sear 2 minutes per side until golden. Turn over and sear on the other side, then remove to a plate.

In a large pot or a casserole, melt the butter with the olive oil over medium heat. Add the garlic, carrots, poblano, red bell pepper, onion, and bay leaf and sauté for about 3 minutes, until the onion turns translucent. Add the cilantro and thyme, then stir in the rice, drained pigeon peas, tomatoes, and currants. Season with salt and pepper and stir to mix.

Add the coconut milk and chicken stock, and lay the chicken on top of the stew. Turn the heat down to low, to keep the ingredients at a simmer, cover, and cook for 25 to 30 minutes, or until the rice is tender and the chicken is cooked through.

Warm the reserved marinade. Spoon the *pelau* onto plates, arranging the chicken breasts on top of the rice and peas. Brush the chicken with the marinade, garnish the dish with the olives, and serve.

recommended wine: An herbal Sauvignon Blanc or earthy California Chardonnay.

pastel de choclo
(Savory Chicken Stew with a Corn Crust)

SERVES 6

Choclo is a type of sweet corn found in Chile. *Pastel* means "pie" or "pastry"—think savory cobbler, more or less. And like a quiche, the filling can be made from an almost infinite variety of ingredients. Here I use chicken.

FOR THE FILLING

One 3 ¹/₂-pound fryer chicken, cut into 6 or 8 pieces
6 cups Chicken Stock (page 267)
2 tablespoons unsalted butter
2 tablespoons vegetable oil
6 cloves garlic, sliced
1 jalapeño, stemmed, seeded, and minced
2 medium Spanish onions, chopped
¹/₃ cup finely chopped scallions (white and green parts)
1 *chayote*, peeled, seeded, and chopped (you can substitute zucchini)
Kosher salt and freshly ground black pepper to taste
1 ¹/₂ teaspoons brown sugar
1 ¹/₂ teaspoons toasted and ground cumin seeds (see page 9)
A pinch of ground cinnamon
3 medium ripe tomatoes, peeled, seeded, and chopped
²/₃ cup Spanish dry sherry
2 tablespoons tomato paste
2 tablespoons chopped cilantro
1 tablespoon tiny capers, rinsed and roughly chopped
12 small pimiento-stuffed olives, rinsed and roughly chopped

¹/₄ cup raisins
2 hard-boiled eggs, coarsely chopped

FOR THE CORN CRUST

2 tablespoons unsalted butter
2 cloves garlic, sliced
2 ¹/₂ cups corn kernels (from 3 to 4 ears)
1 egg
1 egg yolk
¹/₄ cup milk
¹/₂ cup all-purpose flour
¹/₂ teaspoon baking powder
1 teaspoon kosher salt
1 tablespoon minced sage

for the filling

In a large pot, combine the chicken and stock and bring to a boil. Reduce the heat and simmer for about 30 minutes, or until the chicken is cooked through. Remove from the heat.

When the chicken is cool enough to handle, lift it out of the stock and remove the skin and bones. With your fingers, shred the chicken into strips; put them in a large bowl. Reserve 1 ¹/₂ cups of the stock for this dish, and refrigerate or freeze the rest for another use.

In a large sauté pan, heat the butter and oil over medium-high heat until hot. Add the garlic and jalapeño and cook for 1 minute. Add the onions, scallions, and *chayote*, season with salt and pepper, and cook for 5 minutes, stirring occasionally. Add the brown sugar, cumin, cinnamon, and tomatoes, stir, and cook for 2 minutes. Add the sherry, tomato paste, and reserved 1 ¹/₂ cups chicken stock and cook for about 8 minutes. You want the filling to still be juicy. Add the chopped cilantro, capers, olives, raisins, and shredded chicken. Taste for seasoning, and adjust as needed.

Pour the filling into a 4-quart shallow casserole and sprinkle the chopped eggs over it. Set aside.

Preheat the oven to 375 degrees.

for the crust

Melt the butter in a large sauté pan over medium-high heat. Sauté the garlic for about 30 seconds, then add the corn and sauté for 3 to 4 minutes. Remove from the heat and let cool.

In a blender, puree the corn with the egg, egg yolk, and milk. Set aside.

Sift together the flour, baking powder, and salt into a large bowl. Gently fold in the liquid ingredients with a rubber spatula; do this slowly and gradually, so as to retain air in the batter—this gives the crust its fluffiness. Gently spread the batter over the top of the casserole.

Bake for 50 minutes, or until the center of the *pastel* is springy to the touch. Serve.

note: This dish can be reheated very easily in a moderate oven and is wonderful for using up leftovers. Another option is to pour the ingredients into individual casseroles; the *pastels* are quite elegant this way (they will require a shorter cooking time, depending on their size).

recommended wine: The richness of the *pastel* warrants a substantial white like one from the southern Rhône Valley.

poulet à la créole
(Curried Chicken with Pineapple, Cucumber, and Coconut)

SERVES 4

Curry and coconut, star anise and saffron—here is a recipe that demonstrates the powerful union of Caribbean and Asian food so often found in New World cuisine. The coconut milk's richness inclines me toward a simple starch accompaniment. I often serve it with Basic White Rice (page 196).

FOR THE SEASONED FLOUR (or substitute
   1/2 cup all-purpose flour seasoned with kosher salt
   and freshly ground black pepper)

1/2 cup all-purpose flour
1 teaspoon salt
1 1/2 teaspoons freshly ground black pepper
1 tablespoon crushed red pepper
1 teaspoon cayenne pepper

One 4-pound fryer chicken, cut into 8 pieces

2 ounces smoky bacon, cut into medium dice
3 1/2 tablespoons canola oil

FOR THE CURRY SAUCE
4 cloves garlic, thinly sliced
1 Scotch bonnet chile, stemmed, seeded, and
   minced
1 large red onion, chopped
2 tablespoons Madras curry powder
1 cup fresh orange juice
2 star anise
A pinch of saffron threads
1 cup Chicken Stock (page 267)

1 vanilla bean, split lengthwise
1 bay leaf, broken in half
1 1/2 cups unsweetened coconut milk
2 large ripe tomatoes, peeled, seeded, and
   diced

1 European cucumber, peeled, cut lengthwise in
   half, seeded, and cut into small pieces
1 tablespoon kosher salt
Freshly ground black pepper to taste
1 1/2 cups 1/2-inch pieces fresh pineapple
   (golden or regular)

Preheat the oven to 350 degrees.

If you are making the seasoned flour, simply mix all the ingredients together in a bowl.

Dust the chicken with the flour, shaking off any excess. Reserve.

In a large skillet, cook the bacon in the canola oil over medium heat, until it has rendered some of its fat. Add the chicken in batches, skin side down, and sear, 2 minutes per side, turning once, until golden on all sides. Transfer the chicken to a roasting pan; set the skillet aside. Bake the chicken for 25 to 35 minutes.

Meanwhile, make the curry sauce: Set the skillet you seared the chicken in over medium-high heat and add the garlic, Scotch bonnet, and red onion. Stir well to coat and cook until caramelized, about 10 minutes. Add the curry powder, stir well, and cook for 30 seconds.

Add the orange juice, star anise, and saffron and cook, stirring, for 2 minutes, as the juice reduces by half.

Add the chicken stock and stir, then add the vanilla bean, bay leaf, and coconut milk and stir. Bring to a simmer and cook for about 20 minutes until the sauce thickens enough to coat the back of a spoon.

While the sauce is simmering, put the cucumber in a colander and toss with the salt. Let stand for 20 minutes, stirring now and then to distribute the salt. (The salt will pull excess water out of the cucumber.) Rinse the cucumber well under cold running water and drain. Blot with paper towels.

Pass the curry sauce through a fine-mesh strainer into a smaller skillet. Add the tomatoes and heat through. Keep warm over very low heat.

To serve, put 2 pieces of chicken on each plate. Spoon the curry sauce over and scatter the cucumber and pineapple over the top.

recommended wine: An off-dry Riesling will stand up to the spices and heat of this dish.

the asian connection

There are two reasons I am drawn to the silken web that connects New World and Asian cuisines. The first is a man named Tokio Suyehara, a chef I came to admire in my second job as a cook. Toké, as he was known, was Japanese, and ever since working under his guidance I've felt a kinship with all things Asian. The second reason is the beauty, power, and reverence for aesthetics that is integral to all manners of Asian cooking. Since I began to study the influences of Asian cuisine on the New World, and vice versa, I've felt the freedom to pursue this interest but still be true to my pledge to cook within the historical roots of the place I live.

As Toké was one of the first chefs I admired, Raymond Sokolov is a writer whose work influenced me early and often. *Why We Eat What We Eat* has been a spiritual guide for me. Sokolov writes:

> This process of constant evolution in the world's kitchen went into high gear five hundred years ago, when Columbus landed in the West Indies. Even from that first voyage he brought back new foods to Spain. This is not surprising, perhaps, since one of his principal motives in seeking a new westward route to Asia was to seize an advantage in the spice trade, but what is truly surprising about the transoceanic interchange of food and food ideas after 1492 is how fast it happened. Within fifty years, the Spanish had established full-scale European agriculture in the West Indies, Mexico, Peru, and the Caribbean coast of South America (the so-called Spanish Main, which is now divided between Colombia and Venezuela). The Spanish had also opened up a regular trade with China from their base in the Philippines. Food and food ideas flowed freely between Seville and Asia on the same ships that carried goods from China and the Americas to Europe, and on the return trip brought European necessities for the colonists. The so-called Manila galleons took five months to make the passage across the Pacific to Acapulco. Their cargoes were then transported overland to Veracruz on Mexico's Gulf coast, reloaded on shipboard, and sent on to the mother country.

Chinese Influences: Chinese cuisine has played a major role in Peru. To a cuisine already enriched by many ancient cultures, in the nineteenth century the Chinese added a new dimension. Between 1849 and 1874, some ninety thousand Chinese, mostly Cantonese, emigrated to Peru as indentured laborers to work in railroad construction and agriculture. They brought along their traditions, dress, and their five-thousand-year-old cuisine, founded on profound philosophical principles. Many of them settled in Lima's depressed downtown area around Calle Capon, which became the city's Chinatown. Importing ingredients for their cooking from halfway around the world was too costly and cumbersome, so they soon began to grow their own vegetables—snow peas, ginger, and the like—and to raise ducks, chicken, and carp as they had back home. Cuisine proved a strong force in gradually eroding the racial prejudice at first shown by *Limeños* toward the newcomers. First at humble warehouses and cafés and later at family restaurants in and around Calle Capon, Peruvians sampled Chinese cooking and fell in love with it. By the 1940s, the word *chifa* (from the Cantonese *chifau*, "to cook") was applied to these pioneering restaurants.

According to Peruvian food expert Mariella Balbi, there are some basic differences between *chifa* and classic Cantonese cooking. For *chifa* sweet-and-sour sauces, for example, tamarind is preferred to the Cantonese vinegar. Fish and seafood are more plentiful and varied in the New World, and so the menus reflect this. Peruvian-Chinese cooks have an endless choice of hot peppers to choose from, resulting in spicier dishes than in classic Cantonese cuisine. Peruvians love fried wontons and other fried dishes, as well as *chaufa* rice, a richer version of fried rice, and pickled turnip strips. And they can thank the Chinese influence for the popular soft drink Inka Kola, which tastes of lemongrass.

Today the thriving Chinese population is five generations old and numbers almost a million in Peru, and there are more than two thousand *chifas* in Lima alone, from lavishly appointed palaces in plush residential sectors to unpretentious traditional eateries in Chinatown.

Japanese Influences: Peru was also the destination of many Japanese emigrants. In 1899, the first ship arrived, and the Japanese worked on the coastal plantations. Soon, however, they were becoming integrated into all walks of Peruvian life. Superior fishermen, the Japanese dramatically elevated the refinement of seafood dishes throughout Peru. The Peruvian penchant for the pickled seafood dish *ceviche* has found an even more delicate manifestation in *tiradito,* which imitates Japanese sashimi. One can dine on tempura dishes as well in a restaurant in the port city of Callao. And many people know the brilliant cuisine of Nobu Matsuhisa. His daring experimentalism lofted him to the top of the Los Angeles and New York food universes. What most do not realize, however, is that Nobu lived in Peru prior to the United States and that he's fused, with great spirit and intelligence, his Japanese training with South American foods and techniques. In his inimitable style, he reinvented certain Peruvian dishes and they have become part of his delicious repertoire.

The latest phase of culinary creativity in Peru is called *Novoandino*—the new cooking of Peru. It is born out of the fusion of ancient Indian and modern-day Japanese cooking. When one realizes the important influence Japanese cuisine has had on Peru over one hundred years, one can begin to appreciate how significant the Japanese influence in this country—where it has only recently begun to affect mainstream American cooking—may turn out to be.

Indian and Indonesian Influences:

In the 1800s, a number of the islands in the Caribbean became major producers of sugar. After the abolition of slavery in the colonies, indentured labor became the last significant pool of cheap labor to be used by the planters. These laborers were mainly Indian immigrants, and it wasn't long before curries and *roti* began to work their magic throughout the Caribbean. Many other dishes of East Indian heritage commingled with the Caribbean table from the mid-1800s on, particularly on the island of Trinidad.

The Indonesian dish known as *rijstaffel* (Dutch for "rice table") came west via Indonesia in the eighteenth century to the Dutch colonies of the Caribbean, such as St. Maarten, St. Eustatius, Aruba, and Bonaire. It is a highly ritualistic style of dining that consists of hot rice paired with a stunning array of small, tasty dishes that include seafood, meats, vegetables, sauces, and the like. Traditionally servants stood behind the chair of each guest, ready to provide soothing morsels when necessary to cool a burning palate.

The Dutch, attracted by nutmeg and cloves, also waged wars over the Spice Islands of Indonesia and colonized the entire archipelago. Chile peppers were carried there by Dutch traders from Mexico. Peanuts from the Americas provided sauces for satays.

Brave New World:

When I delivered a speech titled "Fusion Cuisine" in 1988, it caused quite a stir; I was the first chef to use that term. Its meaning has been distorted by detractors, but then again, meanings often are. The debate goes on to this day over whether "fusion cooking" is a good or a bad thing. I'd argue that plenty of bad examples of classic cuisine exist, and that the fact that a cuisine is experimental doesn't make it bad until proven otherwise. Culinary experimentation has gone on throughout history and will continue to do so. When I reached the end of that speech, I quoted Walt Whitman, in his "Leaves of Grass": "Do I contradict myself, very well then, I contradict myself; I am large, I contain multitudes."

Well, the multitudes, including those from Asia, are weaving their way into the Americas, and my wish is that this book gives us all the more reason to be thankful for that.

mojo curry chicken

(Marinated, Spice-Rubbed, and Roasted Chicken)

SERVES 4

I've combined the *mojo* sauce ubiquitous in Cuba with the curry spice rub indigenous to the West Indian islands to create one extremely perfumed bird. Note that it has to marinate overnight. I like to serve the chicken with *Arroz con Coco* (page 195) or Red Rice (page 197).

One 3- to 4-pound fryer chicken
Kosher salt and freshly ground black pepper to taste
1 cup Curry *Mojo* (page 285)
¹/4 cup Curry Spice Rub (page 266)

Sprinkle the chicken with salt and pepper and place it in a large resealable plastic bag. Pour the *mojo* over the chicken, seal the bag, and marinate overnight in the refrigerator, turning occasionally to ensure that all of the chicken becomes saturated.

Preheat the oven to 375 degrees.

Remove the chicken from the marinade, discarding the liquid, and place the bird in a large bowl. Sprinkle it evenly all over with the spice rub. Tie the legs of the chicken together with kitchen string to help maintain the natural shape of the bird as it cooks. Place it on a rack set in a roasting pan.

Roast the bird for 1 hour and 25 minutes, or until the juices run clear when the thigh is pierced.

Carve the chicken and serve with rice.

recommended wine: Beer always works with curry, but if you prefer to have wine, go for a big, full-bodied Chardonnay from California.

tamarind barbecued duck
with smoky plantain *crema*

SERVES 6

The tamarind, a tropical shade tree native to India, also grows in Southeast Asia, Africa, Hawaii, Mexico, South America, and, of course, the Caribbean. Its long brown brittle bean-like pods each hold a sweet-sour sticky brown pulp containing up to ten seeds. Its flavor is akin to dates mixed with lemon and peaches.

Just as we in the West often use a squeeze of lemon to lift the richness of a dish, in Asia they use tamarind. The American palate is not accustomed to the tamarind's particular brand of sourness, and so Western dishes using the fruit are usually tempered by ingredients that soften its acidity. In this dish, the heavy cream in the Smoky Plantain *Crema* balances the tamarind's acidity, while the chipotles complement the flavor of the grilled duck meat.

When preparing this, note that the duck should marinate overnight.

3 whole boneless duck breasts, cut in half
    and trimmed (you can ask your butcher
    to do this)
1 recipe Sugarcane Marinade with Tamarind
    (page 281)
1 recipe Smoky Plantain *Crema* (page 291)
Kosher salt and freshly ground black pepper
    to taste

With a sharp knife, score the skin of the duck breasts in a crisscross fashion. Put them in a large resealable plastic bag and pour in the marinade. Refrigerate overnight, turning the bag occasionally.

Prepare a medium-hot fire in a grill.

When the coals are ready, lightly oil the grill rack. Remove the duck from the marinade, allowing the excess to fall away, and place the duck skin side down on the grill. (Be careful, as dripping fat may cause the fire to flare up.) Grill for 6 minutes. Flip the breasts over and grill for an additional 7 or 8 minutes, or until medium-rare in the center. (If the duck begins to brown too much, move it to a cooler part of the grill to finish cooking. Allow the breasts to rest for a few minutes on a platter.

Rewarm the *crema* over low heat and spoon it onto six dinner plates. Cut each duck breast crosswise into thin slices and season with salt and pepper. Lay the duck slices atop the *crema* and serve.

recommended wine: A Malbec from Argentina to go with the tamarind in the barbecue sauce.

picadillo de pavo
(Ground-Turkey Stew with Raisins, Green Olives, and Capers)

SERVES 8

The turkey we know today is native to the New World, but its proliferation in our cuisine comes courtesy of the Spaniards, who turned out to be adept at domesticating the wild birds. *Picadillo* is a dish you will find in every humble Cuban café and in homes as well, but it is traditionally made with ground beef. I serve it with black beans and white rice. Prepare the *picadillo* while the beans and rice cook.

FOR THE *PICADILLO*

¹/₄ cup pure olive oil

1 ¹/₄ pounds ground turkey (breast and leg meat mixed)

1 tablespoon unsalted butter

3 cloves garlic, thinly sliced

1 medium red onion, diced

1 red bell pepper, stemmed, seeded, and diced

1 yellow bell pepper, stemmed, seeded, and diced

Kosher salt and freshly ground black pepper to taste

1 large tomato, peeled, seeded, and chopped

¹/₂ cup tomato paste

1 cup dry red wine

¹/₂ cup Spanish dry sherry

¹/₂ cup small capers, well rinsed and chopped

¹/₂ cup raisins or currants, roughly chopped

5 tablespoons lightly rinsed and roughly chopped green olives

³/₄ cup sliced scallions (green and white parts)

1 recipe Black Beans (page 202), for serving

1 recipe Basic White Rice (page 196), for serving

for the *picadillo*

Heat a large skillet over medium-high heat and add 2 tablespoons of the olive oil. Put the turkey in the skillet and cook, separating the clumps of meat with a spoon or spatula, until crumbly and lightly browned, about 5 minutes. Transfer the turkey and any juices to a bowl. Reserve.

Add the remaining 2 tablespoons olive oil and the butter to the skillet and heat until hot. Add the garlic, onion, and bell peppers, season with salt and pepper, and sauté for 10 to 15 minutes, stirring occasionally.

Stir in the turkey, tomato, tomato paste, red wine, sherry, capers, raisins, olives, and scallions. Lower the heat to medium-low, season to taste, and cook for about 15 minutes until the flavors marry. Remove from the heat.

Spoon the rice into serving bowls, and top with the black beans. Top with the *picadillo* and serve.

recommended wine: A medium-bodied Pinot Noir from Carneros or a Bourgogne Rouge from Burgundy would be seductive with the food's acidity and would sharpen the sweetness of the peppers.

meats

When I think of meat, I think of my father. I grew up near Chicago, and he loved to take my brother, my sisters, and me to dinner at the city's great steak houses. In these places, you'd personally select your own steak from a display case in the restaurant. The big, burly, beef-loving waiters in their gold-braided uniforms would then wield a searing-hot iron and brand your family's initials *right on your meat!*

Back then, the only sauces were sour cream for the baked potatoes and ketchup for the fries. After all, these were American steak houses, in Sandburg's "City of Big Shoulders." The menu choices were porterhouse, T-bone, club steak, rib steak, and, of course, New York strip steak. No *au poivre* or Steak Diane—for those, a French restaurant would have been necessary, and trust me, my dad did not *"parlez-vous?"*

I've often thought, though, that he would have instinctively understood the language of the *gauchos*, the nomadic part-Indian, part-Latin cowboys who herded wild cattle across the endless pampas of Argentina, Uruguay, Venezuela, and southern Brazil. Many visitors to the pampas, among them the naturalist Charles Darwin and the novelist W. H. Hudson, have described the *gauchos'* beef-eating and roasting habits, because their influence on meat in South America has been profound. Hudson writes of coming across a primitive barbecue in the middle of nowhere, hastily set up by a band of cowboys for the purpose of cooking a cow (that only moments before had been wandering the plain with the rest of the herd). Hudson sampled a piece of beef (with the hide still on) and declared it the best roast meat he'd ever eaten.

The *gauchos'* culinary gift to the world is the Argentine technique *asado,* in which meats are broiled over embers, not flames, and slow-cooked, their natural juices preserved. A wood fire is started on one side of the grill, and then just the right amount of embers are gradually pushed underneath the meat to maintain a steady temperature. The distance between grill and embers must be between seven and twelve inches, depending on a complex calculus of wind, sun, and climate conditions. The farther the grill is from the embers, the more evenly the meat will cook. Any meat that is prepared *asado*-style is medium-rare; to cook it well done would be sacrilege.

Traditionally, this is men's work. On Sunday, the head of the family becomes roast master, whether the family is on a huge cattle ranch or in a modest urban backyard. Wives and daughters see to the salads, vegetables, and desserts; sons and other male relatives dispense freshly baked country bread and earthy red wines by the jug. Etiquette is casual.

Dad would have been a happy man in South America. In fact, he would have been in heaven.

CLOCKWISE FROM TOP RIGHT: Potato
Tacos with Avocado Salsa (page 26);
Sopapillas (page 235); Doubles
(page 18); *Acarajé* with Crabmeat
Stuffing (page 17); various empanadas

Black Bean *Muñeta* with
Chipotle-Corn Skillet Bread (page 38)

Black Bean, Tropical Fruit, and
Queso Blanco Salsa (page 37)

Piononos (page 53)

Black Bean Soup with
Roasted Squash (page 62)

FROM THE TOP: *Ajiaco de Pollo*
(page 74); *Pepperpot* (page 176);
Chupe de Camarones (page 66)

pork *carnitas*

MAKES 4 CUPS

Carnitas are braised or fried pork bits. Of Mexican origin, they are often used as filling for tamales and tacos, but they are a natural component of any dish that would benefit from the sweet richness of the meat. I use *carnitas* to enhance my Cuban-inspired Pork and *Boniato Croquetas* (page 25).

¹/₂ cup canola oil
1 large Spanish onion, roughly chopped
2 carrots, peeled and roughly chopped
2 stalks celery, roughly chopped
6 cloves garlic, sliced
12 black peppercorns, toasted (see page 9)
2 bay leaves, broken in half
3 pounds boneless pork butt, shoulder, or
    country ribs, cut into 1 ¹/₂- to 2-inch pieces
10 sprigs thyme
Kosher salt and freshly ground black pepper to
    taste

Heat the canola oil in a large pot over medium heat. When it is hot, add the onion, carrots, celery, and garlic and cook for 5 to 8 minutes, until the vegetables begin to caramelize. Add the peppercorns, bay leaves, pork, and thyme, then add just enough water to cover and bring to a high simmer. As you do, the impurities in the ingredients will rise and foam; skim them off the top. Reduce the heat and cook until the meat is very tender, 1 ¹/₂ to 2 hours.

Strain the braising liquid into a bowl. Pull out the chunks of meat to cool, and discard the vegetables and spices. Separate the fat from the liquid using a fat separator. (Or cool the liquid in the refrigerator; as it solidifies, the fat will rise and congeal so that it can easily be skimmed off.) Transfer the fat to a nonstick skillet; set the braising liquid aside.

By now you should be able to comfortably handle the meat; pull it apart with your fingers.

Heat the fat over medium-high heat almost to sizzling. Add the meat and cook, stirring, until a crisp golden brown. Using a slotted spoon, transfer the meat to a medium bowl lined with paper towels; set aside.

Pour the reserved braising liquid into a saucepan and reduce over medium-high heat until there is just enough liquid left to coat the meat. Pour over the meat and season with salt and pepper. Use immediately, or refrigerate for up to 5 days. (The *carnitas* also freeze well.)

carapulcra

(Pork, Chicken, and Potatoes in Peanut Sauce)

SERVES 6

This rustic and captivating dish was one of the first Quechua Indian dishes that the Spanish integrated into their own cooking. *Carapulcra* derives from the word *kalas,* the hot stones over which the stew was cooked. It may surprise you to see that I use crushed animal crackers in this recipe to thicken it, but my Peruvian friends tell me this is what their mothers do as well! I quickly saw the brilliance of this ingredient when combined with the chocolate and peanuts that also go into making this New World stew. I raced to the store to get them for the first time in, well, a long time.

Carapulcra also calls for *papas secas,* dried Peruvian potatoes, which can be found in specialty markets. It is possible to simply use fresh red potatoes, but it is worth the effort to try to obtain these Peruvian traditional tubers. The dish is more sturdy made with them; they give it a consistency not unlike a risotto.

4 ounces *papas secas* (see headnote; optional)

3 tablespoons Annatto Oil (page 261) or pure olive oil

1 ½ pounds boneless chicken thighs and legs, cut into serving pieces

1 ½ pounds boneless pork loin, cut into ³/₄-inch cubes

Kosher salt and freshly ground black pepper to taste

2 tablespoons unsalted butter

4 cloves garlic, sliced

1 Scotch bonnet chile, stemmed, seeded, and minced

1 large red onion, finely chopped

½ teaspoon cayenne pepper

1 teaspoon toasted and ground cumin seeds (see page 9)

1 cup port

3 cups Chicken Stock (page 267), or as needed

8 ounces red potatoes, peeled and diced

1 tablespoon grated bittersweet chocolate

½ cup raw peanuts, toasted and ground medium-coarse (see page 9)

2 tablespoons finely ground animal crackers

FOR THE GARNISH

3 hard-boiled eggs, sliced

1 large ripe tomato, peeled, seeded, and diced

If you are using the dried potatoes, toast them in a nonstick skillet over medium-high heat for about 3 minutes, tossing now and then. Remove the pan from the heat and cover the potatoes with double their volume of water. Let soak for 30 minutes, then drain.

In a large heavy pot heat the oil over medium-high heat until very hot. Season the chicken and pork with salt and pepper. Sear the chicken first, starting skin side down, until golden brown on all sides. Transfer to a platter, and sear the pork 2 minutes per side. Add the pork to the chicken, and pour the juices from the pot over the meat.

Add the butter to the pot. When it has melted, add the garlic, Scotch bonnet, and onion and cook for about 3 minutes. Stir in the cayenne and cumin, then add the port and reduce it by half. Pour in the chicken stock. Slide the meats, with their juices, into the pot and add the red potatoes. Loosely cover with parchment paper and simmer until the meat is tender, 35 to 40 minutes.

Using a slotted spoon, transfer the chicken, pork, and red potatoes to a platter. Drain the

papas secas, if you have them. Season with salt and pepper, and add to the simmering pot. Take the chicken off the bone and cut the meat into cubes about the same size as the pork. Set aside. (If you want a more delicate texture to the meats you can hand-shred them after they have reached this point.)

Add the chocolate, peanuts, and ground animal crackers to the pot and simmer gently until the dried potatoes and/or the crackers disintegrate and thicken the stew, about 15 minutes.

Add the chicken, pork, and red potatoes to the pot. The sauce should be fairly thick, but add a little more stock if necessary. Simmer just long enough to heat through and blend the flavors.

Spoon the stew onto a warm serving platter and garnish with the hard-boiled eggs and tomatoes.

recommended wine: An optimally ripe Pinot Noir or a Grenache-based wine from the Roussillon.

chilean country ribs
(Chipotle-Marinated Grilled Pork Ribs)

SERVES 4

The Caribe Indians on the island of Hispaniola taught the Spanish how to use green wood lattices to make *barbacoa*—or what we now know as barbecue. A staple of the islanders' diet was the wild hog. The locals called the animals *boucan,* and that French word eventually came to be applied to many of the wild seafaring island men: buccaneers.

Barbecue has become one of the world's favorite foods; few culinary subjects stir such rabid debate, from Texas to Memphis to South Carolina and on down to the Caribbean and South America. Barbecue as we have come to love it—using marinades and/or sauces and carefully slow-

cooking—was perfected in the Caribbean. But some food scholars theorize that barbecue may have originated by accident in China many centuries ago, when a devastating fire burned down a barn, and the pig farmers, who had previously never cooked meat in a fiery fashion, smelled solace in their loss and as a consequence ate well that night. No less an authority on food than Waverly Root stated that cooking in this fashion was "so natural under primitive circumstances that it would practically invent itself everywhere, especially in societies accustomed to living outdoors most of the time."

If you aren't familiar with country ribs, this recipe will introduce you to the cut, also known as split blade chops. You'll love them for all manner of dishes calling for pork ribs, barbecued or otherwise. This is a very easy recipe, though you need to allow the ribs to marinate overnight. These are terrific with Yuca Fries (page 215).

3 cloves garlic, roughly chopped
1 jalapeño, stemmed, seeded, and roughly
    chopped
4 scallions, white and green parts, chopped
One 7-ounce can chipotle chiles in *adobo* sauce
3 tablespoons roughly chopped fresh oregano
1 tablespoon kosher salt, plus more to taste
1 ¹/₂ cups red wine vinegar
1 cup pure olive oil
4 pounds country pork ribs
Freshly ground black pepper to taste

Combine the garlic, jalapeño, scallions, chipotles, oregano, and salt in a food processor and mix until relatively smooth. While the processor is running, gradually pour in the vinegar and then the oil. Transfer this marinade to a bowl.

Season the ribs with salt and pepper. Put them in a large resealable plastic bag, pour 2 cups of the marinade over them, and refrigerate overnight. Cover and refrigerate the remaining marinade.

Prepare a medium-hot fire in a grill.

Remove the ribs from the bag, shake off the excess marinade, and place on the grill. Grill for 15 to 20 minutes, basting with the reserved marinade and flipping them frequently so that they cook evenly. Serve.

recommended wine: A red wine with ripe fruit and hints of spice and black pepper, such as a Malbec from Argentina or the Cahors region in France. Of course, the combination of barbecue and beer never misses.

cerdo picante
(Spiced Pork Chops)

SERVES 6

In Bolivia, the fare is robust and highly spiced to keep people warm and energized at altitudes above 12,000 feet. After a hard day's work in the thin air, this dish does the trick. The split peas offer a soothing, homey touch. As a garnish, I like sliced pimiento-stuffed green olives and lemon wedges.

FOR THE SPLIT PEAS

1 tablespoon olive oil

1 1/2 tablespoons unsalted butter

2 cloves garlic, minced

1/2 large Spanish onion, diced

2 celery stalks, diced

1 carrot, diced

1 teaspoon cayenne pepper

1 teaspoon toasted and ground cumin seeds
 (see page 9)

4 cups Chicken Stock (page 267)

1 smoked ham hock

1 bay leaf, broken in half

12 ounces split peas, rinsed

FOR THE PORK CHOPS

1 1/2 tablespoons toasted ground cumin seeds
 (see page 9)

1 tablespoon ground cardamom

1 tablespoon toasted ground coriander seeds

1 1/2 teaspoons cayenne pepper

1 1/2 teaspoons kosher salt

1 1/2 teaspoons freshly ground black pepper

3 tablespoons grated lemon zest

6 loin pork chops, 1 to 1 1/2 inches thick

3 tablespoons Roasted Garlic Oil (page 262) or
 pure olive oil

for the split peas

Heat the olive oil and butter in a medium saucepan over medium-low heat. When the butter has melted, add the garlic and cook for 30 seconds. Turn the heat up to medium-high, add the onion, celery, and carrot, and cook until they start to turn golden. Add the cayenne and cumin, stir, and add the chicken stock, ham hock, bay leaf, and peas. Bring to a simmer, turn down the heat, and simmer gently until the peas are tender, about 45 minutes. Remove the ham hock and bay leaf and coarsely mash the peas. Set aside; the mixture will thicken as it cools. While it does, prepare the pork chops.

for the pork chops

Preheat the oven to 350 degrees.

Combine the cumin, cardamom, coriander, cayenne, salt, pepper, and lemon zest. Sprinkle over the pork chops, rubbing it into both sides.

Heat a large skillet over medium-high heat. Add the oil and sear the chops on both sides. As they brown, transfer them to a baking sheet.

Put the chops in the oven and bake to desired doneness, 140 degrees for medium, 150 degrees for well-done.

Meanwhile, gently reheat the peas. Serve, using the split peas as a sauce.

recommended wine: A young Crozes-Hermitage red or a Syrah from California's central coast.

jerked pork chops

SERVES 6

Jamaica's native herbs and spices glorify the lush island's most popular meat. I serve this with Golden Pineapple Chutney. These chops need at least 4 hours' marinating time, and if you can let them sit overnight, they'll be even better.

FOR THE MARINADE

1/4 cup allspice berries

1-inch cinnamon stick

1 teaspoon freshly grated nutmeg

1 Scotch bonnet chile, stemmed, halved, and seeded

1/2 medium red onion, diced

1/2 cup finely chopped scallions (white and green parts)

3 cloves garlic, roughly chopped

3 tablespoons peeled and minced ginger

1 tablespoon chopped fresh thyme

1 tablespoon sugar

1 tablespoon soy sauce

2 tablespoons Worcestershire sauce

3 tablespoons fresh lime juice

1/4 cup dark rum

6 loin pork chops, about 1 1/2 inches thick

Kosher salt and freshly ground black pepper to taste

1 1/2 cups Golden Pineapple Chutney (page 265)

for the marinade

Toast the allspice berries in a dry skillet over medium heat until fragrant. Finely grind them with the cinnamon stick in a spice mill. Transfer to a food processor.

Add all of the remaining marinade ingredients to the processor and blend until smooth.

Season the pork chops with salt and pepper, then rub them all over with the marinade. Place on a plate, cover, and refrigerate for at least 4 hours, or, preferably, overnight.

Prepare a medium-hot fire in a grill.

Remove the pork from the marinade, place on the grill, and grill, turning once, for about 7 minutes on each side; the internal temperature of the chop should be 140 degrees for medium, 150 degrees for well-done. The thinner the chops, the less cooking time required.

Serve with the chutney.

recommended wine: A Pinot Noir from Oregon with cherry-cola fruit, soft tannins, and low alcohol.

pork cali-style with herbed *ají* salsa
(Marinated and Buttermilk–Bathed Pork Tenderloin)

SERVES 4

Cali, in the lush Cauca Valley of western Colombia, is considered the country's larder, and pork plays a major role in the valley's regional cuisine. Omar Prunera, who's been with us at the restaurant since our first day, is from Colombia, and early on he took Janet and me to a Colombian restaurant in Miami where we had a version of this powerful dish. Ever since, it has been part of my repertoire. Note that the meat must marinate overnight.

FOR THE MARINADE

1 small red onion, sliced

6 cloves garlic, sliced

1/2 Scotch bonnet chile, stemmed, seeded, and minced

12 black peppercorns, toasted and lightly bruised (see page 9)

1/4 cup fresh sour orange juice (or 2 tablespoons each fresh lime and regular orange juice)

1 cup pure olive oil

1 medium orange, cut in half

1 lime, cut in half, plus 4 lime wedges for garnish

4 pork tenderloins, trimmed

3 tablespoons *Escabeche* Spice Rub (page 266), or kosher salt and freshly ground black pepper to taste

2 cups all-purpose flour

1 egg

1 egg yolk

1 cup buttermilk

1/4 cup canola oil

3/4 cup Herbed *Ají* Salsa (page 277)

for the marinade

Combine the onion, garlic, Scotch bonnet, peppercorns, sour orange juice, and olive oil in a baking dish or large shallow bowl. Squeeze the juice of the orange and lime into the dish, then toss the fruit in. Immerse the meat in the marinade, cover, and refrigerate overnight.

Preheat the oven to 375 degrees.

Take 1 tenderloin out of the marinade and lay it on a cutting board. Slice it open down the center without cutting all the way through, so it opens like a book. Gently pat to flatten the meat. Now, using the center of the pork as a guide, make two more vertical cuts equidistant to the middle of each edge. Now you have butterflied the pork three times. Cover the meat with plastic wrap and, with the smooth side of a meat mallet or the bottom of a small sauté pan, pound the meat to $1/8$ to $1/4$ inch thick. Transfer to a platter and repeat with the other tenderloins. Sprinkle half of the spice rub over the meat, lightly coating both sides.

Put the flour on a baking sheet and season with the rest of the spice rub. In a large bowl, whisk together the egg, yolk, and buttermilk. One at a time, dredge the pork tenderloins in the flour, shaking off any excess, then, dip the tenderloins in the egg and buttermilk mixture; set aside on a plate.

In a large skillet, heat 1 tablespoon of the canola oil over medium-high heat. When it is very hot, sear one pork tenderloin until golden brown, about 2 minutes per side. Transfer to a baking sheet lined with parchment paper. Repeat with the remaining tenderloins and oil.

Roast the pork for 5 minutes. Serve topped with the salsa or on the side.

recommended wine: A Sauvignon Blanc or a dry Sémillon; for a red, a light-acid, full-flavored Freisa from Asti in Piedmont.

pork *colombo* in *roti*
(Curried Pork Stew with West Indian Bread)

SERVES 6

This dish is traditionally served in *roti,* which is wrapped like a tortilla around the *Colombo,* a steaming, fragrant mélange of pork, vegetables, and herbs and spices. If you don't want to make (or buy) the bread, however, you can substitute pitas, or simply serve this very satisfyingly with Basic White Rice (page 196).

3 pounds boneless pork shoulder, cut into
    1-inch pieces
Kosher salt and freshly ground black pepper to
    taste
¹/₄ cup fresh lime juice
¹/₄ cup canola oil
2 tablespoons unsalted butter
1 large Spanish onion, finely chopped
7 scallions, white and green parts, finely
    chopped
3 cloves garlic, minced
1 Scotch bonnet chile, stemmed, seeded, and
    minced
3 tablespoons peeled and minced ginger
3 tablespoons Madras curry powder
1 tablespoon dark brown sugar
3 tablespoons finely chopped Italian parsley
2 tablespoons minced chives
1 tablespoon chopped fresh thyme
1 ¹/₂ cups Chicken Stock (page 267)
1 pound red potatoes, peeled and cut into
    1-inch cubes
3 large carrots, peeled, halved lengthwise, and
    sliced into ¹/₂-inch-thick half-moons
1 pound *calabaza,* peeled, seeded, and diced
    (or substitute acorn squash)

1 lime, halved
12 to 14 *Roti* (page 229)

Preheat the oven to 350 degrees.

Season the pork with salt and pepper. Toss into a large resealable plastic bag with the lime juice and shake well. Marinate, refrigerated, for about 30 minutes.

Heat the oil in a large ovenproof skillet over medium heat. Drain the pork and sear it, in batches, for about 10 minutes, until lightly browned all over. Using a slotted spoon, transfer the pork to a bowl; leave the cooking juices in the skillet.

Melt the butter in the skillet and sauté the onion, scallions, garlic, Scotch bonnet, and ginger until soft, about 3 minutes. Add the curry powder, brown sugar, parsley, chives, and thyme and cook for 2 minutes, stirring continuously.

Return the pork to the skillet and stir to coat well. Add the chicken stock and bring to a simmer. Cook, uncovered, for 15 minutes.

Add the potatoes, carrots, and squash and season with salt and pepper. Cover the pan, place in the oven, and cook, stirring every 30 minutes or so, for 2 to 2 ¹/₂ hours; the meat should be falling apart.

Skim any oil off the top of the stew. Season with salt and pepper and squeeze the lime juice over the top. Serve with the *roti.*

recommended wine or beer: A Rheingau Riesling will pair well with this Jamaican favorite. A Red Stripe beer would too.

carne desmenuzada
(Shredded Meat Stew)

SERVES 10

This is one of the most popular beef dishes throughout Central and South America. It reminds me of the Sloppy Joes (a very soulful version) I ate growing up in Illinois. In Nicaragua, they first sear the meat, then simmer it, and assemble the dish. I've followed their lead. Serve the stew over rice, or with a side of Nicaraguan Tomato and Beet Salad (page 89) and some *Maduro* Plantains (page 211).

FOR THE BEEF

3 pounds boneless beef chuck roast, cut into
    1- to 1 $^1/_2$-inch pieces
Kosher salt and freshly ground black pepper to
    taste
$^1/_4$ cup canola oil
4 cloves garlic, sliced
1 large Spanish onion, sliced
1 red bell pepper, stemmed, seeded, and sliced
2 bay leaves, broken in half
5 cups Beef Stock (page 268)

2 tablespoons pure olive oil
1 tablespoon unsalted butter
4 cloves garlic, sliced
1 medium Spanish onion, sliced
2 red bell peppers, stemmed, seeded, and sliced
2 large ripe tomatoes, peeled, seeded, and chopped
1 tablespoon sugar
$^1/_3$ cup tomato paste
2 $^1/_2$ tablespoons red wine vinegar
$^1/_2$ cup fresh sour orange juice (or $^1/_4$ cup each
    fresh lime and regular orange juice)
Kosher salt and freshly ground black pepper

for the beef

Season the meat with salt and pepper. Heat the oil in a large pot over medium-high heat. When it is very hot, sear the meat, in batches (don't crowd it, or it will steam) until browned all over. Transfer to a platter.

Turn the heat down to medium, add the garlic, onion, and bell pepper, and sauté until soft, 3 to 5 minutes. Add the bay leaves and beef stock, then return the beef to the pot. Bring to a simmer, skimming impurities off the top as needed, then turn the heat down to medium-low. Let simmer gently, uncovered, for 2 to 2 $^1/_2$ hours, until the beef is tender enough that it shreds easily.

Using a slotted spoon, transfer the meat to a platter to cool. Strain the stock and reserve.

When the beef is cool enough to handle, shred it; set aside.

To finish the dish, heat the oil and butter in a large pot over medium heat. When the butter foams, add the garlic, onion, and bell peppers. Sauté until soft, 5 to 8 minutes. Add the reserved stock, the tomatoes, sugar, tomato paste, and vinegar. Cook over high heat, stirring, for 5 minutes. Stir in the shredded beef and the orange juice. Simmer for about 10 minutes. Season with salt and pepper and serve.

recommended wine: A light-bodied Cabernet Sauvignon from Argentina or Chile with a nice level of fruit showing.

braised beef shanks *con maní*

(Beef Shanks with Coconut Milk, Avocado, Currants, and Peanuts)

SERVES 4

The African contribution to the melting pot of Brazilian cuisine is clearly evident in this complex dish. The thick coconut milk provides a background richness not unlike that of heavy cream. The peanuts (*maní*) add texture as well as a certain woodsy quality. I break a bit from tradition and add some avocado and currants or raisins. The dish has some of the power of a great gumbo, another totemic meal of African ancestry.

The long list of ingredients can look intimidating, but the recipe is actually quite easy. The key is to do all your slicing, dicing, and mincing first. Once that's done, it is a simple matter of combining the ingredients and cooking the meat. Serve with Basic White Rice (page 196).

¹/₄ cup all-purpose flour

1 teaspoon kosher salt, plus more to taste

1 teaspoon freshly ground black pepper, plus more to taste

4 beef shanks (about 1 pound each), about 1 ¹/₂ inches thick

2 ¹/₂ ounces smoky bacon, cut into small pieces

¹/₄ cup canola oil

1 tablespoon unsalted butter

1 large red onion, chopped medium-fine

2 carrots, peeled and diced

5 garlic cloves, thinly sliced

³/₄ cup Spanish sherry vinegar

1 ¹/₂ teaspoons grated orange zest

2 tablespoons peeled and minced ginger

2 tablespoons tomato paste

1 teaspoon toasted and ground cumin seeds (see page 9)

1 tablespoon crushed red pepper

6 cups Beef Stock (page 268)

1 cup unsweetened coconut milk

1 large ripe tomato, peeled and cut into 8 wedges

1 tablespoon extra virgin olive oil

1 cup raw peanuts, toasted and roughly chopped (see page 9)

1 ripe avocado, pitted, peeled, and diced

¹/₂ cup dried currants or raisins

Preheat the oven to 325 degrees.

In a shallow bowl, mix the flour, salt, and pepper. Dredge each beef shank in the flour, shaking off the excess. Set aside.

In a large roasting pan, cook the bacon in the canola oil over medium-high heat until beginning to crisp. Slide the bacon over to one side of the pan, and sear the beef shanks, turning until browned. Transfer the shanks to a platter and reserve.

Add the butter to the pan. When it begins to foam, add the onion, carrots, and garlic, season with salt and pepper, and stir to coat. Cook, stirring occasionally, until the vegetables caramelize, 10 to 15 minutes.

Deglaze the pan with the vinegar, stirring until almost all the liquid has evaporated. Add the orange zest, ginger, tomato paste, cumin, and crushed red pepper. Stir in the stock and coconut milk, return the shanks to the pan, and bring to a simmer, skimming off any foam, as necessary.

Cover the pan, transfer to the oven, and braise the shanks for 2 to 3 hours, until the meat is very tender and falling off the bone.

Using a large spoon or ladle, skim off any fat that has risen to the surface of the cooking liquid. Transfer the shanks to a casserole and cover loosely with foil to keep warm. Strain the braising liquid into a saucepan and reduce it over medium-high heat to about 3 cups; it should thickly coat the back of a wooden spoon.

Season the tomato wedges with salt and pepper, arrange them atop the shanks, and pour the reduced braising liquid over them. Sprinkle about two-thirds of the peanuts over the top and put the pan in the oven, uncovered, until the tomatoes wilt, about 20 minutes.

Serve the shanks on warm plates, spooning the sauce over them. Garnish with the avocado, currants, and the rest of the peanuts, and accompany with rice.

recommended wine: An old-vines Zinfandel or a Barossa Valley Shiraz.

hilachas

(Beef Stew Served in an Acorn Squash)

SERVES 6

This is one of the national dishes of Guatemala, but the first time I tasted it I was reminded of my Nana's homemade beef stew. The dish gets its name—which means "threads" in Spanish—from the fact that the cooked meat is shredded. I add a topping of potatoes and pearl onions, and I serve the stew in a "bowl" of acorn squash. It is fine to present it this way, but if you want to skip that step, I'll understand (so would Nana).

FOR THE STEW

2 poblano peppers

About 2 tablespoons canola oil

12 ounces tomatillos, papery husks and cores removed, and rinsed

One 2-pound boneless beef chuck roast

Kosher salt and cracked black pepper to taste

3 tablespoons unsalted butter

2 large carrots, peeled and roughly chopped

2 large stalks celery, roughly chopped

10 cloves garlic, minced

2 medium Spanish onions, diced

6 cups water

1 bay leaf, broken in half

1 tablespoon coriander seeds

1 tablespoon black peppercorns

1 sprig of thyme

1 ancho chile

2 chipotles

2 tablespoons pure olive oil

7 scallions, white and green parts, chopped

$^1/_2$ cup cubed stale bread

$^1/_2$ cup chopped Italian parsley

1 tablespoon chopped fresh oregano

FOR THE POTATOES AND ONIONS

2 cups new potatoes, cut into 1-inch cubes

24 pearl onions, blanched briefly in boiling water, trimmed, and peeled

3 tablespoons unsalted butter, melted

Kosher salt and freshly ground black pepper to taste

$^1/_2$ cup pear or tiny cherry tomatoes, quartered

Kosher salt and freshly ground black pepper to taste

Chopped parsley or other herbs for garnish

3 acorn squash, cut in half and seeded (optional)

for the stew

Preheat the oven to 425 degrees.

Rub the poblanos with a little canola oil. Put them and the tomatillos on a baking sheet and roast for about 25 minutes. Remove them from the oven and let cool slightly.

Peel off the poblano skins and remove the seeds and stems; reserve the poblanos with the tomatillos.

Season the beef chuck with salt and pepper. Heat 2 tablespoons canola oil in a large stockpot over medium-high heat and sear the meat on all sides. Transfer to a platter.

Add 2 tablespoons of the butter to the pot. When it begins to melt, sauté the carrot, celery, half the garlic, and half the onions for 8 to 10 minutes, until lightly browned. Return the meat to the pot and add the water. With a wooden spoon, scrape up all of the drippings from the bottom of the pot. Add the bay leaf, coriander, peppercorns, and thyme. Bring to a boil, reduce the heat, and simmer, loosely covered with aluminum foil, for 2 to 2 1/2 hours, until the meat quite easily pulls apart in threads. Remove from heat and let cool slightly.

Meanwhile, roast the ancho and chipotles in a small skillet over medium heat, then soak in warm water until softened, about 20 minutes. Drain, and remove the stems and seeds; reserve.

When the meat is cool enough to handle, use tongs to scoop it onto a platter. Strain the broth and reserve. Shred the meat, season with salt and pepper, and set aside.

Heat the remaining 1 tablespoon butter and olive oil in a large saucepan over medium heat. Sauté the scallions and the remaining garlic and onions for 3 minutes, or until soft.

Meanwhile, roughly chop the tomatillos, poblanos, and ancho and chipotle chiles. Add them to the vegetables, along with the bread, parsley, oregano, and the reserved broth, and bring just to a simmer. Season with salt and pepper, and remove from heat. Let cool slightly.

for the potatoes and onions
Transfer the vegetables and broth to a food processor and blend until smooth. Return to the pan and set over medium heat. Add the shredded beef and simmer until the liquid thickens to the consistency of a gravy. Season with salt and pepper. Keep warm.

Meanwhile, prepare the potatoes and pearl onions. Preheat the oven to 400 degrees.

Toss the potatoes and pearl onions in the butter and season with salt and pepper. Place them in a roasting pan and roast, uncovered, for 40 to 45 minutes, until the potatoes are tender. If using the acorn squash, put it cut side down on another baking sheet and roast for 40 to 45 minutes or until easily pierced with a fork. Season the squash with salt and pepper.

Season the tomatoes with salt and pepper; reserve.

Spoon the hot stew into the hollowed-out acorn squashes, or into shallow soup bowls. Top with the potatoes and tomatoes. Garnish with the pearl onions and, if you like, some chopped herbs, such as Italian parsley.

recommended wine: This is the perfect dish for a medium-bodied Merlot from Chile or California.

churrasco de sao paulo a la parilla con chimichurri rojo

(Barbecued Steak Brazilian-Style, with Garlicky
Marinade and Dipping Sauce)

SERVES 4

Churrasco is a very primitive form of cooking meat. The *gauchos*, or cowboys, of Brazil would kill and butcher the animals out on the pampas, build a big fire, and barbecue the meat on a spit of some sort, basting it with a vinegary liquid.

As cities developed, however, this recipe too became more civilized—I do ask you to prepare it the way they do in many Brazilian steak houses, with *cebollas fritas* (otherwise known as onion rings).

1 recipe *Chimichurri Rojo* (page 280)
Two 1-pound skirt steaks
Kosher salt and freshly ground black pepper to
  taste
1 recipe *Cebollas Fritas* (page 210)
¹/₄ cup assorted olives, pitted and chopped
1 tablespoon minced Italian parsley

Pour ¹/₂ cup of the *chimichurri* into a large resealable plastic bag. Add the skirt steaks and marinate overnight in the refrigerator. (Reserve the rest of the *chimichurri* for serving.)

Prepare a hot fire in a grill. (Prepare the onions while the grill heats.)

Remove the steaks from the marinade and, turning once, grill to desired doneness. (Because they are thin and have been marinated overnight, they will cook very fast.)

Cut each steak in two, arrange them in the center of four warm plates, and season with salt and pepper. Top with the onions and garnish with the olives and parsley. Serve with the reserved *chimichurri* on the side.

recommended wine: A Nebbiolo d'Alba or a Cabernet Sauvignon from Mendoza, Argentina.

palomilla steak
(Seared Steak Cuban-Style)

SERVES 6

When I ask Cubans to describe the reverence they have for this dish, they look somewhat mystified, as if I am asking them to try to describe faith: it is there or it isn't. *Palomilla* steak is usually served with black beans, white rice, *maduro* plantains (see page 211), white onions, and parsley, and lime is squeezed over the steak at the end. You may be disarmed by the thinness of the steak. Like many beloved down-home dishes, it evolved out of a need for economy. But *palomilla* steak has the soul of beef tenderloin. *Xuxu* Slaw (page 100) goes well with these steaks.

Three large $^1/_4$-inch-thick slices boneless sirloin or top sirloin steak (ask the butcher for slices from the sirloin)
Kosher salt and freshly ground black pepper to taste
1 recipe Classic Sour Orange *Mojo* (page 283)
1 recipe Caramelized Red Onions (page 210)
$^1/_4$ cup chopped Italian parsley
3 tablespoons canola oil

One at a time, lay each piece of steak on a cutting board, cover with a piece of plastic wrap, and pound with the smooth side of a mallet until $^1/_8$ inch thick, then lightly pound all over with the smaller ridged side of the mallet. Cut each steak in half and season with salt and pepper. Put the steaks in a resealable plastic bag and pour 1 cup of the *mojo* over them, shaking the bag so that the marinade thoroughly covers the steaks. Seal the bag and refrigerate for 30 minutes.

(Prepare the onions while the steaks marinate. Stir in the parsley. Keep warm.)

Remove the steaks from the marinade and drain off the excess liquid. Heat two large skillets over high heat until very hot. Add 1 $^1/_2$ teaspoons of the canola oil to each pan and quickly sear 2 steaks on both sides. (In Cuban restaurants, the steak is almost always served well-done; I resist that, but it is up to you and your preference for the doneness of beef.) Wipe out the pans and repeat with the remaining steaks.

Put the steaks on plates and scatter the caramelized onions over them. Serve with the remaining $^1/_4$ cup *mojo* as a drizzle sauce.

recommended beer or wine: A lager beer or a young Spanish Crianza Rioja.

rabo encendido
(Oxtails Braised in Red Wine)

SERVES 4

The literal translation of *rabo encendido* is "tail on fire," yet this dish is not especially spicy-hot. If you want it to live up to its moniker, serve it with *Sauce au Chien* (page 287).

Ask your butcher for oxtails that are big and meaty and have some fat on them. The fat will dissolve and add richness to the broth.

3 1/2 to 4 pounds oxtails, cut into 2-inch-wide
    pieces
1 cup all-purpose flour
Kosher salt and freshly ground black pepper
    to taste
2 tablespoons toasted and ground cumin seeds
    (see page 9)
1/4 cup pure olive oil
5 cloves garlic, minced
1 large Spanish onion, finely chopped
2 poblano peppers, stemmed, seeded,
    and diced
2 red bell peppers, stemmed, seeded,
    and diced
2 medium ripe tomatoes, peeled, seeded,
    and chopped
1 tablespoon minced fresh thyme
1/2 cup Spanish dry sherry
1 1/2 cups dry red wine
2 bay leaves, broken in half
6 cups Beef Stock (page 268)
3 1/2 cups water

Preheat the oven to 300 degrees.

Dust the oxtails with the flour. Sprinkle them with salt and pepper and the cumin. Heat the oil in a large ovenproof pot over medium-high heat. When it is hot but not smoking, brown the oxtails, in batches, on all sides. Transfer them to a platter.

Pour off all but about 2 tablespoons of the oil from the pot. Add the garlic, onion, poblanos and bell peppers and cook over medium heat until tender, about 3 minutes. Add the tomatoes and thyme and stir to mix, seasoning with salt and pepper.

Add the sherry, red wine, and bay leaves and simmer until the liquid has reduced by about one-quarter, approximately 10 minutes.

Return the oxtails to the pot and pour in the beef stock and water. Stir well, and bring to a simmer over medium heat, skimming off the impurities occasionally. Cover loosely with foil pressed directly against the surface of the stew. Transfer to the oven and braise for 3 hours, or until the oxtails are done and the sauce is thick enough to coat a wooden spoon.

Distribute the oxtails among four bowls, spooning the sauce generously over them. Serve.

recommended wine: Surprisingly, the Carignan grape, from one-hundred-year-old vines in Priorato in Spain, will set the tone for this intense dish; an old-vines Grenache from the same region in Spain would also do.

bistec con huevos
(Steak and Eggs Salvadoran-Style)

SERVES 4

Given today's delicate appetites, I suppose I should have put this hearty recipe in the Feasts and Traditions chapter. But I think it belongs in a more regular culinary rotation. Think of it as a paean to protein—and plan on a little nap afterward.

4 teaspoons pure olive oil

4 sirloin strip steaks (8 to 12 ounces each), trimmed well

Kosher salt and freshly ground black pepper to taste

1 recipe *Pico de Gallo* (page 278)

6 ounces mozzarella cheese, grated

Canola oil for frying the eggs

4 eggs

1 avocado, pitted, peeled, sliced, and drizzled with a squeeze of lime (so the slices don't turn brown)

1/2 recipe Red Bean Puree (page 203)

Prepare a hot fire in a grill.

Rub 1 teaspoon of the olive oil over both sides of each steak and season with salt and pepper. Put the steaks on the grill and cook, turning once, until medium-rare. Remove from the grill and cover each steak with *pico de gallo*. Then top with the cheese. Put them back on the grill for a minute or two, with the lid on, to melt the cheese. Transfer the steaks to a platter and let them rest for about 5 minutes while you cook the eggs.

Heat a little canola oil in one large or two smaller nonstick skillets, and fry the eggs sunny-side up. Meanwhile, reheat the bean puree if necessary.

Put each steak on a plate and top with an egg and about 2 tablespoons *pico de gallo*. Season with a little salt and pepper. Put a few slices of avocado on the side of each and serve with the red bean puree.

recommended wine: A Grenache from California with good structure.

vaca frita
(Crispy Beef)

SERVES 4

Cubans often make *vaca frita* from Sunday dinner's leftover pot roast—another example of their creativity and thrift. Here I begin with a savory mixture of spices, bacon, and vegetables, forging a foundation for the underused skirt steak. Less tender than cuts from the loin, skirt steak is deeply flavorful, and when you braise it, as I do here, it becomes perfectly tender too.

Note that the braised steak has to be marinated for at least a few hours, or preferably overnight.

2 ¹/₂ pounds skirt steak, cut (with the grain) into 4- to 5-inch-wide pieces

2 tablespoons *Escabeche* Spice Rub (page 266), or kosher salt and freshly toasted (see page 9) and freshly ground black pepper to taste

3 tablespoons Roasted Garlic Oil (page 262) or pure olive oil

2 ounces smoky bacon, diced

2 tablespoons unsalted butter

1 head garlic, cut horizontally in half

1 large red onion, chopped

1 large carrot, peeled and chopped

2 stalks celery, chopped

1 bay leaf, broken in half

8 cups warm water

8 to 10 cloves garlic, thinly sliced

¹/₂ cup fresh lime juice

2 tablespoons canola oil

Lay the skirt steak on your cutting board and sprinkle on both sides with the spice rub.

Heat the garlic oil in a large pot over medium-high heat. When it is quite hot, quickly sear the steak, in batches, until well browned on both sides. Transfer the steaks to a plate.

Add the diced bacon to the pot and cook until beginning to crisp. When it is almost done, add the butter. When the butter begins to foam, add the garlic, red onion, carrot, celery, and bay leaf. Cook for about 8 minutes, until the vegetables begin to caramelize.

Add the water and the skirt steaks and bring to a simmer, skimming off any impurities, then reduce the heat to medium-low. Braise for about 1 ¹/₂ hours, until the meat is very tender. Remove the steaks from the braising liquid and allow to cool. Strain the liquid (this will be your sauce) and refrigerate.

Meanwhile, mix together a marinade of the thinly sliced garlic and lime juice and set aside to let the flavors marry.

When the meat has cooled, season with salt and pepper and put it in a large resealable plastic bag, pour the marinade over it, and give it a shake, so that it is thoroughly coated. Refrigerate for at least a few hours, or preferably, overnight.

When you are ready to finish the dish, take the steaks and the braising liquid out of the refrigerator. Discard any fat that may have risen to the top of the broth, and pour it into a pot. Bring to a brisk simmer over high heat and reduce it to about ¹/₂ cup.

By now, the meat should have come to room temperature. Discard the marinade. Shred the steaks into somewhat thick strands. Heat the canola oil in a large skillet over medium-high heat. Fry the shredded meat until crispy and golden brown. Season with salt and pepper.

Distribute the meat among four bowls and pour on the sauce.

Serve with Caramelized Red Onions (page 210) if you like, and with a lime wedge. *Tostones* (page 213) and Basic White Rice (page 196) also go well with this.

recommended wine: A fruity red with good acidity, such as a Dolcetto from Piedmont.

creole mustard–glazed calves' liver with *escabeche* onions

SERVES 4

When I first began frequenting the little Latin cafés of Key West, I was surprised to see, over and over, a dish called "Calves' Liver, Italian-Style." I could divine nothing specifically Italian about the dish—except for the red wine that everyone seemed to order to drink with it. I've since come to understand how fundamentally Italy bestowed her warm culinary influences on South America.

I like to serve this with *Boniato* Mash (page 205), but if you want something a little richer and more unusual, try *Papas Chorreadas* with Romaine (page 207).

1 recipe Caramelized Red Onions (page 210)
4 slices (about 5 ounces each) calves' liver
  (see note)
Kosher salt and freshly ground black pepper to
  taste
¼ cup all-purpose flour
¼ cup canola or peanut oil
2 tablespoons Creole mustard
1 ½ tablespoons unsalted butter
4 teaspoons *Escabeche* Spice Rub (page 266)

Put the caramelized onions in a saucepan (if they aren't still in one); reserve. Season the liver with salt and pepper on both sides. Dredge in the flour, shaking off any excess.

Heat the oil in a large heavy skillet over medium-high heat. When it is good and hot, add the liver and sear for about 1 minute, then turn and sear for about 30 seconds on the other side. Transfer the liver to a warm platter and spread the Creole mustard on one side of each slice.

Meanwhile, heat the caramelized onions until hot, and stir in the butter and spice rub.

Place each liver slice on a plate. Top with the onions, and serve.

note: True calves' liver should not be bright red, but pale, as veal is in general.

recommended wine: An earthy Cabernet Sauvignon from California.

grill-roasted rack of lamb in red *mole*

SERVES 4

The grill adds a sophisticated smoky quality to this dish, but you can make it from beginning to end using only the oven. *Maduro* Plantains (page 211) would make an excellent side dish.

Two 7- to 8-bone racks of lamb, trimmed and
    Frenched (the butcher can do this)
2 ¹/₂ cups Red *Mole* (page 286)
1 to 2 tablespoons canola or grapeseed oil
Kosher salt and freshly ground black pepper to
    taste

Cut the racks of lamb in half so that you have four 3- or 4-boned sections of meat.

Place on a platter or in a baking dish and cover the meat with 1 ¹/₂ cups of the *mole* (try to avoid wasting the *mole* on the bones). Cover and refrigerate for at least 4 hours, and for as long as overnight. Refrigerate the remaining *mole* for when you serve the dish.

Prepare a medium fire in a grill. Preheat the oven to 475 degrees.

Brush off any excess marinade from the lamb. Oil the grill rack, lay the racks of lamb on it, and grill, turning once or twice, until nicely browned on all sides. Be mindful that the fat on the lamb can drip and cause the flames to flare; if this happens, simply turn the lamb over or move it away from the hottest flames.

Transfer the meat to a small roasting pan and put it in the oven. Check it after 10 minutes, and discard any fat that may have accumulated in the bottom of the pan. Cook the lamb until it has reached the desired doneness. In my opinion, lamb from the rack is best served medium-rare. (When it is rare, the texture can be too springy; when medium-well to well-done, it often will be disagreeably dry.) An internal temperature of 130 degrees will be right—especially when you take into account that the temperature will rise another few degrees once it comes out of the oven. Allow the lamb to rest for a few minutes.

Meanwhile, warm the reserved *mole* in a small saucepan.

Cut the lamb into chops, or serve the half-racks as they are. Offer the *mole* on the side, with salt and pepper.

recommended wine: A Zinfandel from Sonoma (but not a high-alcohol one) will offer restraint to complement the gentle gaminess of the lamb and the power of the red *mole*.

feasts and traditions

If you reject the food, ignore the customs, fear the religion, and avoid the people, you might better stay home. You are like a pebble thrown into the water; you become wet on the surface but you are never part of the water.

—JAMES A. MICHENER

Some of our strongest emotions are bound together with our memories of food. The quest for food-as-survival unites us with the animal kingdom, but what elevates us is our love of ceremony, our need for ritual, and our passion for sharing tradition with others. A feast meets these definitions, and the New World, particularly Latin America, reveres its feast days and food traditions.

In this chapter, I've highlighted the foods of these places that speak of the recurring themes of structure and order—for which, in this modern world, we still have a deep need. The days of feasting and meals of tradition in this section echo those we know from our American holidays. But they are different because of the permutations of experience that shaped the hands that held the spoons; people who came from Africa, from Europe, and from Asia, and who bravely made the New World their home.

When you look over the recipes in this chapter, you will be seeing some of the foods that are most important to the peoples of Latin America and the Caribbean. They may stir the same yearnings and memories in you as would a Thanksgiving Day turkey or a July Fourth rib cookout. Or they may evoke such standards as fried chicken with candied yams, deep-dish apple pie and vanilla ice cream, or grilled T-bone steaks and fried onion rings. People the world over have their versions of such dishes, which are always as much about history and family as they are about food.

gnocchi for the 29ᵗʰ of the month

SERVES 8

In Argentina and Uruguay, where the cuisines have been strongly influenced by Italy, there is a curious tradition involving this pasta: It is said that if you eat gnocchi on the 29th of each month, you'll have plenty of cash for the next thirty days. (No one addresses what happens in February, which has only twenty-eight days except in leap years.) Some people place their wallets on their laps while they eat or put a couple of bills under their plates to reinforce their luck. Restaurant chefs and housewives alike have invented all kinds of recipes to support this tradition. Mine is adapted from the version served by a prominent Montevideo hostess.

FOR THE GNOCCHI

1 pound Yukon Gold potatoes, peeled
Kosher salt and freshly ground black pepper to taste
1 extra-large egg, lightly beaten
About 1 cup all-purpose flour
1 ounce Parmesan cheese, grated

FOR THE "29ᵀᴴ CHEESE SAUCE"

8 tablespoons (1 stick) unsalted butter
4 cloves garlic, sliced
2 large shallots, finely chopped
1 cup diced fennel
Kosher salt and freshly ground black pepper to taste
1/4 cup virgin olive oil
1/2 pound cremini (or "baby bella") mushrooms, roughly chopped
2 tablespoons Spanish sherry vinegar
2 tablespoons chopped Italian parsley
2 tablespoons chopped fresh basil
2 tablespoons all-purpose flour
1 1/2 cups Chicken Stock (page 267)
8 ounces Manchego cheese, grated
1/2 cup sour cream

for the gnocchi

Cook the potatoes in boiling salted water until tender; drain. Put the potatoes in a bowl and season with salt and pepper. Pass them through a ricer or mash them. Set aside to cool while you make the cheese sauce.

for the sauce

Melt 6 tablespoons of the butter in a large heavy skillet over medium-high heat. Sauté the garlic, shallots, and fennel for about 3 minutes. Season with salt and pepper. Add the olive oil and mushrooms and sauté for 3 minutes, or until the mushrooms are tender. Add the vinegar, parsley, and basil, and transfer to a bowl.

Wipe out the pan, and melt the remaining 2 tablespoons butter. Whisk in the flour. Remove from the heat for a moment to allow the flour to cook gently, then return to the heat and whisk in the chicken stock. Continue whisking until the sauce thickens slightly and there are no more lumps. Stir in the Manchego cheese. When it has melted, stir in the sautéed mushroom mixture. Remove from the heat and stir in the sour cream. Reserve.

To make the gnocchi dough, add the egg, 3/4 cup of the flour, and the Parmesan cheese to the mashed potatoes. Knead the dough only enough to combine. You want the dough to hold its shape when pinched; add only as much additional flour as needed to achieve this—potatoes vary in terms of how much water they contain, but if you add too much flour, the gnocchi will be heavy.

Lightly flour a wooden board or marble slab. Cut off a small piece of the dough and, with the palms of your hands, roll it into a rope between $^1/_2$ and $^3/_4$ inch thick. With a knife, cut the rope into $^1/_2$-inch pillow shapes. With the back of a fork, lightly score each dough pillow; the little grooves will make it easier for the gnocchi to hold the sauce. Repeat with the remaining dough, putting the gnocchi on a floured baking sheet.

Set a large pot of salted water over medium-high heat. While you wait for it to come to a boil, gently reheat the sauce.

When the water is boiling, slowly lower the dumplings into the pot and stir gently until they surface, then let them cook for another 8 to 10 seconds. Remove them from the boiling water with a slotted spoon or skimmer and drain well. Spoon the hot cheese sauce onto a serving platter and top with the gnocchi.

recommended wine: A Tocai from Friuli or a Pinot Grigio from Trentino.

papas a la huancaina
(Potatoes in Creamy Cheese Sauce)

SERVES 6

This dish drops down to us from 11,000 feet, up in the Peruvian Andes, home to many varieties of potato. The Peruvian comfort-food equivalent of macaroni and cheese, *papas a la Huancaina* gets its name from a town there called Huancayo, the last stop on the world's highest single-gauge railroad line. I can imagine that when you get to the end of the line you might want some *papas a la Huancaina*.

Often served as halved potatoes in lettuce leaf cups topped with corn cob rounds, the dish stands in handsomely on any occasion at which you might serve potato salad. And, considering its potato and cheese components, *papas a la Huancaina* tastes amazingly light.

3 medium Yukon Gold potatoes, diced

FOR THE SAUCE (MAKES 3 CUPS)
$^1/_3$ cup pure olive oil
2 cloves garlic, sliced
1 Scotch bonnet chile, stemmed, seeded, and minced
$^1/_2$ medium Spanish onion, roughly chopped
Kosher salt and freshly ground black pepper to taste
$^1/_4$ teaspoon ground turmeric
$^1/_4$ cup white wine vinegar
1 cup Chicken Stock (page 267)
$^3/_4$ cup heavy cream
$^3/_4$ cup coarsely chopped *queso blanco*
12 ounces cream cheese

$^1/_4$ teaspoon minced Scotch bonnet chile
2 medium ripe tomatoes, peeled, seeded, and chopped
$^1/_4$ cup Arbequina or Niçoise olives, pitted and coarsely chopped
1 tablespoon chopped cilantro
1 $^1/_2$ teaspoons chopped Italian parsley
3 scallions, white parts only, chopped
1 tablespoon pure olive oil
2 hard-boiled eggs, diced
Kosher salt and freshly ground black pepper to taste

18 romaine leaves, for garnish
1 recipe Pickled Red Onions (page 211), for garnish

Cook the potatoes in boiling salted water until tender; drain. Transfer to a bowl and set aside at room temperature.

for the sauce

Heat the oil in a skillet over medium-high heat. Add the garlic, Scotch bonnet, and onion, stir to combine, and season with salt and pepper. Sauté until the onion just begins to caramelize, about 4 minutes. Add the turmeric, vinegar, and chicken stock and reduce to about ³/₄ cup.

Remove the skillet from the heat and mix in the cream. Pour into a blender and process until almost smooth. Add the cheeses and puree. Season with salt and pepper. Set aside, covered to keep warm.

To assemble the dish, put the potatoes in a medium bowl and fold in the Scotch bonnet, chopped tomatoes, olives, cilantro, parsley, scallions, olive oil, and eggs. Season with salt and pepper.

Quickly arrange 3 romaine leaves on each plate. Fold about three-quarters of the sauce into the potato mixture and mix well. Scoop the potatoes onto the centers of the plates. Ladle some of the remaining sauce onto the plates and top the potatoes with the pickled onions. Dress with more sauce, if desired, to taste.

recommended wine: A clean, crisp Rhône white, such as a Sablet Blanc.

pepperpot
(Mixed Meats, Shrimp, and Plantain Stew)

SERVES 6 TO 8

This dish goes back to the times of slavery, colonialism, and the roots of the sugar industry in the islands. In the early nineteenth century on Grenada, it was quite common for people to drop by the cane plantations, and showing them hospitality with a good, filling meal was considered not only kind but necessary to sustaining commerce.

Amazingly, the plantation cooks had discovered that they could wring out the poisonous substance in *cassava* (also known as *casabe*, *caçabi*, *yuca*, and *manioc*), a starchy root that grows all over the Caribbean and in abundance on Grenada. They would boil it and reduce it to a treacly black substance called *cassareep*. This was the base of the pepperpot, and whenever a guest arrived, the cook would add freshly killed game to the huge, eternally simmering black cauldron called a *canaree*. The *canaree* was wrapped in white napkins and set directly on the dining table. On some plantations, they boasted of keeping their pepperpots going for more than twenty years at a stretch.

In my adaptation, I've substituted pork for freshly killed game. And, I prepare our pepperpot with blackstrap molasses, as *cassareep* is not readily available.

This stew is intense enough to be reduced a little and served as a sauce. In my restaurant, I serve a pork osso buco atop this sauce, with some grits on the side.

2 pounds boneless pork shoulder, cut into
 1-inch cubes
Kosher salt and freshly ground black pepper to
 taste

FOR THE MARINADE

1 cinnamon stick

5 cloves

2 teaspoons cumin seeds, toasted (see page 9)

1 teaspoon black peppercorns, toasted (see
 page 9)

2 cloves garlic, minced

$^1/_3$ cup red wine vinegar

$^1/_4$ cup pure olive oil

2 tablespoons blackstrap molasses or $^1/_4$ cup
 packed dark brown sugar

2 tablespoons fresh lime juice

FOR THE STEW

1 ancho chile

2 tablespoons pure olive oil

4 ounces smoky bacon, diced small

1 medium Spanish onion, thinly sliced

2 Scotch bonnet chiles, stemmed, seeded, and
 minced

1 tablespoon chopped fresh thyme

1 teaspoon toasted and ground cumin seeds
 (see page 9)

7 $^1/_2$ cups Chicken Stock (page 267)

Kosher salt and freshly ground black pepper to
 taste

2 medium-ripe plantains (yellow but turning
 black), peeled and diced

2 tablespoons unsalted butter, melted

12 ounces kale or collard greens, stemmed and
 chopped

8 ounces spinach or *callaloo*, tough stems
 removed, thoroughly washed, and chopped

1 to 1 ¼ pounds medium shrimp, shelled,
   deveined, and cut into bite-sized pieces

Season the pork cubes with salt and pepper.

for the marinade

In a spice mill, grind the cinnamon, cloves,
cumin, and peppercorns to a powder. In a
large bowl, combine the spices, garlic, vinegar,
olive oil, molasses, and lime juice. Whisk to
combine. Add the pork, turning to coat in this
mixture, cover, and marinate for an hour in
the refrigerator.

for the stew

Toast the ancho in a small skillet over medium
heat, then soak in warm water to cover until
soft, about 20 minutes. Drain, remove the
stem and seeds, and finely chop.

Add the olive oil to a large stockpot and
sauté the bacon over medium heat until it begins to crisp. Turn up the heat to medium-
high, add the onion and Scotch bonnets and
sauté, stirring frequently, until the onion is
softened and translucent, about 4 minutes.

Stir in the pork, marinade and all, then add
the thyme, cumin, and chopped ancho chile.
Add the chicken stock and bring to a simmer.
Season with salt and pepper. Turn the heat
down to low, cover the pot, and simmer for 1
hour and 15 minutes, or until the pork is just
shy of falling apart when pierced. Season
again to taste.

While the pork is cooking, preheat the oven
to 375 degrees.

Toss the plantains with the butter and salt
and pepper to taste. Put them in a baking pan
and roast for 20 to 25 minutes, tossing about
halfway through to prevent sticking. Reserve
in a warm place.

When the pork is cooked, add the greens,
cover, and continue to cook for another 20
minutes, or until the greens are tender.

Stir the plantains and shrimp into the stew
and cook for another 2 to 3 minutes, until they
are just cooked. Serve.

recommended wine: This big dish calls
for a medium-bodied red with plenty of spice
and flavor, such as an old-vines Monastrell
from Spain.

braised duck legs with orange-chocolate sauce

SERVES 4

In Caracas, Venezuela, there was once an incredible cook and housekeeper named Juanita. She was a true gourmet in a country not yet internationally known for its excellent agriculture. Venezuela produces marvelous fruits, vegetables, livestock, and, of course, chocolate. (In fact, its cacao is of the highest quality in the world.)

This recipe, which was born in Juanita's kitchen, became so popular in Caracas that it has been imitated in homes and even in the city's upscale restaurants. One of the children she helped raise, Paola Gaitan Petrella, eventually came to work at NORMAN'S, and she taught me how to make Juanita's signature dish.

I like to garnish the duck legs with additional orange segments and serve with a side of Corn-Turmeric Rice (page 196).

FOR THE DUCK

2 oranges

8 duck legs

Kosher salt and freshly ground black pepper

2 tablespoons canola oil

4 large Spanish onions, cut in half and thinly sliced

4 cloves garlic, thinly sliced

2 leeks, white parts only, washed well and cut into thin strips

2 stalks celery, cut into thin strips

1/4 cup chopped fresh thyme

2 bay leaves, broken in half

5 cups Chicken Stock (page 267)

FOR THE SAUCE

2 cups sugar

1 1/2 cups fresh orange juice

1 1/2 cups fresh lime juice

1/4 cup heavy cream

5 ounces extra-bitter Venezuelan chocolate (or any excellent-quality extra-bitter European chocolate), chopped into small pieces

1 tablespoon unsalted butter, diced

Dash of red wine vinegar (optional)

Preheat the oven to 300 degrees.

Grate the zest from the oranges; reserve. Peel the oranges and separate them into segments, discarding any seeds. Reserve.

With a sharp knife, score a crisscross pattern in the skin of the duck legs. Season them with salt and pepper. Heat the canola oil in a large roasting pan over medium-high heat. When the oil is very hot, add the duck legs, in batches, skin side down, and sear, turning once, until browned on both sides. As they brown, transfer them to a platter lined with paper towels. If necessary, drain off some of the excess oil between batches. Once the legs are brown, pour off the excess fat from the pan.

Spread half of the sliced onions in the bottom of the pan and place the duck legs on top. Scatter the garlic, leeks, celery, orange segments, thyme, and bay leaves. Season with 1 tablespoon pepper, and cover with the remaining onions.

Pour 4 cups of the chicken stock over the onions. Cover the pan with aluminum foil, and braise in the oven for 1 hour.

Stir the onions in the pan, cover again, and braise, stirring every 20 minutes, for another 1 1/2 to 2 hours, until the duck is very tender.

While the duck cooks, make the sauce: In a medium saucepan, combine the sugar, orange juice, lime juice, and the reserved orange zest. Bring to a boil, then reduce the heat to medium and cook for 40 to 45 minutes, until the liquid has turned dark amber and thickly coats a wooden spoon. Remove from the heat and slowly whisk in the heavy cream, and then the chopped chocolate. Set aside.

Remove the pan from the oven. Set the duck aside and keep warm. Skim the fat off the top of the pan. Lift the onions out of the braising liquid and set aside. Put the pan on a medium-high heat and reduce until there is only enough liquid to coat the onions. Return the onions to the braising liquid and keep warm.

Heat the remaining 1 cup chicken stock in a small saucepan. Very slowly, whisking constantly, gradually add stock to the chocolate sauce, which will have become very thick. Take care not to add too much stock: The stock and chocolate sauce mixture should be shiny and thick enough that it coats the back of a spoon. Finally, whisk in the diced butter. Taste; if the sauce is too sweet for you, add a dash of red wine vinegar.

To serve, spoon the braised onions onto a large serving platter. Season the duck with salt and pepper and place it on top of the onions. Drizzle the sauce over the duck and around the platter.

recommended wine: A full-bodied Napa Cabernet with cocoa flavors and a firm structure.

chicken tamales with *mole verde*

MAKES 20 TO 25 TAMALES

Tamales are often given short shrift, perhaps because few people north of Mexico have ever had the pleasure of homemade tamales. What's the difference? Imagine judging Italian cuisine by the merits of a bowl of boxed pasta topped with a jar of bland sauce.

I include these chicken tamales in the Feasts and Traditions chapter because the mere making of tamales can create a generational love fest. In Mexico, the family gathers for the holidays and at some time early on the day of the big feast, everyone forms an assembly line in the kitchen and festively prepares dinner. There's even a name for this, *la tamalada,* and many a Mexican has fond memories of the holiday ritual. Duties vary each year as age and expertise change and it is not uncommon for a family to make two hundred tamales in an afternoon. Some will be served at the dinner, but tamales freeze well and others will be consumed later.

This version is very simple and easily adapted to your favorite fillings; I like to sprinkle finely chopped toasted ancho chiles on the *masa* dough. Serve these with *Gallina Rellena* (page 182) or *Nochebuena* (page 189).

FOR THE DOUGH (MAKES ALMOST
    4 POUNDS)

5 ¹/₂ cups *masa harina* (available in many grocery stores and in Latin American markets)

2 teaspoons baking powder

5 teaspoons kosher salt

4 cups Chicken Stock (page 267), heated until hot

12 tablespoons (1 ¹/₂ sticks) unsalted butter, softened

1 cup vegetable shortening

FOR THE FILLING (MAKES 2¹/₄ CUPS)

8 ounces tomatillos, papery husks and cores removed, and rinsed

2 tablespoons canola oil

¹/₂ large Spanish onion, chopped

¹/₄ teaspoon ground allspice

¹/₄ teaspoon freshly ground black pepper, plus more to taste

¹/₈ teaspoon ground cloves

1 tablespoon mashed Roasted Garlic (page 262)

1 canned chipotle chile in *adobo* sauce

¹/₄ cup chopped cilantro

Kosher salt to taste

1 ³/₄ cups Chicken Stock (page 267)

8 ounces cooked chicken, shredded

¹/₄ cup pumpkin seeds, toasted and ground to a powder (see page 9)

2 tablespoons fresh lime juice

Roughly 30 large fresh corn husks, thoroughly washed and patted dry (see Note)

for the dough

Combine the *masa harina,* baking powder, and salt in the bowl of an electric mixer fitted with the paddle attachment. Add about half of the hot chicken stock and blend well. Beat in the butter and shortening. Beat in the rest of the stock. Let the dough rest for at least 30 minutes at room temperature.

for the filling

Preheat the oven to 450 degrees.

Put the tomatillos in a baking pan and roast for 20 minutes. Let cool slightly.

Meanwhile, heat the canola oil in a sauté pan over medium-high heat. Add the onions and cook for about 5 minutes, until it starts to turn golden. Stir in the spices, remove from the heat, and set aside.

In a food processor, combine the tomatillos, sautéd onions (set the pan aside), roasted garlic, chipotle, and cilantro, and puree until smooth. Season with salt and pepper.

Add the puree, chicken stock, and chicken to the onion pan, bring to a simmer over medium heat, and simmer, uncovered, for about 30 minutes, stirring occasionally, until most all of the liquid has cooked off; the mixture should resemble a thick stew. Stir in the ground pumpkin seeds and lime juice, and season with salt and pepper. Let cool.

To assemble the tamales, pull apart a few corn husks so that you have strings for tying up the ends (you can also use butcher's string for this). Lay a corn husk flat on your work surface. Spread about 2 tablespoons of the *masa* dough down the center of the husk. Spoon a tablespoon of the chicken mixture on top of the *masa,* and top that with about 2 table-spoons more *masa,* spreading it over the chicken mixture, so it is sandwiched in dough.

Fold the top of the husk over the *tamal,* then fold the sides of the husk over, and, finally, fold the bottom over, enclosing the dough completely. Secure the *tamal* by tying one or two corn husk strings around it, just as you would a ribbon on a package. Repeat the process until all the tamales are made. (You can see why the assembly line technique works well in tamale preparation.)

Fill a deep steamer pot with an inch or so of water; there should be 1 inch between the water and the bottom of the steamer insert. Set the tamales on the steamer rack, place it in the pot, and cover tightly. (You can stack the tamales, but allow them more time to cook.) Steam over medium-high heat for about 1 hour; you'll know the tamales are done when the husks pull easily away from them. Let them rest for 5 minutes before serving. Open and enjoy.

note: Dried corn husks are available at some grocery stores and at specialty and gourmet food markets; you can also substitute banana leaves, which are available frozen at Latin markets and some grocery stores.

recommended wine: New World Viognier or a single batch bourbon served neat.

gallina rellena

(Roasted Chicken Stuffed with Beef, Pork, Potatoes, Raisins, and Olives)

SERVES 6 TO 8, WITH LEFTOVERS

This roasted chicken is one beautiful bird at the table. In Nicaragua, *gallina rellena* is the dish families gather around in the same way we in America commune over turkey at Thanksgiving and roast prime ribs of beef at Christmas. It conveys that same spirit of generosity and abundance, and celebration of life.

Note that both the marinated chicken and the stuffing have to stand overnight.

FOR THE MARINADE

2 tablespoons ground annatto seeds

1 tablespoon red wine vinegar

1 cup diced golden pineapple (or substitute regular pineapple)

1 cup dry red wine

$^1/_2$ cup Worcestershire sauce

$^1/_2$ cup ketchup

$^1/_2$ cup fresh sour orange juice (or substitute $^1/_4$ cup each fresh lime and regular orange juice)

1 large Spanish onion, roughly chopped

Kosher salt and freshly ground black pepper to taste

One 6- to 7-pound chicken

4 tablespoons unsalted butter, softened

Kosher salt and freshly ground black pepper to taste

FOR THE STUFFING

3 tablespoons canola oil

1 $^1/_2$ pounds beef for stew, cut into $^1/_2$-inch cubes

1 $^1/_2$ pounds boneless pork shoulder, cut into $^1/_2$-inch cubes

Kosher salt and freshly ground black pepper

8 ounces smoky bacon, diced

3 tablespoons pure olive oil

4 cloves garlic, minced

1 large Spanish onion, diced

4 carrots, peeled and diced

3 *chayote,* diced (you can substitute 3 zucchini)

1 $^1/_2$ pounds Red Bliss potatoes, peeled and diced

4 cups Chicken Stock (page 267)

$^3/_4$ cup ketchup

$^3/_4$ cup Worcestershire sauce

1 bay leaf, broken in half

1 tomato, peeled, seeded, and diced

$^1/_2$ cup raisins

2 pimiento-stuffed ripe green olives, sliced into thin rounds

1 cup diced golden pineapple (or substitute regular pineapple)

1 tablespoon cracked black pepper

1 $^1/_2$ cups diced stale white bread

$^1/_4$ cup milk

for the marinade

Combine the annatto seeds and vinegar in a cup, stirring to make a paste. In a bowl, combine the pineapple, wine, Worcestershire, ketchup, sour orange juice, onion, and salt and pepper, and add the paste.

Rub the chicken's breast with the softened butter. Season the cavity and skin of the bird all over with salt and pepper. Put the chicken in a large resealable plastic bag and pour in the marinade, making sure some of it coats the bird's cavity as well as its exterior. Tie the bag closed and marinate overnight in the refrigerator, turning occasionally to ensure that all of the chicken is well coated.

Meanwhile, make the stuffing, which also has to stand overnight:

In a large skillet, heat the canola oil over high heat. When it is hot, season the beef and pork with salt and pepper and sear them, in batches, until browned on all sides. Transfer to a bowl and let cool.

In a large heavy roasting pan or skillet, cook the bacon in the olive oil over low heat until it begins to crisp. Turn the heat up to medium-high, add the garlic and onion, and cook until they begin to caramelize. Add the carrots, *chayote,* and potatoes and cook for 3 minutes. Add the chicken stock, Worcestershire, ketchup, and bay leaf, then stir in the tomato, raisins, olives, pineapple, 2 tablespoons salt, and the cracked pepper. Remove from the heat and set aside to cool.

Add the seared meats to the stuffing, cover, and refrigerate overnight.

The next day, preheat the oven to 375 degrees.

Put the bread in a medium bowl, drizzle it with the milk, and let stand until it absorbs the milk, about 10 minutes. Add 2 cups of the stuffing and mix well. Reserve the rest of the stuffing.

Take the chicken out of the bag (discard the marinade), and put it breast side up in a large roasting pan. Fill its cavity with the soaked bread and stuffing mix. Truss it, then scatter the reserved stuffing over it. Cover with a foil tent and roast for 1 hour.

Remove the foil and push the stuffing mixture off the chicken so that you can baste the bird with the pan juices. Put the foil back on the bird and roast for another hour.

Remove the foil, turn up the heat to 450 degrees, and roast the chicken for another 35 to 45 minutes, until golden brown. Allow it to rest for 10 minutes.

Carve the chicken and serve on a large platter with the stuffing and the pan juices around it.

note: There will probably be a good amount of leftover stuffing. Because it is filled with so much meat, it makes a terrific sandwich. It is also nice served over rice.

recommended wine: A fruity, young Italian Dolcetto from Dogliani in Piedmont.

asado negro

(Blackened Roast of Beef in Savory Caramel Sauce)

SERVES 6

This beef dish is the traditional way in which Venezuelans break the Lenten fast at Easter. Families gather at the holiday and eat *asado negro*—so called because the roast is made dark, and glistening, by the *papelón* brown sugar and almost savory caramel—with white rice and plantains. The distinct flavor of the *papelón* gives the meat a complex identity, yet as feasts go, this one is relatively simple to prepare.

Serve the beef with Basic White Rice (page 196) and *Maduro* Plantains (page 211). If you think you'll have room for dessert, make a batch of Candied Papaya (page 233).

Note that the meat must marinate overnight.

One 4-pound beef bottom round roast (called *boliche* in Latin markets and some grocery stores)
5 cloves garlic, slivered
2 large Spanish onions, thinly sliced
2 stalks celery, thinly sliced
1 leek, white and light green parts only, washed well and thinly sliced
2 bay leaves, broken in half
$^1/_2$ cup pure olive oil
$^1/_2$ cup Worcestershire sauce
1 cup water
1 cup sugar
1 tablespoon grated *papelón* (you can substitute 1 $^1/_2$ teaspoons brown sugar) (see Note)
2 cups white wine vinegar
1 cup dry red wine
2 tablespoons canola oil
2 tablespoons unsalted butter
2 green bell peppers, stemmed, seeded, and thinly sliced
Kosher salt and freshly ground black pepper to taste

With the tip of a sharp knife, make incisions all over the steak meat, and insert the slivers of garlic into them. In a bowl, mix the onions, celery, leek, bay leaves, oil, and Worcestershire. Put the meat in a large resealable plastic bag and add the marinade. Tie tightly and refrigerate overnight.

The next day, combine the water and sugar in a deep heavy saucepan and heat over medium-high heat until the sugar dissolves and becomes a very dark caramel. Carefully add the *papelón*, vinegar, and red wine and stir and cook only until all the caramel lumps dissolve. Set aside.

Preheat the oven to 375 degrees.

Heat a casserole large enough to hold the meat over medium-high heat. Add the canola oil and butter and heat until very hot. Remove the meat from the marinade, reserving the marinade, and place it fat side down in the pan. Sear, turning once, until dark golden brown on both sides. Transfer the meat to a plate.

Pour the marinade into the pan and cook until the onions turn translucent, 8 to 10 minutes. Slide the meat back into the pan, cover with the green pepper slices, and bathe it all in the marinade. Pour the caramel sauce over it and season with salt and pepper.

Cover the pan, transfer to the oven, and cook for 1 hour. Baste the meat and cook for 1 1/2 more hours, basting every 30 minutes. Remove the pan from the oven. Let the meat stand for 30 minutes. (Leave the oven on.)

Transfer the steak to a cutting board and slice it into 1/2-inch-thick slices. Put the meat back into the pan and spoon the sauce over, and adjust the seasoning. Put back in the oven for 30 minutes.

If the sauce hasn't reduced enough by then—it should be almost syrupy—transfer the meat and vegetables to a platter, letting any excess sauce drain back into the pan. Put the pan on a burner over medium-high heat and reduce the sauce as necessary, then return the meat and vegetables to the pan, mixing them in the sauce. Serve.

note: *Papelón* is a dark brown Latin American sugar sold in bricks or cones; look for it in Latin markets.

recommended beer or wine: Xingu Black Beer from Brazil or a California Petite Sirah.

matambre

("Kill-Hunger" Flank Steak, Marinated and Stuffed)

SERVES 4 TO 6

This is a famous steak dish with an evocative name—from whence that name comes will be evident once you make it. The butterflied beef (sometimes pork loin is used) is rolled up around a stuffing of sausage, eggs, and vegetables, tied into a neat cylinder, and roasted until nicely browned. It can be served hot or cold. After it is roasted and cooled, you can press it into a very firm cylinder, wrap tightly, and refrigerate it until well chilled. Slice it quite thin, and present it as an elegant cold cut. Ask the butcher to butterfly the steak for you if you prefer.

FOR THE MARINADE

$^1/_4$ cup Spanish sherry vinegar

$^1/_4$ cup pure olive oil

1 tablespoon medium-fine-chopped fresh sage

1 teaspoon toasted and ground cumin seeds (see page 9)

6 cloves garlic, minced

Kosher salt and freshly ground black pepper to taste

One 1 $^1/_2$-pound flank steak

FOR THE STUFFING

3 tablespoons pure olive oil

3 shallots, minced

2 $^1/_2$ cups packed stemmed spinach

Kosher salt and freshly ground black pepper to taste

1 large carrot, peeled, halved lengthwise, and each half cut lengthwise into 3 pieces

6 ounces cooked crumbled chorizo

4 hard-boiled eggs, peeled

$^1/_4$ cup canola oil

1 recipe Chimichurri Verde (page 280)

for the marinade

Mix all the ingredients together in a bowl. Set aside while you prepare the steak.

If you did not get the butcher to butterfly the steaks, starting from one long side, slice the steak horizontally almost in half so you can open it like a book. Place the opened-up meat on a large cutting board and cover it with plastic wrap. Using a meat mallet or a small sauté pan, pound the meat until it is a uniform $^1/_4$-inch thickness.

Put the steak in a large dish and add the marinade. Turn the meat over once so that both sides are coated in the marinade, cover, and refrigerate for 2 to 4 hours.

About an hour before you want to cook the steak, prepare the stuffing: In a large skillet, heat the olive oil over medium-high heat. Add the shallots and sauté for about 30 seconds, then add the spinach, seasoning with salt and pepper. Sauté until the spinach is wilted, then transfer the spinach and shallots to a fine-mesh strainer and let drain for about 10 minutes.

While the spinach cools, bring a saucepan of salted water to a boil. Prepare an ice-water bath.

When the water is boiling, add the carrots and blanch for 1 1/2 to 2 minutes, until tender yet still al dente. Drain the carrots and immediately plunge into the ice-water bath. Remove them as soon as they are cool; drain.

Preheat the oven to 425 degrees.

Lift the steak out of the marinade and put it on a cutting board. Open it out flat, with a short side facing you, and season well with salt and pepper. Spread the spinach over the meat, leaving a border all around, followed by the chorizo. Lay the carrots, evenly spaced in three rows across the meat, and arrange the eggs lengthwise in a row between the two lower rows of carrots. Season again to taste. Roll the steak into a tight cylinder, starting from the bottom. Tie the beef crosswise in 5 or 6 places with butcher's string, then tie it once lengthwise to keep the stuffing from seeping out.

Heat a heavy skillet over high heat, and add the canola oil. When it is very hot, sear the steak roll on all sides. Transfer to a roasting pan and roast for 30 minutes.

Let the meat rest for about 15 minutes before slicing it. Serve with the *chimichurri* sauce at the table.

recommended wine: If you serve it hot, go with an earthy but jammy Argentinean Malbec; if cold, try a Cabernet Franc–based wine such as Chinon (slightly chilled) from the Loire Valley.

feijoada

(Black Bean and Meat Stew)

SERVES 6 TO 8

Feijão is the Brazilian word for "bean," and beans are the heart of the matter in this recipe. A Brazilian woman once told me that black beans are so important to her country's men and women "they are like oxygen." Interestingly, *feijoada* was originally considered a meal fit only for the slaves who worked the sugar plantations near Rio de Janeiro. But because of its irresistible aromas and flavors—in addition to its beloved beans, *feijoada* is prepared with a veritable orgy of smoked, roasted, and simmered meats—the plantation masters could not resist the dish. Now it is a treasured part of the Brazilian table, traditionally served for Saturday's midday meal. It takes three or four hours and several bottles of red wine to consume *feijoada* properly—not to mention the time you need to allow for sleeping off the meal afterward.

The custom is to top this lusty, hearty stew with a salad. I like to serve it with Orange, Hearts of Palm, and Fennel Salad (page 88) with Pickled Red Onions (page 211).

2 tablespoons pure olive oil
1 pound chorizo or Italian pork sausage links
3 cloves garlic, thinly sliced
1 medium-to-large Spanish onion, diced
1 poblano pepper, stemmed, seeded, and cut
    into small dice
1 cup Spanish dry sherry
Freshly ground black pepper to taste
1 smoked ham hock
1 $^1/_2$ cups dried black beans, rinsed, soaked
    overnight in water to cover, and then
    drained

2 bay leaves, broken in half
9 cups Chicken Stock (page 267)
6 cups chopped kale
Kosher salt to taste
$^1/_2$ recipe Chilean Country Ribs (page 150)

In a large pot, heat the oil over medium-low heat. Add the sausage and cook, turning frequently, until cooked through. Transfer to paper towels to drain. Turn up the heat to medium-high, add the garlic, onion, and poblano, and sauté for 5 minutes. Add the sherry, season with pepper, and simmer until reduced by half. Add the ham hock, beans, bay leaves, and chicken stock. Bring to a simmer, skimming any impurities from the surface. Turn the heat down to low and cook, uncovered, for 1 $^1/_2$ to 2 hours, or until the beans are tender. During the last 15 minutes of cooking, add the kale. Remove the ham hock and bay leaves from the pot and discard. Season the stew with salt and pepper.

Meanwhile, cut the sausage and ribs into bite-sized pieces (discard any bones).

Add the sausage and ribs to the stew and heat through. Ladle into bowls and serve.

recommended wine: A Syrah from Cornas or an old-vines Mourvèdre from Bandol will complement the smoked and roasted characteristics of this intense, slow-cooked dish.

nochebuena

(Roast Pork Havana-Style with White Beans)

SERVES 8 TO 10

Nochebuena—"the Good Night"—is what Latin Americans call Christmas Eve. And in Cuba, Christmas Eve without pork would be like an American Thanksgiving without turkey. This is but one of literally dozens of recipes to uphold such an honored tradition.

Note that the pork needs to marinate for at least 2 days. You can make the white beans several days in advance; refrigerate, and gently reheat to serve.

Serve this with Basic White Rice (page 196), *Maduro* Plantains (page 211), and Pickled Red Onions (page 211).

3/4 cup fresh sour orange juice (or substitute 6 tablespoons each lime and regular orange juice)

1/4 cup fresh lime juice

3/4 cup olive oil

2 bay leaves, broken in half

1 tablespoon toasted and ground cumin seeds (see page 9)

1 tablespoon freshly ground black pepper

3 large cloves garlic, thinly sliced

One 9-pound fresh pork butt (not smoked), skin removed

1 recipe White Beans (page 204)

Whisk together the juices, oil, bay leaves, cumin, pepper, and garlic. Put the pork in a large heavy resealable bag and pour in the marinade. Seal the bag tightly and marinate in the refrigerator for at least 2 and up to 4 days, turning it occasionally.

Preheat the oven to 325 degrees.

Put the pork fat side up in a Dutch oven or roasting pan; discard the marinade. Cover and bake for 1 1/2 hours.

Turn the pork fat side down, cover, and cook for another 1 1/2 hours.

Turn the meat one last time, cover, and cook for about 1 hour more, or until it is almost falling off the bone.

Turn up the heat to 375 degrees. Cook the pork uncovered, for 30 minutes to brown it. Transfer the roast to a cutting board and allow it to rest for 10 minutes.

Meanwhile, reheat the beans. Pull the pork apart with two big forks and place it on a platter. Skim off the grease from the drippings in the roasting pan, and pour the drippings over the pork. Toss and serve with the prepared white beans on the side.

recommended wine: A New World Pinot Noir, such as one from the Santa Lucia Highlands in California or a Beaujolais from Fleurie.

xinxim

(Chicken and Seafood Stew with Coconut Milk and Nuts)

SERVES 6

This is one of the more complex recipes included in the book, but if you have the time to devote to it, you'll be more than satisfied with the results; when I cook this for people at the restaurant, they are blown away by the intensity of flavors. Mixing fish and meat is common in Brazilian cuisine, and *xinxim* (pronounced *sheen-sheem*) is almost paella-like in its diversity and ingredients. It is also similar to the Brazilian *vatapá* (page 122).

I like to serve this with rice, either Basic White Rice (page 196) or richer Saffron Rice (page 200). I garnish the dish with toasted unsweetened shredded coconut, cilantro leaves, and lime.

6 boneless chicken breasts, skin-on

Kosher salt and freshly ground black pepper
    to taste

$1/4$ cup Annatto Oil (page 261) or pure olive oil

$1/4$ cup pure olive oil

2 ounces smoky bacon, diced

4 tablespoons unsalted butter

5 cloves garlic, thinly sliced

$1/2$ Scotch bonnet chile, stemmed, seeded,
    and minced

1 medium red onion, diced

2 red bell peppers, stemmed, seeded,
    and diced

2 stalks celery, diced

1 cup diced fennel

1 bay leaf, broken in half

5 large ripe tomatoes, peeled, seeded,
    and chopped

1 $1/2$ cups fresh orange juice

6 small clams, scrubbed

6 mussels, scrubbed and debearded

1 cup heavy cream

$1/4$ cup toasted and finely ground cashews
    (see page 9)

$1/4$ cup toasted and ground *pepitas* (hulled
    pumpkin seeds) (see page 9)

$1/4$ cup dried shrimp, softened in $1/4$ cup warm
    water for 10 minutes, drained, and ground
    or finely chopped

2 tablespoons peeled and minced ginger

12 sea scallops

Preheat the oven to 400 degrees.

Season the chicken breasts with salt and pepper.

In a large ovenproof skillet, heat the annatto oil over medium-high heat until hot. Add the chicken breasts and cook, turning once, until golden on both sides. Pour off any excess oil. Place the chicken in the oven and cook for about 20 minutes, or until juices run clear when pierced. Set aside in a warm place.

Meanwhile, heat a large skillet over medium-low heat. Add 2 tablespoons of the olive oil and then the bacon, and sauté until it is beginning to crisp. Add 3 tablespoons of the butter and allow it to melt, then add the garlic and Scotch bonnet and cook for 30 seconds. Turn the heat up to medium-high, add the onion, bell peppers, celery, fennel, and bay leaf, and sauté until the vegetables are softened, about 5 minutes. Add the tomatoes and remove from the heat. Season to taste; set aside.

To make the sauce, pour the orange juice into a large saucepan. Add the clams and mussels, cover, and steam them open over medium-high heat; transfer them to a bowl as they open. When they are all cooked, add the cream, nuts, dried shrimp, and ginger, and cook for about 2 minutes. Add the tomato and vegetable mixture, season with salt and pepper, and keep warm over very low heat.

Pat the scallops dry and season with salt and pepper. Heat the remaining 2 tablespoons olive oil and 1 tablespoon butter in a large nonstick skillet over medium-high heat until quite hot. Sear the scallops, turning once, until golden brown on each side, 1 1/2 to 2 minutes on the first side and 45 to 60 seconds on the second side. Remove from the heat.

To serve, ladle the sauce into six bowls. Put a chicken breast and 2 scallops in each bowl, followed by a clam and a mussel. Season with salt and pepper.

recommended wine: A white Rhône, a Roussanne, or, perhaps, an Alsatian Pinot Gris.

rice, starches,
and other sides

During the Columbian Exchange, when ingredients and cooking techniques began to crisscross the ocean on the ships of the European explorers, rice was one of the most powerful gifts from the Old World to the New. (The only rice native to the Caribbean and the Americas is wild rice, *zizania aquatica,* which is not a rice at all but the root of a marine grass—and not a part of Latin and Caribbean diets.) It took a long time for rice of Spanish and Asian origins to establish a place in the cuisines of the New World, but ultimately it did, notably in such dishes as *asopao, arroz con pollo,* and the Southern American classic chicken and rice.

Beans, on the other hand, have been a staple here for thousands of years. Turtle beans (also known as black beans), kidney beans, and navy and pinto beans, all extremely important to Latin and Caribbean cooking, were already being farmed in Central America by 5000 B.C. The Brazilian feast, *Feijoada* (page 188), is a rich stew based on black beans. At the same time, beans accompany rice throughout the region in myriad everyday but nourishing dishes. In Mexico and Central America, a third partner, corn, is a mainstay.

Another column in the gastronomy of Latin American and Caribbean cuisine is the potato. Archeologists have discovered signs of its cultivation as early as 7000 B.C., in the Andean valley. Researchers believe that people first domesticated the wild tuber on the shores of Lake Titicaca, along the borders of modern-day Peru and Bolivia. These early inhabitants bred yellow potatoes and white potatoes, fat ones and skinny ones, and gave them memorable names: "Flat like a cow's tongue," "Like a woman with the colors of a condor's neck," and "Makes the daughter-in-law weep." By the time Conquistadores arrived in the sixteenth century, the potato was the basic staple of the Andes. It was the stuff of legends: a god covered in dirt but endowed with magical powers.

In the United States you rarely find more than half a dozen varieties of potato in even the most sophisticated supermarkets. In Lima's International Potato Center, about four thousand domesticated and wild varieties are registered as adaptable to all climates and soils, and some are resistant to insects and plagues. It was the ancient dwellers of the Andes who discovered how to freeze-dry potatoes: They exposed them to frigid nighttime temperatures at high altitudes and stamped on them to squeeze out the tubers' water, then thawed them in the potent mountain sun. The result of the discovery is *chuño*, a dehydrated product that keeps indefinitely. The Inca emperors kept warehouses filled with *chuño*, ready to feed the people in times of famine. Today you'll still find it used in recipes for pre-Columbian dishes that date back some six thousand years.

After the Spanish conquest, potatoes were introduced into Europe, but at first they were ignored, even despised. Sicilians would write down the name of an enemy, fix it to a potato, and bury it in hopes that the enemy would meet an early demise. The Spanish used potatoes for medicinal purposes. British Protestants wouldn't plant potatoes, because they were not mentioned in the Bible. (Irish Catholics found a way around that dilemma by sprinkling the potatoes with holy water and planting them on Good Friday.) But Queen Elizabeth I (1533–1603) received a few sample seedlings from her protégé, Sir Walter Raleigh, with instructions on how to plant them. She handed them over to one of her gardeners and a few months later, they were growing in the valleys of the Thames. Her Majesty then ordered up a grand banquet, at which she would introduce the potato to noblemen and merchants. But the royal cooks had no notion of how to prepare the New World tuber. They discarded the sweet flesh and instead steamed the bitter leaves and stems, serving them on silver plates. Soon news of this terrible food reached all of the courts of Europe, and the potato became an outcast, fit to be fed to only to pigs.

It took almost two hundred years for the tuber to be rehabilitated, when the respected French agronomist and gourmet Auguste Parmentier began to include it in his delicious recipes. The taste for potatoes in Europe soon spread to the masses, as an inexpensive and nutritive staple, and great chefs like Carême, Escoffier, and Maxim created potato recipes that have circled the globe.

arroz con coco
(Coconut Rice)

MAKES 8 CUPS

Arroz con coco, another gift from Africa to New World cuisine, is immensely popular in the Caribbean as an accompaniment to meat, fowl, and, most particularly, fish.

2 cups unsweetened coconut milk
4 ounces smoky bacon, finely diced
3 cups long-grain white rice
$^1/_4$ cup packed dark brown sugar
6 cups water
Kosher salt and freshly ground black pepper to taste
$^3/_4$ cup raisins

In a medium-to-large saucepan, reduce the coconut milk over medium heat until all the liquid evaporates and you are left with the dark brown coconut solids that appear to be frying in the remaining coconut oil. Add the bacon and cook until crispy, about 2 minutes.

Add the rice and sugar and stir, then add the water and a pinch each of salt and pepper and stir. Bring to a boil over medium heat and cook, uncovered, stirring occasionally, until most of the water has evaporated. (Cooking the rice uncovered causes the liquid to evaporate faster and concentrates the coconut flavor in the rice.)

Add the raisins, put the lid on, reduce the heat to low, and cook for 5 to 8 minutes, or until the rice is soft. Season with salt and pepper, and serve.

basic white rice

MAKES 3 CUPS

You may be tempted to add various ingredients to this comforting staple dish of many nations, but I advise you not to. This plain rice is suggested as an accompaniment in so many of my dishes because its simplicity provides a welcome foil to the intensity of many New World ingredients. Think of Basic White Rice as a culinary security blanket.

2 cups water
$1/2$ teaspoon kosher salt
1 cup long-grain white rice
1 tablespoon unsalted butter (optional)

Wash the rice by placing it in a bowl of cool water and swishing the grains around a dozen times or so. Drain and repeat once.

In a medium saucepan, bring the 2 cups water to a boil over high heat. Add the salt, rice, and, if desired, the butter, and stir. Cover, reduce the heat to low, and cook for 20 minutes, or until the rice has absorbed most of the water and is tender. Remove the rice from the heat and allow it to stand, covered, for 5 minutes, or until all the remaining liquid is absorbed.

corn-turmeric rice

MAKES $3^{1}/_{2}$ TO 4 CUPS

The golden hues of corn and turmeric work in tandem in this dish, which is found in various forms throughout the Andean highlands and the Caribbean.

2 tablespoons olive oil
2 tablespoons unsalted butter
4 cloves garlic, thinly sliced
2 teaspoons ground turmeric
1 carrot, peeled and diced
1 stalk celery, diced
$1/2$ red onion, diced
2 cups corn kernels (from about 3 ears)
1 cup long-grain white rice
1 $1/2$ cups Chicken Stock (page 267)
Kosher salt and freshly ground black pepper
    to taste

Heat the olive oil and butter in a medium saucepan over medium-low heat. When the butter foams, add the garlic and turmeric and stir for about 2 minutes. Add the carrot, celery, and onion, stir, and cook for 6 minutes, stirring occasionally. Stir in the corn and rice. Add the stock, season with salt and pepper, stir once, and bring just to a boil. Turn the heat down very low, cover, and cook until the rice has absorbed all the liquid and is tender, about 15 minutes. Let stand, covered, for 5 minutes, then serve.

red rice

MAKES 3 ¹/₂ CUPS

Red rice gets its color from annatto seeds, also called *achiote*, a word that comes from Náhuatl, the Aztec language. *Achiote* comes from a plant native to Mexico, and it gives this rice a subtle vegetal flavor.

This goes well with *Poulet à la Créole* (page 136). It can be kept warm, covered, in a warm spot, for 20 to 30 minutes before serving.

2 tablespoons unsalted butter
2 tablespoons Annatto Oil (page 261)
1 Scotch bonnet chile, stemmed, seeded, and minced
4 cloves garlic, minced
¹/₂ medium Spanish onion, diced
1 carrot, peeled and diced
1 stalk celery, diced
2 small bay leaves, broken in half
1 cup long-grain white rice
Kosher salt and freshly ground black pepper to taste
1 ¹/₂ cups Chicken Stock (page 267), warmed

Melt the butter with the annatto oil in a medium saucepan over medium-high heat. Add the Scotch bonnet and garlic, stir, and cook for 15 seconds. Add the onion, carrot, celery, and bay leaves and stir well. Allow the vegetables to cook, stirring frequently, until well glazed, about 10 minutes.

Stir in the rice and salt and pepper. Add the chicken stock, stir once and bring to a simmer, then immediately turn the heat down to very low. Cover and cook until the rice has absorbed the stock, 12 to 15 minutes. Cover and let stand for 5 minutes, then serve.

rice and peas

MAKES 7 CUPS

A highly popular household staple on the English-speaking Caribbean islands, this dish is a worthy rival of Cuba's *congri* (page 208).

1 tablespoon unsalted butter
1 tablespoon olive oil
3 cloves garlic, thinly sliced
1 Scotch bonnet chile, stemmed, seeded, and minced
1/2 medium Spanish onion, diced
1 large carrot, peeled and diced
2 large stalks celery, diced
1 1/2 cups long-grain white rice, rinsed
2 bay leaves, broken in half
1 1/2 cups unsweetened coconut milk
1/2 cup water
1 tablespoon chopped fresh thyme
4 scallions, white parts only, thinly sliced
2 cups cooked red kidney beans
1 teaspoon kosher salt
1 teaspoon freshly ground black pepper

In a medium saucepan, melt the butter with the olive oil over low heat. Sauté the garlic and Scotch bonnet, letting them flavor the oil, for about 1 minute. Turn the heat up to medium-high, add the onion, carrot, and celery, and cook for 5 minutes. Add the rice and bay leaves and stir to coat. Add the coconut milk and water and bring to a simmer, then lower the heat, cover, and cook until all the liquid is absorbed, 15 to 20 minutes. Remove from the heat.

Fluff the rice with a fork. Add the thyme, scallions, beans, salt, and pepper, and mix well. Cover and let stand for 5 minutes to heat through. Serve.

rice and potatoes with tiny shrimp

MAKES 8 CUPS

Rice was brought from Spain to South America, and in Peru it found endless partnerships with the bounteous seafood produced by the Humboldt Current, which runs along the country's coastline. My contribution is to add the beautiful purple potatoes native to the Andean highlands to this side dish.

I've also served this cold as a salad, with the addition of diced ripe avocado, mango, and/or orange segments.

3 tablespoons canola oil

1/2 Scotch bonnet chile, stemmed, seeded, and minced

3 cloves garlic, minced

1 large red onion, finely chopped

2 large ripe tomatoes, peeled, seeded, and finely chopped

2 bay leaves, broken in half

1 tablespoon fresh chopped oregano

1/2 cup dry white wine

1 cup Chicken Stock (page 267)

2 red bell peppers, stemmed, seeded, and chopped

1 pound peeled rock shrimp or other shrimp, cut into bite-sized pieces

Kosher salt and freshly ground black pepper to taste

2 cups cooked long-grain white rice

1 pound Peruvian purple potatoes, peeled, cooked in boiling salted water until tender, and diced

3 tablespoons chopped cilantro

In a large skillet, heat the canola oil over medium heat. Add the Scotch bonnet and garlic and sauté for 30 seconds. Add the onion, tomatoes, bay leaves, and oregano. Cook, stirring occasionally, until the onion is softened, about 10 minutes.

Pour in the wine and cook until it evaporates, about 5 minutes. Add the chicken stock, bell peppers, and shrimp and cook for another 5 minutes until the shrimp are just cooked.

Stir in the rice, potatoes, cilantro, and salt and pepper. Cook for 5 minutes. Remove from the heat, cover, and let stand for about 15 minutes to allow the flavors to marry. Serve.

saffron rice

MAKES 3 1/2 TO 4 CUPS

Saffron is one of the most expensive ingredients in the world. That makes this the most aristocratic of rices.

1 1/2 cups Chicken Stock (page 267), warmed
A pinch of saffron threads, preferably Spanish
2 tablespoons olive oil
2 tablespoons unsalted butter
4 cloves garlic, minced
1 Scotch bonnet chile, stemmed, seeded, and minced (optional)
1/2 medium Spanish onion, diced
1 carrot, peeled and diced
1 stalk celery, diced
2 small bay leaves, broken in half
1 cup long-grain white rice
Kosher salt and freshly ground black pepper to taste

In a small bowl, pour the chicken stock over the saffron. Set aside for 15 to 20 minutes to infuse. In a medium saucepan, heat the olive oil and butter over medium-high heat. Add the garlic, and the Scotch bonnet, if you're including it, stir, and cook for 15 seconds, then add the onion, carrot, celery, and bay leaves and stir well. Allow the vegetables to cook, stirring frequently, until well glazed, about 10 minutes.

Stir in the rice and salt and pepper. Add the chicken stock and saffron, stir once, and bring to a boil, then immediately reduce the heat to very low. Cover and cook until all of the stock is absorbed, 10 to 15 minutes. Let stand, covered, for 5 minutes. Serve.

black bean, sweet pea, and cilantro rice

MAKES ABOUT 4¹/₂ CUPS

Three Latin American favorites blend harmoniously in flavor and texture. This pilaf-style rice, with its pungent, grassy vinaigrette, can serve as a light lunch on its own, or it can be an elegant accompaniment to other dishes, particularly roasted and broiled meats. I even serve it with hamburgers and barbecue.

FOR THE RICE

2 ¹/₃ cups chilled cooked long-grain white rice

2 cups chilled cooked black beans (see page 202) or well-rinsed canned beans

¹/₃ small red onion, cut into medium dice

¹/₂ cup green peas, cooked in boiling salted water until tender and chilled

¹/₂ teaspoon kosher salt

¹/₂ teaspoon freshly ground black pepper

1 jalapeño, stemmed, seeded, and minced

4 cloves garlic, minced

FOR THE VINAIGRETTE

2 tablespoons extra virgin olive oil

¹/₂ tablespoons Spanish sherry vinegar

1 ¹/₂ teaspoons fresh lime juice

¹/₄ cup mashed Roasted Garlic (page 262)

2 tablespoons minced cilantro

2 tablespoons minced Italian parsley

¹/₄ teaspoon kosher salt

¹/₂ teaspoon freshly ground black pepper

for the rice
Mix all of the ingredients together in a bowl.

for the vinaigrette
Put the olive oil in the blender. Pulsing the machine at a low speed, slowly add the vinegar and lime juice. Add the roasted garlic and blend well. Pour this mixture into a small bowl, add the rest of the ingredients, and mix well. Toss with the rice and serve.

black beans

MAKES 3 1/2 CUPS

The countries of Latin America and the Caribbean each favor a particular bean in their cooking. In Brazil, the be-all is the black bean.

1 ounce smoky bacon, diced

1 1/2 teaspoons pure olive oil

1 tablespoon unsalted butter

3 cloves garlic, minced

2 jalapeños, stemmed, seeded, and minced

1/2 medium red onion, diced

1 large stalk celery, diced

1 carrot, peeled and diced

1 1/2 teaspoons toasted and ground cumin seeds (see page 9)

1 1/2 teaspoons freshly ground black pepper, plus more to taste

1 bay leaf, broken in half

1/4 cup Spanish sherry vinegar

1 cup dried black beans, rinsed, soaked overnight, and drained

2 smoked ham hocks

5 cups Chicken Stock (page 267), or more as necessary

Kosher salt to taste

In a medium saucepan, cook the bacon in the olive oil over medium heat until beginning to crisp. Add the butter. When it foams, add the garlic and jalapeños, stir, and allow them to cook for about 30 seconds. Add the onion, celery, and carrot, stirring to coat, turn the heat to medium-high and, stirring occasionally, cook until the vegetables are nicely caramelized, about 10 minutes.

Add the cumin, black pepper, and bay leaf, then add the vinegar, drained beans, ham hocks, and chicken stock and bring to a boil, skimming off any impurities that float to the surface. Reduce the heat to medium-low and cook the beans, uncovered, until soft, 1 1/2 to 2 hours; add more stock or water as necessary.

Season with salt and pepper and serve.

red bean puree

This rustic puree can be used in many ways. I like to serve it with Steak and Eggs Salvadoran-Style (page 165), or to top *cachapa* cakes as a base for grilled chicken.

2 cloves garlic, sliced
1 small Spanish onion, diced
1 tablespoon pure olive oil
1 teaspoon toasted and ground cumin seeds
    (see page 9)
1 bay leaf, broken in half
One 12-ounce package small red beans, rinsed
6 cups Chicken Stock (page 267)
2 1/2 tablespoons brewed espresso
Kosher salt and freshly ground black pepper to
    taste

In a medium saucepan, sauté the garlic and onion in the oil over medium heat for 2 to 3 minutes. Stir in the cumin and bay leaf. Add the beans and stock and bring to a simmer. Cook until the beans are soft, 1 1/2 to 2 hours. Remove from the heat.

Puree the beans in a food processor. Add the espresso, then salt and pepper, and serve.

white beans

MAKES 10 CUPS

Homey and rustic, this *ragù* is very versatile and easy to make. We serve it as part of our *Nochebuena* feast (see page 189).

2 tablespoons pure olive oil

2 ounces smoky bacon, diced

8 ounces chorizo or other spicy sausage, pierced in a few places with a fork

6 cloves garlic, thinly sliced

1 large Spanish onion, diced

2 poblano peppers, stemmed, seeded, and diced

1 tablespoon toasted and ground cumin seeds (see page 9)

2 bay leaves, broken in half

2 tablespoons Spanish sherry vinegar

2 tablespoons tomato paste

1 smoked ham hock or ham bone

8 cups Chicken Stock (page 267)

2 cups dried white beans, rinsed, soaked overnight in water to cover, and drained

Kosher salt and freshly ground black pepper to taste

Heat a large heavy soup pot over medium-low heat and add the olive oil. When it is warm, add the bacon and chorizo. Cook, turning to brown, until the sausage is firm enough to cut into rounds when cooled. Remove the sausage from the pot and drain on paper towels, then place it in the refrigerator to firm up. (Leave the bacon in the pot.)

Add the garlic to the pot and sauté over low heat for 30 seconds. Turn the heat up to medium, add the onion and poblanos, and cook for 7 to 8 minutes, stirring occasionally. Stir in the cumin, bay leaf, vinegar, and tomato paste, then add the ham hock, stock, and drained beans. Turn up the heat and bring to just a simmer, skimming off the foam as necessary. Simmer (lower the heat if necessary) until the beans are tender, about 1 1/2 hours. Stir occasionally, taking care not to let the beans stick to the bottom of the pot.

Meanwhile, cut the chorizo into 1/4-inch rounds.

When the beans are tender, season with salt and pepper. Remove 1 1/2 cups of the beans, put them in a bowl, and mash well, then return to the pot. Add the chorizo and cook for 20 minutes more. Remove the ham hock, season to taste, and serve.

boniato mash

MAKES 5 CUPS

Boniato is the Spanish word for a white sweet potato grown in the Caribbean. You can find it in South America as well; in Colombia, it is known as *batata*, in Peru as *camote*. I serve this alongside Snapper *a la Veracruzana* (page 114), and I also use it in Pork and *Boniato Croquetas* (page 25).

2 pounds *boniato*, peeled and cut into 2-inch cubes
4 tablespoons unsalted butter
$^1/_2$ cup heavy cream
2 teaspoons mashed Roasted Garlic (page 262)
Kosher salt and freshly ground black pepper to taste

Put the *boniato* in a large pot, add water to cover generously, and bring to a boil. Boil for 35 minutes, or until the *boniato* is tender when tested with a knife. Drain, transfer to a large bowl, and let cool slightly, then mash with a potato masher.

In a small saucepan, heat the butter, cream, and garlic to a simmer. Mash this mixture into the *boniato,* and season with salt and pepper.

calabaza mash

MAKES 6 CUPS

The word *calabaza* means "squash" in Spanish, and this giant bright orange, speckled member of the *Curcubita* family tastes like pumpkin. In fact, it is often referred to as West Indian pumpkin. *Calabaza*'s soft flavor and orange color makes it appealing on the table. Try it the next time you are thinking of making mashed potatoes or baked acorn squash. You'll find out how easy cooking a *Nuevo Latino* vegetable can be.

6 pounds *calabaza*, peeled, seeded, and cut into 1-inch pieces
$^1/_2$ cup packed brown sugar
4 teaspoons kosher salt, or to taste
1 teaspoon freshly ground black pepper, or to taste
12 tablespoons (1 $^1/_2$ sticks) unsalted butter, diced

Preheat the oven to 400 degrees.

In a large bowl, toss the squash with all of the remaining ingredients, mixing well. Transfer to a large baking pan and bake, uncovered, for about an hour, or until the squash is very tender when pierced with a knife and beginning to fall apart. Remove from the oven, transfer to a bowl, and mash.

Scoop the squash into a colander or medium-mesh strainer and let it stand for 2 to 3 minutes to allow most of the excess liquid to drain. Adjust the seasonings and serve.

purple potato mash

MAKES 4 CUPS

Of the thousands of varieties of potato classified by the folks at the International Potato Center, the distinctive purple Peruvian potato has become perhaps the most familiar here in the United States.

2 ¹/₂ pounds Peruvian purple potatoes
4 tablespoons unsalted butter
1 medium red onion, sliced paper-thin
1 tablespoon sugar
1 tablespoon Spanish sherry vinegar
Kosher salt and freshly ground black pepper
    to taste
1 cup heavy cream
2 tablespoons mashed Roasted Garlic
    (page 262)

Preheat the oven to 350 degrees.

Put the potatoes in a roasting pan, without crowding them, and bake for 1 hour, or until tender when pierced with a knife.

While the potatoes are baking, caramelize the onions: Melt 1 tablespoon of the butter in a small skillet. Add the onion and sauté over medium heat until beginning to soften, about 2 minutes. Add the sugar and sherry vinegar and continue to cook, stirring occasionally, until the onions are a deep caramel color and all of the liquid has evaporated, 4 to 5 minutes. Season with salt and pepper, remove from the heat, and reserve.

Remove the potatoes from the oven and allow them to cool slightly, then peel them and transfer to a bowl. In a small saucepan, bring the cream and roasted garlic to a simmer. Mash the potatoes with a potato masher, then add the cream mixture a bit at a time, incorporating it with the masher, until completely blended into the potatoes. Add the remaining 3 tablespoons butter, then fold in the onions. Season with salt and pepper if needed. Serve.

papas chorreadas with romaine
(Potatoes in Cheese Sauce)

SERVES 4

Papas chorreadas is a staple of Colombian cuisine. The combination of potatoes and cheese works the world over. This dish adds style to simple grilled steaks, chicken breasts, or pork chops.

4 large Idaho potatoes, scrubbed and quartered lengthwise
3 tablespoons unsalted butter
1 red onion, finely chopped
3 large ripe tomatoes, peeled, seeded, and diced
Kosher salt and freshly ground black pepper to taste
²/₃ cup heavy cream
6 ounces pepper Jack cheese, grated
Two handfuls of thinly sliced romaine lettuce
Extra virgin olive oil to taste

Cook the potatoes in boiling salted water until tender, about 30 minutes. Drain.

While they are cooking, make the sauce: In a large sauté pan, melt the butter over medium-high heat. When it is foaming, add the onion and cook until lightly caramelized, about 8 minutes. Add the tomatoes, season with salt and pepper, and cook for 7 minutes, or until the tomatoes start to break down. Add the cream, bring to a simmer, and sprinkle in the cheese. Allow it to melt, and cook for another 3 minutes. Pour half the sauce into a small pot and keep warm.

In a bowl, toss the romaine with the remaining sauce until the lettuce is warm. Arrange on a large platter. Place the potato wedges on top, drizzle them with extra virgin olive oil, and season with salt and pepper. Spoon the remaining sauce over the potatoes. Garnish with chopped fresh herbs, if you like.

congri
(Red Bean and Rice Hash)

MAKES 3 QUARTS

This simple Cuban hash goes well with most meat and chicken dishes. When prepared with black beans, it is known as *Moros y Cristianos* (Moors and Christians) in the Spanish-speaking countries of the Caribbean. You'll find *congri* tastes even better as leftovers, as its flavors seem to blossom after a day or two.

1 ¹/₂ tablespoons pure olive oil

4 ounces smoky bacon, cut into small dice

4 cloves garlic, minced

1 medium red onion, diced

1 red bell pepper, stemmed, seeded, and diced

2 bay leaves, broken in half

2 cups long-grain white rice

1 tablespoon minced fresh thyme

1 teaspoon toasted and ground cumin seeds
   (see page 9)

3 cups Chicken Stock (page 267)

1 cup diced smoked ham

4 cups cooked kidney beans

Kosher salt and freshly ground black pepper to
   taste

In a large pot, sauté the bacon in the olive oil over medium heat until beginning to crisp. Add the garlic, onion, bell pepper, and bay leaves and cook for about 5 minutes. Add the rice, thyme, and cumin, stirring to coat. Add the chicken stock, ham, and cooked beans and bring to a simmer. Turn the heat down to low, cover, and cook for about 20 minutes, or until all the stock is absorbed.

Remove the lid, season with salt and pepper, and fluff with a fork. Cover and let stand for 5 minutes. Serve.

tropical tuber hash

MAKES 6 CUPS

I love to serve this lusty, homey hash with fish and poultry dishes. It is a sort of Latin succotash.

FOR THE TUBERS

1 sweet potato
1 *boniato* (you can substitute sweet potato)
1 yuca (you can substitute an Idaho potato)
1 tablespoon unsalted butter
1 teaspoon kosher salt
$^1/_2$ teaspoon freshly ground black pepper

FOR THE VEGETABLES

3 ounces smoky bacon, diced
2 tablespoons canola oil
$^1/_3$ cup diced yellow bell pepper
$^1/_3$ cup diced red bell pepper
$^1/_4$ cup diced seeded poblano pepper
1 jalapeño, stemmed, seeded, and minced
$^1/_3$ small red onion, diced
Kosher salt and freshly ground black pepper to
 taste

FOR THE CONDIMENT

$^1/_4$ cup mashed Roasted Garlic (page 262)
1 $^1/_2$ tablespoons Spanish sherry vinegar
2 tablespoons chopped Italian parsley
2 tablespoons chopped cilantro

for the tubers

Preheat the oven to 350 degrees.

Peel the sweet potato, *boniato,* and yuca and cut into small dice. Blanch in boiling salted water for about 10 minutes. Drain well and toss with the butter, salt, and pepper.

Spread the tubers on a baking sheet or in a large baking pan. Roast for 15 minutes, or until they are easily pierced with a knife. Transfer to a bowl; reserve.

Meanwhile, prepare the vegetables: Cook the bacon in a sauté pan until it starts to crisp. Add the canola oil and vegetables, season with salt and pepper, and sauté until tender but still a little firm. Add the vegetables and the tubers, and spoon into a warm serving dish.

for the condiment

Mix together the garlic mash, vinegar, parsley, and cilantro. Serve on top of or beside the hash.

cebollas fritas
(Fried Onions)

SERVES 4

These egg-battered onions have a sweetness that marries well with rich dishes such *Churrasco de Sao Paulo a la Parilla* (page 162).

2 extra-large eggs, beaten
1 cup milk
1 large Spanish onion, thinly sliced
1 1/2 cups all-purpose flour
Kosher salt and freshly ground black pepper to taste
1 cup grated Manchego cheese
Canola or peanut oil for frying

Whisk together the eggs and milk in a medium bowl. Toss in the sliced onion and let stand for 30 minutes, stirring occasionally.

Preheat the oven to 400 degrees.

In a large bowl, season the flour with salt and pepper.

Pour an inch of oil into a deep skillet and heat it to 350 degrees. Lift the onions out of the egg mixture and toss them in the flour. Fry, in batches, until golden brown, and transfer to paper towels to drain.

Place the onions in a casserole, sprinkle with the cheese, and bake for 10 minutes. Serve.

caramelized red onions

SERVES 4

I've used these onions for years to perk up many dishes, among them *Vaca Frita* (page 166), Creole Mustard–Glazed Calves' Liver (page 168), and *Palomilla* Steak (page 163).

2 tablespoons pure olive oil
2 tablespoons unsalted butter
2 large red onions, cut lengthwise into thin slices
Kosher salt and freshly ground black pepper to taste
1 tablespoon sugar
1/4 cup Spanish sherry vinegar

Heat a very large sauté pan over high heat. Add the olive oil and butter. When the butter begins to foam, add the onions, season with salt and pepper, and stir well. Cook, stirring occasionally, until the onions are nice and golden, 8 to 10 minutes. Turn the heat down to medium, sprinkle the sugar over the onions, stir gently, and cook for 1 minute. Add the vinegar, stir, and reduce until almost no liquid remains, 1 to 2 minutes. (For a little more flavor, you can add some fresh herbs.)

Season with salt and pepper and serve.

Tortilla Soup with Sugarcane-
Marinated Chicken (page 72)

Carbonada en Zapallo (page 76)

Sea Bass *Ceviche* with Jicama and Avocado Slaw (page 93)

Pastel de Mariscos
(page 108)

Deviled Lobster (page 110)

Fish in Foil with Sweet Onions,
Tomatoes, and *Mojo Verde*
(page 111)

pickled red onions

MAKES 2 TO 2¹/₂ CUPS

A charming alchemy takes place when you "quick-pickle" red onions. They act very sweetly with a wide range of birds, meat, and fish, and I also use them in *Papas a la Huancaina* (page 174) and Conch Salad (page 95).

1 large red onion, sliced into ¹/₄-inch rounds
1 ¹/₂ teaspoons kosher salt
³/₄ cup red wine vinegar
2 ¹/₂ tablespoons sugar
¹/₂ teaspoon freshly ground black pepper

Separate the onion rings and put in a large bowl. Sprinkle with the salt, tossing to distribute it evenly. Let stand for 30 minutes.

Rinse the onions and drain well. Lay the rings between paper towels and pat them dry. Put the onions in a bowl.

In a small bowl, whisk together the vinegar, sugar, and pepper. Pour over the onions, toss and marinate for 1 hour. Serve, or refrigerate until ready to use. (This will keep for 1 day.)

maduro plantains
(Caramelized Very Ripe Plantains)

SERVES 6

When I am away from Miami for more than a few days and I begin to miss the food, this dish of plantains is likely to stir my memory palate. In the tropical belt of the New World, most people would forgo their meat and potatoes before they'd miss their daily ration of plantains, be they green skinned or blackened and overripe—*maduro*. *Maduro* plantains go with almost every kind of dish; I've offered them with seared foie gras, black beans, and everything in between.

2 very ripe plantains (their skins should be extremely dark, almost black), peeled
Kosher salt and freshly ground black pepper to taste
Canola or peanut oil for panfrying

Slice each plantain on the bias into nine ¹/₄-inch-thick ovals. Season with salt and pepper.

Pour ¹/₄ inch of oil into a large skillet and heat over medium-high heat. Add the plantains, several at a time, leaving yourself room to flip them, and cook for 1 to 1 ¹/₂ minutes on each side, until golden with black edges. Transfer to a plate lined with paper towels to drain. Sprinkle with salt and pepper and serve.

plátanos en tentacion
(Plantains Glazed with "Temptation" Caramel)

SERVES 4

As corn is to the people of Mexico, plantains are to Venezuelans: an elementary truth and sustenance. In Caracas and Maracaibo, they are served almost every day on the dinner table with a protein and, of course, white rice. This delightful recipe has been a tradition for generations in many Venezuelan households. Once you try it, you'll realize why it is called "Plantains with Temptation Sauce."

This dish is excellent with roast pork, *Carne Desmenuzada* (page 157), or a simple roasted chicken.

Canola oil for panfrying
2 very ripe plantains, peeled and cut into 1-inch rounds
3/4 cup sugar
3/4 cup Spanish sherry vinegar
1 teaspoon ground cinnamon
1 teaspoon ground cloves
1 1/2 teaspoons grated lime zest
3/4 cup water
2 1/2 tablespoons unsalted butter, diced

Pour 1/2 inch canola oil into a medium pot and heat until hot. Add the plantain rounds and fry, in batches, until dark golden brown all over. Remove and drain on paper towels.

In a medium saucepan, melt the sugar over medium-high heat, stirring until it becomes a dark brown caramel. Very gradually add the vinegar, stirring until any bits of caramel are dissolved; be careful, this will splatter. Add the cinnamon, cloves, lime zest, and water and boil until reduced to a dark amber caramel. Reduce the heat to medium-low, carefully fold in the plantains, and cook, constantly basting the plantains with the caramel, for 2 minutes. Add the butter and stir until it melts. Serve.

tostones

(Twice-Fried Plantains)

MAKES 20 TO 24 *TOSTONES*

How somebody figured out that frying plantains, smashing them, and frying them again would make them taste great is a mystery to me.

3 large green plantains
Canola oil for frying
Kosher salt and freshly ground black pepper
    (optional)

With a sharp knife, cut the ends from each plantain and then slice lengthwise several times through the skin. Put them in a deep bowl, cover with very hot water, and allow to sit for about 10 minutes (this helps loosen the peels).

Drain the plantains, peel them, and cut into 1-inch-thick rounds.

Pour 1 1/2 inches of oil into a pot or deep skillet and heat over medium heat until just hot enough to sizzle when a plantain piece is added. Fry the slices, in batches, without crowding, until tender and golden. Transfer to paper towels to drain. Set the pot aside.

While the plantains are still warm, put a damp towel over them and smash each one with the heel of your hand. (You can keep them wrapped for a few hours in the damp towel before serving.)

Reheat the oil over medium heat until it is very hot but not smoking. Cook the flattened plantains, in batches, without crowding, until golden brown. You've created *tostones*. Transfer them to paper towels to drain, and season with salt and pepper, if desired. Serve immediately.

crispy potato and *boniato* cakes

MAKES 16 CAKES

I started my cooking career in an all-American diner, where I made plenty of hash brown potatoes for the hard-working clientele who came in to fuel up before work. These potato and *boniato* cakes are a step south of those hash browns, and they are an easy way to add a New World dimension to your table.

1 ¼ pounds chef's potatoes (also called Maine or Kennebec potatoes; if you cannot find these medium-starch white potatoes, substitute new potatoes), scrubbed

1 ¼ pounds *boniato*, scrubbed

4 tablespoons unsalted butter

1 large Spanish onion, chopped medium-fine

1 small bunch scallions, green and white parts, minced

¼ cup mashed Roasted Garlic (page 262)

3 tablespoons chopped fresh basil

1 teaspoon chopped cilantro

1 teaspoon chopped fresh thyme

2 extra-large egg yolks

Kosher salt and freshly ground black pepper to taste

Cayenne pepper to taste

Canola or peanut oil for deep-frying

Put the potatoes and *boniato* in a pot, cover them with cold salted water, and bring to a high simmer. Cook until almost but not quite tender. Drain well and refrigerate uncovered, for at least 3 hours.

Melt the butter in a large heavy skillet and sauté the onion, scallions, and garlic for 3 to 5 minutes, stirring occasionally, until translucent. Drain the excess butter from the pan. Add the herbs, and let cool slightly.

In a large bowl, combine the vegetable mixture with the egg yolks, salt and black pepper, and cayenne, mixing well.

Peel the *boniato* and potatoes and shred on the large holes of a grater. Add to the vegetable egg mixture, and season with salt and pepper.

Preheat the oven to 375 degrees.

Form the potato mixture into 16 cakes or patties about 2 inches in diameter and 1 inch thick, placing them on a baking sheet.

Heat the oil in a large deep skillet over medium-high heat until hot. Add the potato cakes, in batches, without crowding, and fry until golden brown on both sides. Transfer to a baking sheet lined with parchment paper.

Heat the cakes in the oven for 8 to 10 minutes. Serve.

yuca frita with mojo ketchup
(Yuca Fries)

SERVES 4

This dish combines three popular foods: french fries, *mojo* sauce, and ketchup—yes, the fast food chains have brought ketchup to the Caribbean and Latin America. The sour orange *mojo* gives it a Latin/Caribbean luster. Yuca fries are my preferred way to go here, but then again, regular fries will work fine too.

2 pounds yuca, peeled and cut lengthwise into planks 3 inches long and about $^1/_3$ inch thick

FOR THE *MOJO* KETCHUP
$^1/_2$ cup ketchup
2 tablespoons Classic Sour Orange *Mojo* (page 283)
Canola or peanut oil for deep-frying
Kosher salt and freshly ground black pepper to taste

Put the sliced yuca in a large pot and cover it with water. Bring to a boil, then lower the heat and simmer for 15 to 30 minutes—the time can vary a great deal, because yuca can vary greatly in its woodiness; the yuca should still be a little firm, so you can just barely pierce it with a fork. Drain the yuca and let cool for a few minutes on a cutting board.

When you can handle the yuca, cut it into $^1/_2$- to $^3/_4$-inch-wide fries. (If there are any woody cores, discard them.)

For the ketchup: Whisk the ketchup and *mojo* in a small bowl; reserve.

Heat the oil in a large skillet or deep-fryer to 360 degrees. Fry the yuca, in batches, and transfer to paper towels to drain. Season and serve with the *mojo* ketchup.

breads

A Catalonian saying goes, "With bread and wine, you can walk your road." No food in history is more important than bread, as both a source of sustenance and a symbol. In sixteenth-century Spain, neither nobleman nor peasant would do without his daily bread, olive oil, and wine.

It was Spain that introduced wheat—and hence European-style bread—to the New World. In fact, wheat's arrival in Latin America can be traced to a single moment, according to Luis Zalamea. In Peru, in 1547, he says, "The noblewoman Maria de Escobar first cultivated wheat of Spanish origin on her farm in the dales of the Rimac River, near Lima. So, you see, by the time the Pilgrims had settled in Plymouth, the Spaniards had long been making many varieties of bread."

I don't want to mislead you: the indigenous civilizations of the New World did enjoy their own bread. But maize (corn) was their wheat, their gift from and to the gods. In Mexico and Central America, rough corn dough was flattened and seared on hot rocks, giving birth to the tortilla. Ancient Peruvians used maize to make corn mash, cakes, and more elaborate dishes such as tamales. Sometimes they enriched the dough with quinoa and *quañigua,* another native grain.

The tribes of the Amazon Basin made their own bread too, from wild *manioc* (also known as yuca or *cassava*), strained to remove its lethally toxic elements and then pounded into a flour. In Colombia, Ecuador, and Venezuela, fluffy *pandeyuca* buns are the heirs of this rain-forest staple. Trinidadians make a stuffed *roti* called "buss-up-shut" (the name derives from the bread's resemblance to a "busted up-shirt"), a *ghee*-brushed bread, almost a pastry.

It comes as little surprise, then, that the breads of Latin America and the Caribbean today are remarkably varied, and always a noble complement to the cuisine. Whether made from wheat, maize, or *manioc,* whether the fruit-encrusted South American Christmas bread called *panetón* or the Mexican Day of the Dead *Pan de Muerto* (page 227), the bread almost always tells the story of the culture's influences, past and present.

almojábanas
(Cheese Corn Rolls)

MAKES 22 ROLLS

The original recipe for these rolls, and their Arabic name, date back to the long period (711 to 1492) when the Moors occupied a substantial part of Spain. The recipe then made its way to the New World via the Conquistadores, and it is still served today in Colombia, with the addition of New World corn. Families gather to have a hot cup of chocolate milk with warm *almojábanas* (pronounced *al-mo-YAH-bah-nas*).

The best way to eat these *is right out of the oven.* Try them with butter . . . maybe some orange marmalade too.

2 cups corn kernels (from 2 to 3 ears)

1 ¼ pounds *queso blanco*, grated

½ cup ricotta cheese

1 tablespoon sugar

1 ½ teaspoons kosher salt

3 tablespoons unsalted butter, diced, softened

2 egg yolks

1 ½ teaspoons baking powder

One 12-ounce package potato starch (also called potato flour; look in the kosher food or baking section of your grocery store)

In a food processor, combine the corn, cheeses, sugar, salt, butter, and egg yolks and process until the mixture resembles creamy scrambled eggs. Transfer to a large bowl. Add the baking powder to the potato starch, then fold them into the batter until incorporated and free of any lumps. Cover the dough with a damp towel and let rest for 15 minutes.

Preheat the oven to 375 degrees. Grease two baking sheets.

Pull off large pieces of dough and roll into balls 1 ½ inches in diameter (grease your hands with butter to prevent sticking if necessary). Arrange the balls about 1 inch apart on the baking sheets.

Bake for 35 minutes, or until puffed and golden.

arepas

(Cheese Corn Cakes)

MAKES FIFTEEN TO SIXTEEN 3-INCH *AREPAS*

Arepas are rich, cheese-topped cornmeal cakes and wonderful in a rather hedonistic way, though you might not know it if your only prior experience of them comes from Latin American street fairs and carnivals. I adore these cakes and look for all manner of ways in which to use them. Try them with a lean bowl of chicken soup or *Sopa de Pavo* (page 71), or a bowl of chili.

Arepa flour, also called *masarepa, harina de pan,* and *areparina* is finely ground precooked white cornmeal, available in Latin American markets.

1 ¹/₂ cups milk

¹/₃ cup (5 ¹/₃ tablespoons) unsalted butter, melted, plus about 2 tablespoons for sautéing the cheese

1 ¹/₂ cups *arepa* flour

1 ¹/₂ teaspoons kosher salt

Canola oil for panfrying

10 ounces *queso blanco*, cut into ¹/₄-inch-thick slices

Pour the milk into a medium saucepan, add the butter, and bring to a boil. Remove from the heat.

When the milk is just warm enough for you to touch, put the flour and salt in a medium bowl and add a little of the warm milk. Knead briefly, then add some more milk and knead again, continuing the process until all the milk is incorporated and you have a smooth dough. Cover the dough with a damp cloth and let rest for 5 to 10 minutes.

Place a small bowl of water by your work surface. Pull off large pieces of dough and roll into balls approximately 1 ¹/₂ inches across; keep shaped balls covered with the damp cloth as you work. Flatten each ball into a disk about ¹/₄ inch thick, dipping your fingers in the bowl of water and smoothing the frayed edges of the disks as you go. Place on a baking sheet and cover with a damp cloth until ready to cook.

In a large nonstick sauté pan, heat just enough canola oil to cover the bottom of the pan and heat over medium heat until hot. Cook the disks, in batches, turning once, until golden and crisp. Drain on paper towels.

Wipe out the pan and add just enough butter to coat the bottom. Sauté the cheese slices, in batches, turning once, until golden brown on both sides. Lay each slice atop an *arepa,* and serve immediately.

cachapas
(Corn Cakes)

MAKES THIRTY 2¹/₂-INCH PANCAKES

I've collected pancake recipes since I was a breakfast cook in the Midwest, and these quickly became one of my all-time favorites. In Venezuela, they are often served wrapped around mild white cheese; I often pair them with shrimp or foie gras.

6 cups corn kernels (from 8 to 10 ears corn)
1 tablespoon sugar
¹/₂ cup yellow cornmeal
1 teaspoon kosher salt
Canola oil for panfrying

In a food processor, process the corn kernels until you have achieved a coarse puree. Add the sugar, cornmeal, and salt and mix well.

In a large nonstick skillet, heat just enough canola oil to cover the bottom over medium heat. Working in batches, drop heaping tablespoonfuls of the *cachapa* batter into the skillet and cook for about 1 minute on each side, until golden. Serve hot.

corn

I was working in the kitchen at NORMAN'S one day when I got a phone call from a friend, an aspiring author, who specializes in food writing, and also, shall I say, *sensual* writing. As I was listening to her read one of her latest passages, a sous-chef set a pan of freshly roasted corn down on the counter to cool beside me. He'd cooked the ears in their husks, and I absentmindedly tore off a little of a ridged, pliant wrapper and pressed it to my lips. "Oh, man," I blurted helplessly into the receiver.

My friend on the other end of the line said, "Norman likes that part, eh?"

It was the corn that had elicited my moan of pleasure, but I didn't wish to disillusion her, so I kept that bit of information to myself. And while limbs were writhing in the story being read over the phone, the ears I was longing to nibble were coming into view through the lens of memoryland.

It was a dusky evening in a late summer of my childhood in rural Illinois. My mother was driving us to church, and, as the car windows were always rolled down in the summer, when we pulled into the parking lot it was as if a shaft of air from sweet Heaven was pouring directly onto that patch of asphalt. It was Corn Roast Night—I couldn't get out of the car fast enough. The men and women of the congregation were passing along bushel upon bushel of the corn that grew in the fields all around us, working feverishly over huge, glowing charcoal braziers to meet the crowd's demands. Whatever else was served that night escapes me.

When I was working on the recipes for this book, I realized how many of them included corn. I knew that I had to carefully choose the ones I wanted or I might find myself writing a whole book on corn! Betty Fussell, who in fact did write such a book—*Crazy for Corn*—says:

> We don't just eat and drink corn as a vegetable and a grain. We eat it converted through fodder into pork chops and beef steaks, chickens and eggs, milk and cheese. We drink it as beer and whiskey and soda pop. Corn is the base not just of our food chain but of our industrial chain. Industry eats corn chemically as an oil, a starch, and a sugar. Anything petroleum can do, corn

can do better. We use this industrially converted corn in thousands of different products from cradle to grave, from talcum powder to embalming fluid. Every one of our lives is touched every day by an invisible network of corn.

We are keenly appreciative of how central rice is to the Asian diet, and how the quest for its grains moved kingdoms to explore the globe. And we make much of the European introduction of wheat to the New World diet (the civilizing properties of bread). But when Columbus arrived in the New World in 1492, it was a world of corn. It was the Conquistadores' and the Pilgrims' acceptance and adaptation of corn into their diets that allowed for their very survival in the often-harsh new land. Indians in the Mexican state of Pueblo speak of corn as the fifth element: there is earth, air, fire, water—and corn.

pan cubano
(Cuban Bread)

MAKES 2 LONG LOAVES

The New World had not known yeast-raised doughs until the Colombian Exchange, the arrival of Columbus in the New World and exchange of goods—and slaves—that then ensued between Europe and the Americas. But wheat, raised to the heavenly texture of bread, quickly took hold in Cuba.

1 ounce fresh yeast or two $1/4$-ounce packets active dry yeast

1 tablespoon kosher salt

1 tablespoon sugar

4 tablespoons unsalted butter, melted

1 $1/2$ tablespoons extra virgin olive oil

1 $1/2$ cups warm water (about 110 degrees)

4 cups bread flour

In the bowl of a mixer fitted with the dough hook, combine the yeast, salt, sugar, butter, olive oil, and warm water and mix on low speed. Let stand for a few minutes, until you see the yeast bubble.

With the machine on low, add the flour 1 cup at a time. When all the flour has been incorporated, knead the dough on medium-low speed for 8 minutes.

Transfer the dough to a large lightly oiled bowl (one that will allow the dough to double in bulk without overflowing), cover the bowl tightly with plastic wrap, and place in a warm, draft-free place. Let the dough rise for about 45 minutes, or until doubled in bulk.

To shape the dough, remove it from the bowl and knead a few times on a lightly floured surface to deflate it and get rid of any air bubbles. Divide it into 2 equal pieces. With the palm of your hand, flatten the one piece of dough into about a 6-inch-square. Fold the dough in thirds, as you would a business letter, and press firmly to seal the seam. Then turn the dough in on itself again, doing one more letter fold.

Flip the dough over so that it is seam side down. Gently, using your fingertips, roll the dough back and forth, moving your hands from the center of the dough out toward the ends, to elongate the dough into a baguette shape. Don't force it: if it becomes too elastic and resists, cover it and let rest for several minutes before proceeding. (What you are letting rest, in fact, is the dough's gluten—the substance that gives bread its texture.)

When the dough is 14 to 16 inches long, gently transfer it to a floured or parchment-lined baking sheet and cover loosely with parchment paper. Repeat with the remaining dough, placing it on a separate floured baking sheet. Let the dough rise in a warm, draft-free place for 45 minutes to 1 hour, until doubled in bulk.

Preheat the oven to 450 degrees.

Yeast dough expands dramatically once it hits a hot oven, so bakers cut designs into the tops of their loaves to ensure that the dough will maintain the desired shape during baking; this scoring is always done immediately before baking: Sift a little flour over each loaf. Then, using a very sharp paring knife or a razor blade, score each loaf with three or four parallel slashes, depending on the length of your bread (dipping the blade in flour will help keep it from sticking): Begin about $^{1}/_{2}$ inch from the right end of the dough and, holding the blade at a 45-degree angle, cut an incision about $^{1}/_{2}$ inch deep diagonally from one side of the bread to the other. Begin the next incision about $^{1}/_{2}$ inch from the end of the first one. Continue until you are $^{1}/_{2}$ inch from the other end of the dough.

Bake for 25 to 35 minutes, until the tops are golden and the loaves sound hollow when tapped on the bottom.

crushed red chile and *annatto* flatbread

MAKES 2 FLAT LOAVES

I love to serve spicy bread when I am entertaining. This flatbread gets a New World buzz from the crushed red chile and a rosy hue from the annatto oil. It is a natural for bean dips and salsas such as Black Bean, Tropical Fruit, and *Queso Blanco* Salsa (page 37).

1 cup warm water (about 110 degrees)
¹/₂ ounce fresh yeast or one ¹/₄-ounce packet active dry yeast
6 tablespoons Annatto Oil (page 261)
1 teaspoon sugar
3 ¹/₄ cups all-purpose flour
1 tablespoon plus 2 teaspoons kosher salt
¹/₃ cup cornmeal, plus extra for dusting
1 tablespoon crushed red pepper
Extra virgin olive oil for brushing

In the bowl of an electric mixer fitted with the dough hook, combine the water, yeast, annatto oil, and sugar. Let stand for a few minutes, until you see the yeast bubble.

Combine the flour, salt, cornmeal, and red pepper flakes in a medium bowl and mix well.

With the mixer on low speed, gradually blend the dry ingredients into the wet ingredients. Then knead for 9 minutes, or until the dough comes away from the sides of the bowl.

Remove the bowl from the mixer, cover, and set in a warm, draft-free place to rise for about 45 minutes, until doubled.

Punch down the dough and allow to rise again for 30 minutes.

Preheat the oven to 400 degrees. Generously dust two baking sheets with cornmeal.

Turn the dough out onto a well-floured surface and divide it into 2 pieces. One at a time, roll out each piece of dough as thin as possible, using flour as necessary to prevent the dough from sticking. Place one flatbread on each baking sheet.

Bake for 12 to 15 minutes, or until just golden. Brush with olive oil, and serve.

pan de muerto
(Day of the Dead Bread)

MAKES 1 LOAF

Every year on November 1, Mexicans celebrate *El Dia de los Muertos*, the Day of the Dead. All over the country, in kitchens sophisticated and humble, this bread is baked, a symbol of mankind's rebirth through eternity, a celebration of life and a remembrance of the dead. Families often make a picnic at the gravesite of a loved one, and this bread is part of the feast. An old custom is to bake a toy skeleton inside the loaf; whoever bites on it is said to be in for some good luck. It is common to see a sugar glaze on this bread, but I find it overly sweet and omit it.

2 teaspoons finely chopped orange zest

1 1/2 tablespoons anise seeds

One 1/4-ounce packet active dry yeast

1/2 cup warm water (105 to 115 degrees)

1/2 teaspoon ground cinnamon

3/4 cup sugar

6 1/4 cups all-purpose flour

1 tablespoon kosher salt, plus a pinch

8 tablespoons (1 stick) unsalted butter, melted and cooled to room temperature

7 extra-large eggs, at room temperature

In the bowl of an electric mixer fitted with the dough hook attachment, combine the orange zest, anise seeds, yeast, and water and mix on low speed. Let stand for a few minutes until you see the yeast start to bubble.

In a small bowl, combine the cinnamon with 2 tablespoons of the sugar. Set aside. Sift the flour with the remaining 1/2 cup plus 2 tablespoons sugar and the 1 tablespoon salt and set aside.

In a medium bowl, lightly beat 6 of the eggs. Add the beaten eggs and butter to the yeast mixture, then gradually add the flour, mixing well. Then knead on low speed for 5 to 7 minutes, until the dough comes away from the sides of the bowl; it should be smooth and elastic. Turn it out into a large oiled bowl, cover with plastic wrap, and let rise in a warm, draft-free place for 1 hour, or until doubled.

Punch down the dough and turn it out onto a floured surface. Cut off one-quarter of the dough and set aside. Form the remaining dough into a ball (this will be the skull) and place on a greased baking sheet pan. Divide the reserved dough into 7 pieces. Roll 3 of them under the palm of your hand into thick ropes and shape them like bones. Drape the "bones" over the sides of the "skull"; they should meet at the top. Roll the other 4 pieces of dough into balls. Put one at the base of each "bone." The last one at the top where the "bones" meet. Cover and let rise in a warm, draft-free place for 40 minutes or until doubled.

Preheat the oven to 350 degrees.

In a small bowl, beat together the remaining egg and the pinch of salt. Brush the dough with this egg wash and sprinkle with the reserved cinnamon-sugar. Bake for 45 to 50 minutes, until the bread sounds hollow when tapped on the bottom. Let cool.

medianoche bread
(Midnight Bread)

MAKES 2 LONG LOAVES

The name of this soft bread comes from the wildly popular sandwiches eaten around *medianoche*, midnight, by late-night partygoers in Old Havana, and now from Miami to New York to L.A. In fact, the sandwiches are served at all hours. *Medianoche* bread is often used for sandwiches prepared *a la plancha*, in a sandwich press.

1 1/2 cups warm water (110 degrees)

1 ounce fresh yeast or two 1/4-ounce packets active dry yeast

1/4 cup sugar

4 teaspoons kosher salt

4 extra-large egg yolks, beaten

2 tablespoons unsalted butter, melted

2 tablespoons Annatto Oil (page 261), or
    2 tablespoons unsalted butter, melted

4 1/2 cups bread flour

In the bowl of an electric mixer fitted with the dough hook, combine the water, yeast, sugar, salt, egg yolks, butter, and annatto oil and blend on low speed. Let stand for a few minutes until the yeast begins to bubble.

Add the flour, blending on low speed, then knead the dough for 8 minutes. Transfer to a large lightly oiled bowl, cover the bowl tightly with plastic wrap, and let rise in a warm, draft-free place for 45 minutes, or until doubled in bulk.

To shape the dough, remove it from the bowl and knead a few times on a lightly floured surface to deflate it and get rid of any air bubbles. Divide it into 2 equal pieces.

With the palm of your hand, flatten one piece of dough into a 6-inch square. Fold the dough in thirds, and press firmly to seal the seam. Then turn the dough in on itself again, doing one more fold. Flip the dough over so that it is seam side down. Gently, using your fingertips, roll the dough back and forth, moving your hands outward from the center of the dough to the ends to elongate it into a baguette shape. Don't force the dough; if it becomes too elastic and resists, cover it and let rest for several minutes. When the dough is 8 to 12 inches long, transfer it to a parchment-lined baking sheet and cover with parchment paper. Repeat with the remaining dough, putting it on a separate floured baking sheet. Let the dough rise in a warm, draft-free place for 1 hour, until doubled in bulk.

Preheat the oven to 450 degrees.

Yeast dough expands dramatically once it hits a hot oven, so bakers cut designs into the tops of their loaves to ensure that the dough will maintain the desired shape during baking; this scoring is always done immediately before baking. Using a very sharp paring knife or a razor blade, score each loaf with three or four parallel slashes, depending on the length of your bread: Begin about 1/2 inch from one end and, holding the blade at a 45-degree angle, cut an incision about 1/2 inch deep diagonally from one side of the bread to the other. The slashes should be approximately 1 1/2 inches apart. Continue until you are 1/2 inch from the other end of the dough.

Bake for 30 to 35 minutes, until the tops are golden and the loaves sound hollow when tapped on the bottom.

roti

(West Indian Flatbread)

MAKES TWENTY 3- TO 4-INCH ROUNDS

When nearly four hundred Asian Indians came to Trinidad as indentured servants in the mid-1830s, they brought their customs and flavors with them. Soon many other islands welcomed their cuisine, and now this delightful, slightly puffy bread is a staple of Trinidad and found increasingly across the Caribbean.

3 cups all-purpose flour
1 tablespoon baking powder
1 tablespoon kosher salt
$^1/_2$ pound (2 sticks) unsalted butter, diced
$^1/_2$ cup cold water
Canola oil for cooking the roti

Set up an electric mixer with the paddle attachment. Sift the flour, baking powder, and salt into the bowl. With the mixer on the lowest speed, gradually incorporate the butter, about 1 minute (you can also use a pastry cutter or a fork or potato masher). The dough should resemble coarse crumbs. With the mixer still on low speed, drizzle in the water, mixing until the dough comes together, then knead for 30 seconds. Remove the dough from the bowl, wrap it tightly in plastic wrap, and chill for 1 hour.

Divide the dough into 20 portions and shape each one into a ball. Dust your work surface generously with flour. Roll out each portion into a $^1/_6$-inch-thick round. Set aside on baking sheets.

Lightly grease a large nonstick skillet with canola oil and set over medium-high heat. Cook, one or two roti at a time, depending on the size of the skillet, for 60 to 75 seconds per side, until beginning to turn golden brown. Serve hot.

desserts

The transference from Old World to New and vice versa of dessert ingredients and cooking methods had surely begun by the time Hernando Cortés conquered Mexico in 1519. Two years before, Francisco Hernández de Córdoba had led a group of Spaniards to the Mayan island of Cozumel to show off the Indians' exquisite white honey.

It is now well known that chocolate was not a delicacy in Europe until the Columbian Exchange. The same holds true for vanilla. But it was the Europeans who treasured the dessert course much more than the natives of the New World, who typically feasted on the locally abundant, tantalizing fruits. Yet the Europeans' technical proficiency, knowledge of yeast doughs, and their eventual adoption of chocolate and addiction to sugar, married with the sensual produce of the New World, turned the Caribbean and Latin American dessert repertoire into a powerful union. Never had the Old and New worlds met more seductively than at dessert.

beijinhos de coco

(Coconut Kisses)

MAKES 45 TO 50 KISSES

You'll love these sweet, heady kisses the way you love a favorite candy bar from your childhood. Sometimes I offer them with fruit purees for a light contrast.

(Note: To prepare this recipe, you'll need an instant-read thermometer.)

2 extra-large egg yolks
1 vanilla bean, split lengthwise
One 14-ounce can sweetened condensed milk
1 tablespoon unsalted butter, softened
1 pound unsweetened grated coconut
1 pound bittersweet chocolate, finely chopped
2 cups unblanched almonds, toasted (see
    page 9) and chopped

In a large heatproof bowl, beat the egg yolks. Using the back of a knife, scrape the seeds from the vanilla bean and add the seeds and bean pod to the eggs. Add the milk and butter and stir.

Set the bowl over a large pot of simmering water (or use a double boiler); the bottom of the bowl should not touch the water. Whisk constantly, frequently checking the temperature of the mixture with an instant-read thermometer, until it registers 140 degrees. Remove from the heat.

Discard the vanilla bean. Add the coconut and stir until incorporated. (The mixture will look like the filling of a Mounds candy bar.)

To shape the kisses, use about 1 tablespoon per morsel—I like to form them into little pyramids, but you may prefer little spheres. Set them on a platter and refrigerate for at least 30 minutes.

Spread the almonds on a plate. Put the chocolate into another large heatproof bowl and melt it over simmering water, stirring occasionally until smooth. Pour a little of the melted chocolate into a shallow cup. With a fork (a cocktail or fondue fork works great), gently skewer each kiss and dip it into the chocolate, then quickly roll it in the chopped almonds and place on a platter. Continue this process, adding more chocolate to the cup as necessary, until all are dipped and rolled. Let the chocolate set in a cool place before serving. (Stored in an airtight container at room temperature, these will keep for up to a week.)

candied papaya

SERVES 8

In most Latin American countries, the Christmas holidays are a time for celebrations abundant with food. A typical Christmas spread in Venezuela might consist of a meaty steak, *hallacas* (large, elaborate tamales), potato salad, *torta negra* (a rum-soaked fruitcake), and this incredible candied papaya. What is great about this dessert is that it keeps for a very long time in the refrigerator, and you can eat it with anything—a soft white, slightly salty cheese would balance its sweetness.

To serve this, you'll need 8 martini glasses or similarly festive glassware.

6 cups water

$1/2$ teaspoon baking soda

One 2-pound *not quite ripe* papaya, halved, seeds scraped out, peeled, and cut into strips 2 inches long by $1/2$ inch thick

5 baby coconuts (*coquitos;* see Source Guide, page 310), thinly sliced and toasted (see page 9) (or substitute $1/2$ cup unsweetened grated coconut)

$1 1/2$ cups coarsely grated *papelón* brown sugar (available in Latin markets; you can substitute $3/4$ cup packed dark brown sugar)

1 cup granulated sugar

5 cloves, toasted and lightly crushed

1 cinnamon stick, cracked in half

$1/2$ cup heavy cream

2 tablespoons confectioners' sugar

$1/4$ cup sour cream

1 cup crumbled *queso blanco*

Mint leaves for garnish

Combine the water and baking soda in a medium pot and bring to a boil. Add the papaya pieces and let cook for 5 minutes over medium heat. With a slotted spoon, carefully transfer the fruit strips to a platter lined with paper towels; set aside.

Add the *papelón,* granulated sugar, cloves, and cinnamon to the pot and cook over medium-high heat until the syrup is thick enough to thinly coat the back of a wooden spoon.

Add the papaya and cook for 30 minutes over medium heat. The syrup will turn a very dark amber. Let the papaya cool in the syrup, then transfer it, along with the syrup, to a bowl, cover, and refrigerate overnight.

The next day, put the heavy cream in a cold mixing bowl and whisk or beat, slowly adding the confectioners' sugar, until it holds soft peaks. Fold in the sour cream.

Drop 1 tablespoon of the *queso blanco* into each of eight chilled martini glasses. Then lay 4 slices of candied papaya on top, add another tablespoon of crumbled *queso blanco,* and then 4 more papaya slices. Drizzle some of the syrup over each, then spoon a dollop of whipped cream on top. Garnish each with toasted coconut or mint leaves, as desired.

churros

(Crispy Doughnut Sticks)

MAKES TWENTY-FOUR 3-INCH *CHURROS*

These deliciously addictive fried-dough sticks, dusted with sugar and cinnamon, are traditional in many Latin American countries. If you have ever been to Mexico, you've probably seen them sold by the food vendors who work the plazas of every city. *Churros* make a great coupling with *cajeta* or a cup of frothy Mexican hot chocolate.

2 cups water
2 teaspoons kosher salt
2 cups all-purpose flour
Canola or peanut oil for deep-frying
Cinnamon-sugar for dusting
1 recipe *Cajeta* (page 255) (optional), warmed

In a medium saucepan, combine the water and salt and bring to a boil. Remove from the heat, stir in the flour, and continue stirring until the dough pulls away from the sides of the pan.

Transfer the dough to a work surface and allow it to cool enough to handle, then knead it several times, until smooth. Wrap it tightly in plastic wrap and set aside to cool.

When the dough has cooled to room temperature, put it in a pastry bag fitted with a large star tip.

Pour 1 inch of oil into a deep-fryer or deep pot and heat it to 350 degrees. Squeeze out 3-inch-long *churros* onto a work surface, then drop them, a few at a time, into the hot oil, and cook for 5 to 10 minutes, until dark golden. Transfer to a plate lined with paper towels and immediately dust with cinnamon-sugar. Serve hot, with *cajeta* for dipping, if desired.

sopapillas

(Pastries with Honey and Cinnamon)

MAKES 24 *SOPAPILLAS*

In Mexico, *sopapillas* (pronounced *soh-pah-PEE-yahs*) are served before meals in place of bread, or bought piping-hot from street vendors. In New Mexico, it is customary to enjoy *sopapillas* with a breakfast of black beans, chiles, and eggs. In all cases, they are served with honey.

3 $1/2$ cups sifted all-purpose flour
$1/2$ teaspoon kosher salt
1 tablespoon ground cinnamon, plus more
   for sprinkling
$1/4$ cup vegetable shortening
1 cup water at room-temperature
Canola oil for deep-frying
Confectioners' sugar for dusting
$1/2$ cup honey

Combine the flour, salt, and cinnamon in a large bowl. Work in the shortening with your fingertips or a pastry cutter until the mixture resembles coarse crumbs. Stir in the water until the dough comes together, then knead until the dough is smooth and pulls away from the sides of the bowl. Wrap tightly in plastic wrap and let rest in the refrigerator for at least 1 hour, or for as long as 24 hours.

Let the dough stand at room temperature for at least 30 minutes before rolling it out.

Dust your work surface with flour. Cut the dough in half. One at a time, roll out each piece to a thickness of $1/4$ inch, periodically lifting up the dough so it doesn't stick and dusting the work surface with more flour if necessary. Cut each sheet of dough into 12 rustic-looking 4-inch triangles, placing them on a floured baking sheet.

In a deep-fryer or deep pot, heat the canola oil to 350 degrees. Drop in the pieces of dough, in batches, taking care not to overcrowd them, and fry until they puff up (a matter of seconds) and are golden and crispy. Using a slotted spoon, transfer to paper towels to drain. Arrange on a platter, sprinkle with confectioners' sugar and cinnamon, and drizzle with honey.

tropical fruit *beignets*

SERVES 10

These *beignets,* hot, crisp feather-light batter wrapped around perfectly lucious ripe fruit, are a staple all over the Caribbean. Cooks on the island of Martinique excel at making the French-based delectations.

The *beignets* are dusted with confectioners' sugar and served with whipped cream; for even more flavor, drizzle them with *Almibar* syrup (page 254).

FOR THE BATTER

2 cups sifted all-purpose flour

One ¹/₄-ounce packet active dry yeast

1 teaspoon kosher salt

¹/₄ cup plus 1 tablespoon sugar

1 teaspoon ground mace or nutmeg

1 teaspoon ground cinnamon

¹/₄ cup grapeseed oil

2 extra-large eggs, separated

1 ¹/₄ cup light beer, cold

1 extra-large egg white

1 cup heavy cream

Canola oil for deep-frying

1 cup all-purpose flour

1 teaspoon ground cinnamon

1 teaspoon ground mace

1 tablespoon granulated sugar

5 small bananas, peeled and cut crosswise in half, or 3 regular bananas, peeled, cut lengthwise in half and then crosswise

1 ripe mango, peeled, pitted, and cut into 10 strips

10 thick strips pineapple

Confectioners' sugar for dusting

20 mint leaves, shredded, for garnish

for the batter

Combine the sifted flour, yeast, salt, ¹/₄ cup of the sugar, and the spices in a large bowl. In another bowl, combine the grapeseed oil, egg yolks, and beer. Add the wet ingredients to the dry and whisk until smooth.

In a large bowl, with an electric mixer on medium-high speed, whip the 3 egg whites with the remaining 1 tablespoon sugar to medium-soft peaks. Carefully fold the egg whites into the batter. Let stand covered at room temperature for 1 hour.

In a medium bowl, whip the heavy cream to stiff peaks. Transfer to a serving bowl, cover, and refrigerate.

In a deep-fryer or deep pot, heat the oil to 375 degrees. Combine the flour, cinnamon, mace, and granulated sugar in a shallow bowl. One by one, working in batches, coat the fruit with the flour mixture, shaking off the excess, then dip into the batter, and drop into the hot oil. Cook the *beignets* until golden brown, then drain on a large plate lined with paper towels; gently pat them to soak up the excess oil.

Dust with powdered sugar and serve immediately, with the whipped cream, topped with mint leaves, on the side.

the banana bread man's banana bread

MAKES 1 LOAF CAKE

There was a guy in Key West who used to sell his homemade banana bread off the back of his bicycle. Every night at the famous sunset celebration on Mallory Docks, where locals congregated to drink and watch the street performers as the sun went down, he would pedal up with his wares. Not once did I see him leave with any unsold bread. Maybe that is because in the Caribbean, banana bread is considered a man's bread. Or maybe it was the hefty dose of rum in his recipe. Either way, this is one satisfying dessert.

I like to slice and toast it and serve with ice cream.

2 cups all-purpose flour

$^1/_4$ teaspoon kosher salt

1 teaspoon baking soda

8 tablespoons (1 stick) unsalted butter, softened

1 cup packed dark brown sugar

2 extra-large eggs

1 vanilla bean, split lengthwise, or
   1 $^1/_2$ teaspoons pure vanilla extract

3 tablespoons dark rum

2 cups mashed ripe banana (2 to 3 bananas)

1 $^1/_2$ teaspoons ground cinnamon

$^1/_4$ teaspoon ground mace

$^1/_4$ teaspoon ground cloves

3 tablespoons buttermilk

2 $^1/_2$ ounces bittersweet chocolate, chopped, or
   $^1/_2$ cup chocolate chips

$^1/_3$ cup pecans, toasted (see page 9) and
   chopped

$^1/_3$ cup cashews, toasted (see page 9) and
   chopped

1 cup pitted dates, chopped

$^1/_3$ cup dried cherries

$^1/_3$ cup diced dried papaya

Preheat the oven to 350 degrees. Grease an 8 $^1/_2$-by-4 $^1/_2$-inch loaf pan with butter and dust it with flour. Set aside.

In a medium bowl, whisk together the flour, salt, and baking soda. Set aside.

In a large bowl, cream together the butter and brown sugar. Beat in the eggs one at a time, mixing until fully incorporated. Scrape the seeds from the vanilla bean, if using, and add to the bowl, or add the vanilla extract. Add the rum, mashed bananas, and spices and beat until blended. The batter may look as if it is separating, but don't worry, the flour will bring it all together.

Alternately add the dry ingredients and the buttermilk to the batter, beating until fully incorporated. Fold in the chocolate, nuts, and fruits.

Pour the batter into the prepared loaf pan and bake for 10 minutes. Then reduce the temperature to 315 degrees and bake for another 1 hour and 10 minutes, or until the bread pulls away slightly from the sides of the pan and a toothpick inserted into the center comes out clean. Let cool in the pan on a wire rack for 10 minutes. Then invert onto the rack and turn right side up to cool completely.

panqueques de manzana
(Apple-Stuffed Crêpes with *Dulce de Leche*)

SERVES 6

I learned this recipe from an Argentine woman of Italian extraction named Yami Carattini, whose mother taught it to her.

FOR THE CRÊPES

3 extra-large eggs

1 ¹/₂ cups milk

1 teaspoon kosher salt

1 teaspoon sugar

1 ¹/₃ cups all-purpose flour

2 tablespoons unsalted butter, melted, plus 2 to 3 tablespoons melted butter for frying the crêpes

FOR THE FILLING

¹/₃ cup sugar

1 vanilla bean, split lengthwise

6 Granny Smith apples, peeled, cored, and thinly sliced

4 tablespoons unsalted butter

¹/₄ cup dark rum, for deglazing

1 cup *Dulce de Leche* (page 257)

¹/₂ cup chopped toasted pecans for garnish (optional)

for the crêpes

In a medium bowl, whisk the eggs lightly. Whisk in the milk, salt, and sugar. Sift in the flour and whisk until just blended. Add the melted butter. Allow the batter to rest at room temperature for 30 minutes.

Brush a 7-inch nonstick skillet lightly with clarified butter and set over medium heat. Ladle 3 tablespoons batter into the skillet, swirling to coat the bottom evenly, and cook for 1 minute, or until the crêpe easily comes away from the skillet. Flip it and cook for 10 to 15 seconds more. Remove the crêpe from the skillet and reserve. Repeat with the remaining batter; you should have 12 crêpes in all.

for the filling

On a cutting board, sprinkle the sugar over the split vanilla bean and then, with the back of a knife, scrape out the seeds, rubbing them into the sugar (this will distribute the vanilla seeds evenly). Discard the bean. In a bowl, toss the apple slices with the vanilla sugar. Set aside.

In a large nonstick skillet, melt the butter over medium heat. Sauté the apples, stirring gently—and only occasionally—until they are soft. Deglaze the skillet with the rum, being very careful, because it may ignite—if this happens, simply cover the skillet with a lid to put out the flame. Continue to cook for about 1 minute, then remove the skillet from the heat.

Preheat the oven to 350 degrees.

To assemble the crêpes, spread about a tablespoon of *dulce de leche* over one crêpe. Spoon the apple filling across the center of the crêpe and roll it up. Place seam side down on a baking sheet lined with parchment paper, and repeat with the remaining crêpes.

Warm the crêpes in the oven for about 3 minutes. Drizzle with the remaining *dulce de leche,* and, if you like, sprinkle with chopped toasted pecans. Serve.

warm chocolate *buñuelos*

(Chocolate-Filled Doughnuts with Vanilla-Cinnamon *Almibar*)

This is such a humble-looking pastry, yet it delivers so much pleasure. The key to the recipe is the *almibar* syrup, which came to Latin America from the Arab world by way of Spaniards with roots in Moorish Spain. *Buñuelos* are usually made as round balls, but it's easier simply to fold them over so that they are pillow-shaped. I think it is crucial to serve *buñuelos* fresh and still warm, but if you must make them in advance, they do reheat well.

6 ounces bittersweet chocolate, chopped into small pieces

6 ounces cream cheese, softened

3 1/2 cups all-purpose flour, or more as needed

2 teaspoons baking powder

1 tablespoon kosher salt

1/3 cup sugar, plus 1/4 cup for dusting

1 extra-large egg yolk

1 1/4 cups milk

Canola or peanut oil for deep-frying

1 recipe Vanilla-Cinnamon *Almibar* (page 254)

Put the chocolate in a heatproof bowl and set it over a pot of simmering water; the bottom of the bowl should not touch the water. Stir the chocolate frequently until melted. Remove from the heat and whisk in the cream cheese. Set aside.

In a large bowl, combine the flour, baking powder, salt, and 1/3 cup sugar. In a small bowl, combine the egg yolk and milk and blend well. Make a well in the center of the dry ingredients, pour in the wet ingredients, and mix thoroughly, first with a fork and then with your hands, until the dough comes together and forms a tight ball. Add a little more flour if the dough is too sticky. Wrap in plastic wrap and refrigerate for at least 15 minutes.

Sprinkle your work surface with flour. Divide the dough into 16 equal pieces. Roll out each piece into a rectangle about 1/8 inch thick, using additional flour as necessary.

Drop a tablespoon of the chocolate mixture onto the center of the bottom half of each rectangle. Fold the dough over the filling and seal by pressing the edges together with your fingers. (Don't worry too much how uniform they are; the pastries should look rustic.) If necessary, dust with additional flour to prevent the dough from sticking to your hands or to the work surface.

In a deep-fryer or deep skillet, heat the oil to 350 degrees. Drop in the *buñuelos* two or three at a time and cook for 1 1/2 minutes on each side, until golden brown. Transfer to paper towels to drain for a moment, then toss in sugar, drizzle with the *almibar,* and serve warm.

guava cheesecake with ginger cookie crust

MAKES ONE 9-INCH CHEESECAKE

Guava is one of the defining flavors of Latin pastries. In this recipe, the cheesecake itself is redolent of guava, but the icing on the cake, as it were, is the intensification of the flavor in the glaze. Be sure you cool the cheesecake completely before spreading the glaze, or the top will crack.

FOR THE CRUST

$3/4$ cup all-purpose flour

$1/8$ teaspoon ground allspice

$1/8$ teaspoon baking soda

$1/8$ teaspoon kosher salt

$1/8$ teaspoon freshly ground black pepper

$2 1/2$ tablespoons unsalted butter, softened

$1/3$ cup packed brown sugar

1 extra-large egg yolk

$1 1/2$ tablespoons molasses

1 tablespoon peeled and grated ginger

2 tablespoons granulated sugar

$2 1/2$ tablespoons unsalted butter, melted

FOR THE CHEESECAKE

1 pound cream cheese

$3/4$ cup granulated sugar

4 extra-large egg yolks

1 cup sour cream

1 vanilla bean, split lengthwise

12 ounces guava marmalade (see Source
   Guide, page 310)

for the crust

Preheat the oven to 350 degrees. Line a baking sheet with parchment paper.

Sift together the flour, allspice, baking soda, salt, and pepper into a bowl. Set aside.

In the bowl of an electric mixer fitted with the paddle attachment, on medium speed, cream together the softened butter and brown sugar. Beat in the egg yolk, then the molasses and ginger. With the mixer on low speed, beat in the dry ingredients until completely incorporated.

Divide the dough into 5 pieces. Roll each one into a ball, and roll in the granulated sugar to coat. Arrange 3 inches apart on the parchment-lined baking sheet.

Bake for 12 minutes. Let cool completely on a rack.

Put the cookies in a food processor and grind them into crumbs. Drizzle in the melted butter and pulse to mix. Generously butter and flour a 9-inch springform pan. Press the crumbs evenly into the bottom of the pan. Set aside.

for the cheesecake

Preheat the oven to 275 degrees.

In the bowl of an electric mixer, using the paddle attachment, beat the cream cheese at medium speed for 4 minutes, or until it is soft and no lumps remain; scrape down the bowl frequently. Beat in the sugar and process until smooth. Beat in the egg yolks one at a time, then beat in the sour cream, scraping down the bowl as necessary.

Using the dull side of a knife, scrape the seeds from the vanilla bean and add to the mixer bowl. Beat to combine. Add half of the guava marmalade and beat until smooth.

Pour the batter into the prepared pan and bake for 15 minutes. Turn the oven down to 250 degrees and bake for another 45 minutes, or until set. Turn off the oven, but leave the cake in it for 45 minutes.

Let the cheesecake cool completely at room temperature, then refrigerate, covered, until chilled and firm.

Spread the cheesecake with the remaining guava marmalade, and refrigerate until ready to serve.

warm guava *buñuelos*

(Guava Marmalade–Filled Doughnuts with Vanilla-Cinnamon *Almibar*)

MAKES 16 *BUÑUELOS*

I like the Warm Chocolate *Buñuelos* (page 239) so much that I decided to experiment with guava marmalade. I am glad I did. If you want to keep things simple, you can skip the *almibar* and gently roll the fried *buñuelos* in cinnamon-sugar.

1 tablespoon cornstarch

2 tablespoons cold water

8 ounces guava marmalade (see Source Guide, page 310)

3 ¹/₂ cups all-purpose flour

2 teaspoons baking powder

1 tablespoon kosher salt

¹/₃ cup sugar

1 extra-large egg yolk

1 ¹/₄ cups milk

¹/₃ cup cream cheese

Canola or peanut oil for deep-frying

Cinnamon-sugar for dusting

1 recipe Vanilla-Cinnamon *Almibar* (page 254)

In a small bowl, whisk the water and cornstarch until smooth (this is called a slurry). In a small saucepan, whisk the guava marmalade over medium heat making sure it does not burn. When the marmalade begins to boil, whisk in the slurry. Cook, watching closely and still whisking often, until the mixture becomes glossy and thickens. Remove from the heat and let cool.

In a large bowl, combine the flour, baking powder, salt, and sugar. In a small bowl, combine the egg yolk and milk and mix well. Make a well in the center of the flour mixture, pour in the wet ingredients, and mix thoroughly, first with a fork and then with your hands, until the dough comes together and forms a tight ball. Wrap in plastic wrap and refrigerate for at least 15 minutes.

Flour your work surface. Divide the dough into 16 equal pieces. Roll each one out into a rectangle about ¹/₈ inch thick, using additional flour as necessary. Place a scant teaspoon of cream cheese and a tablespoon of the thickened guava marmalade in the center of the bottom half of each rectangle. Fold the dough over the filling and seal by pressing the edges together. (Don't worry about being too precise; the pastries should look rustic.)

In a deep-fryer or deep pot, heat the canola oil to 350 degrees. Drop in the *buñuelos* two or three at a time and cook for 1 ¹/₂ minutes per side, or until golden brown. Transfer to paper towels to drain for a moment, then roll in cinnamon-sugar and drizzle with the *almiba*

Scallops and *Papas Chorreadas*
with Romaine (page 118)

African *Adobo*-Rubbed Tuna Steaks
(page 116)

Poulet à la Créole (page 136)

Cerdo Picante (page 152)

Braised Beef Shanks *con Maní*
(page 158)

Bistec con Huevos (page 165)

Grill-Roasted Rack of Lamb
in Red *Mole* (page 169)

Gallina Rellena (page 182)

mama's mocha melting love cake

MAKES 1 LOAF CAKE

It is almost imperative that you offer the very best vanilla ice cream, homemade or store-bought, with this melting wonderment that my mother made for us when we were children. (The coffee is my addition to the recipe, a nod to my coffee-connoisseur son.)

1 tablespoon unsalted butter

1 1/4 cups granulated sugar

1/2 cup heavy cream

1 cup all-purpose flour

1 teaspoon baking powder

1/4 teaspoon kosher salt

5 1/2 tablespoons unsweetened cocoa powder

1/2 cup packed brown sugar

1 cup pecans, chopped

1 1/4 cups hot coffee

Preheat the oven to 350 degrees. Butter and flour a 9-by-5-inch glass or nonstick loaf pan, and set aside.

In the bowl of an electric mixer, using the paddle attachment on medium speed, cream the butter with 3/4 cup of the granulated sugar. Beat in the cream, flour, baking powder, salt, and 1 1/2 tablespoons of the cocoa. Using a rubber spatula, spread the batter evenly in the prepared pan.

In a small bowl, combine the remaining 1/2 cup granulated sugar, the brown sugar, pecans, and the remaining 1/4 cup cocoa. Sprinkle over the batter. Pour the coffee over the top.

Bake the cake for 1 hour. The cake will be crunchy on top and gooey in the middle.

Let cool on a rack for 30 minutes, then, while it is still warm, scoop the cake out with a large spoon and serve with ice cream.

chocolate

Almost everything in life seems to have two sides, its ups and downs. Love almost inevitably suffers loss. Salt finds its way into the sugar bowl. Men are from Mars and women from Venus. Is there such a thing as a pleasure that never causes pain? Yes, there is, and it is chocolate.

It is fitting that chocolate has been the elixir of Aztec emperors and Illinois country boys alike. If sex, love, and music were food, they would be chocolate! When asked to describe chocolate, even the most loquacious individuals find themselves resorting to the language of groans, shudders, moans, and sighs. So here are some *hard facts* on the subject.

The cacao tree is native to Central and South America, but it now grows in the countries of the Caribbean, Africa, Southeast Asia, and even the South Pacific. The common thread is that the tree thrives in the vicinity of the equator, between the tropics of Cancer and Capricorn. This belt, known for its rain forests with their wet, windless climates and steady heat, provides ideal conditions for the growth and well-being of the cacao tree. The sensitive tree flourishes in the shade of other taller trees, making the rain forest canopy its perfect protector. Nevertheless, the tree grows tall, about forty feet on average, and its leaves are usually a foot long. Its fruit pods are more-or-less football-shaped and dangle from various areas of both branches and trunk. A mature tree bears fifty to seventy pods each year, and each pod contains twenty-five to fifty seeds, or cocoa beans. The beans are harvested twice a year. It takes about four hundred beans to make a pound of chocolate.

The process of making chocolate begins when workers cut the ripe cacao bean pods from the tree, split them open with axes, and scrape out the pulp contained inside. After the mass of pulp has fermented for a few days, the workers spread it in the sun to dry, then separate the dried seeds from the remainder of the pulp and bag them for shipment to the market. The seeds are roasted, then ground under heavy steel (or, traditionally, stone) rollers, which release the fat (cocoa butter) within, transforming the mass into chocolate liquor, a thick substance that, upon hardening, produces the chocolate used in recipes for baking and for candy making.

While the Ivory Coast and Brazil are today the most productive cacao-growing areas in the world, the oldest plantations are found in northern areas of South America. The Latin name for chocolate is *Theobroma cacao*—and *theobroma* translates as "food of the gods." Even before the Europeans deified it, the Mayans and Aztecs had anointed it as an aphrodisiac, and its legendary powers did not evaporate as it crossed the Atlantic on its way to reinvention in Europe. An officer serving with Hernando Cortés observed the Aztec emperor Montezuma, who had scores of wives, drinking fifty flagons of chocolate a day. The chocolate of these Mesoamerican civilizations was a bitter-tasting drink made of ground cacao beans mixed with a variety of local ingredients that could include chiles, allspice berries, annatto seeds, and vanilla.

Of all the foods that moved from the New World to the Old, it was chocolate that went through the most serious transformation. The Spanish, like the Aztecs, served chocolate as a beverage, but in the sixteenth century they improved the drink's taste by adding sugar, and then kept the recipe a secret for almost a hundred years. In the seventeenth century, the Spanish princess Anna married France's Louis XIII. On some romantic evening, she must have enlightened her husband, because the European nobility soon began to mimic the Aztec kings, drinking chocolate with great ceremony and fuss.

The first "chocolate house" opened in England in 1657. By 1700, there were nearly two thousand in London alone—very similar to the phenomenon of today's coffee shop explosion—and other European countries followed suit. According to some sources, the chocolate bar was invented in 1849 by a Swiss named Francois-Louis Cailler. Ten years later, Conraad J. van Houten, a Dutchman, invented a press that extracted all the cocoa butter from heated chocolate liquor, leaving behind cocoa powder. In 1875, milk chocolate was invented by another Swiss, named Daniel Peter. But perhaps the real hero in the evolution of ecstasy emerged in 1879, when Rudolph Lindt invented conching, a process in which the sugar is ground with the cacao beans. Before his discovery, chocolate had been delicious but a little rough in texture. When chocolate candy began to be made in Switzerland using Lindt's method, the stuff really did melt in one's mouth.

Soon the French, English, and Dutch were cultivating cacao in their colonies in the Caribbean and elsewhere. As the cost of producing chocolate began to drop, it became a confection for the masses. During World War II, the American government contracted with Hershey Chocolate to provide candy bars for the troops. At the height of production, Hershey was producing chocolate bars at a rate of 500,000 a day.

Given the dual roles of New World and Old in the journey of chocolate, it's emblematic that Christopher Columbus was the first European to come into contact with cacao. The date of this fateful meeting, most likely in what is now Nicaragua, was August 15, 1502. Columbus was on his fourth and final voyage to the Americas, and in the way that he'd come upon the chile pepper nine years earlier just as he was about to sail back to Europe, he similarly stumbled upon chocolate in the eleventh hour. The man certainly had a knack for locating the goods.

a perfect flan

SERVES 8 TO 12

Someone once said that nothing is more perfect than an egg undisturbed. Surely he'd never tasted this flan.

1 cup sugar

1 vanilla bean, split lengthwise

One 14-ounce can sweetened condensed milk

One 12-ounce can evaporated milk

1 1/2 cups whole milk

5 extra-large eggs

1/4 teaspoon pure almond extract

Preheat the oven to 250 degrees.

Melt the sugar in a saucepan over medium-high heat and cook until it turns into a smooth dark amber caramel. Pour into the bottom of an 8-inch soufflé dish or other round mold.

Using the back of a knife, scrape the seeds from the vanilla bean and add to a blender. Add the three milks, the eggs, and almond extract and blend well. Pour this into the caramel-lined mold.

Set the mold into a larger baking pan and pour enough very hot water around the mold to come halfway up the sides. Bake until set, 2 1/2 to 3 hours—a toothpick inserted in the center should come out clean.

Let cool, then cover and refrigerate overnight.

When you are ready to serve, run a knife along the inside of the mold to loosen the flan. Pour about 1/2 inch of hot water into a large pan and set the mold in it for 10 minutes so that it will unmold more easily. Take it out of the water, wipe dry, and place a shallow bowl or small platter over the top. Invert the flan into the bowl, and serve.

cheese flan

SERVES 8 TO 12

After making A Perfect Flan, I was flooded with ideas, both my own and from many of the wonderful people who worked with me on this book. My assistant's mother, Gianna Bergonzini-Pedron, who is from Italy but lived in Mexico and Argentina for many years, told us of this delicacy. After tasting only one spoonful of her cheese flan, I knew it needed to be here for you to try at home.

1 cup sugar
1 vanilla bean, split lengthwise
5 extra-large eggs
5 ounces cream cheese
One 14-ounce can sweetened condensed milk
One 12-ounce can evaporated milk
1 1/2 cups whole milk
1/4 teaspoon pure almond extract

Preheat the oven to 250 degrees.

Melt the sugar in a saucepan over medium-high heat and cook until it turns into a smooth dark amber caramel. Pour into the bottom of an 8-inch soufflé dish or other round mold.

Using the back of a knife, scrape the seeds from the vanilla bean and add to a blender. Add the three milks, the eggs, cream cheese, and almond extract. Blend until smooth, then pour through a strainer into the caramel-lined mold.

Set the mold into a larger baking pan and pour enough very hot water into the pan to come halfway up the sides of the mold. Bake until the flan has set, 2 1/2 to 3 hours—a toothpick inserted in the center should come out clean.

Let cool, then cover the mold and refrigerate overnight.

When you are ready to serve, run a knife along the inside of the mold to loosen the flan. Pour about 1/2 inch of hot water in a pan large enough to hold the mold and set the mold in it for 10 minutes, so it will unmold more easily. Remove it from the water, wipe dry, and place a shallow bowl or a small platter over the top. Invert the flan into the bowl, and serve.

tres leches

(Cake Drenched In Three Milks, with Passion Fruit and Pineapple)

MAKES ONE 9-BY-13-INCH CAKE

The passion that the Latin countries have for nearly lethally sweet desserts sometimes stuns me. Such a dessert is the classic *tres leches*, which is akin to Key lime pie, but far sweeter. I've worked up my own rendition, using passion fruit juice as well as a little fresh pineapple to lift the thick richness of the three milks.

FOR THE CAKE

5 extra-large eggs, separated

1 cup sugar

2 1/2 teaspoons pure vanilla extract

3 1/2 tablespoons spiced rum

1/4 cup whole milk

1 1/2 teaspoons baking powder

1 cup plus 2 tablespoons sifted cake flour

1/4 teaspoon fresh lemon juice

One 14-ounce can sweetened condensed milk

One 12-ounce can evaporated milk

2 cups diced pineapple

1/4 cup passion fruit juice (if using fresh fruit juice, sweeten with a little sugar to taste)

FOR THE MERINGUE TOPPING

1/3 cup water

1 cup sugar

3 extra-large egg whites

1/4 teaspoon fresh lemon juice

for the cake

Preheat the oven to 350 degrees. Butter a 9-by-13-inch baking pan.

In a large bowl, with an electric mixer on medium speed, whisk the egg yolks and 3/4 cup of the sugar until light and fluffy. Add 1 teaspoon of the vanilla extract, 1 tablespoon of the rum, and the whole milk and mix well. Add the baking powder and flour and mix until just incorporated. Set aside.

In a large bowl, with clean beaters, whip the egg whites at medium-high speed until frothy. Beat in the lemon juice. Slowly add the remaining 1/4 cup sugar, beating until you have stiff peaks. Fold the whites into the batter, then pour the batter into the cake pan and gently smooth the top.

Bake the cake for about 40 minutes, until a toothpick inserted into the center comes out clean. Let cool completely on a rack.

Meanwhile, combine the condensed milk, evaporated milk, and the remaining 1 1/2 teaspoons vanilla and 2 1/2 tablespoons rum in a bowl. Set aside.

When the cake is cool, pierce it all over with a sharp knife. Pour the milk mixture slowly and evenly over the top. Cover with plastic wrap and refrigerate overnight.

The next day, toss the diced pineapple with the passion fruit juice, then spoon it all over the cake.

For the topping: Preheat the broiler. Set a small bowl of cold water for testing the caramel near the stove. In a small saucepan, combine 3 tablespoons of the sugar and 2 tablespoons of the water over medium-high heat and bring to a boil. Cook until it begins to smoke lightly—it should be a dark caramel. Slowly add the rest of the water—be careful, it will spatter—and then the remaining 3/4 cup plus 1 tablespoon sugar. Boil until the caramel forms a ball (240°F) when you drop a little bit of it in the bowl of cold water.

Meanwhile, in a large bowl, beat the egg whites with an electric mixer at medium-high speed until frothy. Beat in the lemon juice. Very slowly pour in the caramel while you continue to beat. When all the caramel is incorporated, turn the mixer to high speed and beat until the meringue has formed shiny peaks.

Spoon the meringue over the top of the cake. With the back of the spoon, dab at the meringue to form peaks all over. Put the cake under the broiler until the meringue peaks turn golden, being careful not to burn it. Cover and refrigerate for at least 1 hour but no longer than 3 hours, or the meringue will begin to break down.

leche cocinada with calabaza caramel
(Coconut Custard with Sweet Squash Caramel)

SERVES 4

"Cooked milk" is the literal translation of *leche cocinada*, but I've done a New World translation of my own. Working on the popular panna cotta model, I include tapioca, coconut milk, and rum in the preparation. This dish is an utterly comforting dessert.

1 ¹/₂ teaspoons gelatin

1 ¹/₂ cups heavy cream

1 vanilla bean, split lengthwise

³/₄ cup unsweetened coconut milk

2 tablespoons coconut rum

¹/₂ cup confectioners' sugar

2 tablespoons quick-cooking tapioca

1 recipe *Calabaza* Caramel (page 256), at room temperature

In a small cup, sprinkle the gelatin over ¹/₄ cup of the heavy cream and set aside to soften.

Using the back of a knife, scrape the seeds from the vanilla bean. In a small saucepan, combine the remaining 1 ¹/₄ cups cream, the coconut milk, rum, vanilla bean and seeds, confectioners' sugar, and tapioca. Bring just to a light simmer, then remove from the heat and whisk in the gelatin. Remove the vanilla bean and discard.

Using a ladle, distribute the liquid equally among six 6-ounce ramekins or coffee cups. Press plastic wrap directly against the surface of each custard, to prevent a skin from forming. Refrigerate for at least 3 hours.

When the custards are thoroughly chilled, run a knife around the inside of each ramekin and turn each custard out onto a dessert plate. (If they don't pop right out, set them in a pan of hot water for a minute and try again.) Serve with the *calabaza* caramel.

dulce de leche ice cream

MAKES 1 QUART

It won't be long before *Dulce de leche* surpasses vanilla as America's favorite ice cream. Now you can make it at home.

8 extra-large egg yolks
¹/₄ cup sugar
1 ¹/₂ cups half-and-half
1 recipe *Dulce de Leche* (page 257)

In a large bowl, whisk together the egg yolks and sugar.

In a medium saucepan, bring the half-and-half almost to a simmer over medium-high heat. Add the *dulce de leche,* reduce the heat to medium-low, and stir until smooth.

Temper the egg yolks by whisking in just a small amount of the hot cream mixture, then whisking in a little bit more at a time until the eggs are warm. Pour the mixture into the remaining *dulce de leche* mixture and heat over medium-low heat, stirring, for 30 seconds, or until it coats the back of a spoon. Remove from the heat and strain into a bowl. Put the bowl in an ice-water bath to cool or refrigerate.

When the ice cream base is cool, churn in an ice cream maker, following the manufacturer's instructions.

syrups and sauces

The following syrups and sauces are used so often in New World cuisine that I decided they merited their own section. They are simple to prepare and delicious on many foods. Use your imagination and combine them with your favorite cookies, cakes, and fruits.

almibar

(Andalusian Dessert Syrup)

MAKES 1 ¹/₂ CUPS

Almibar is made by boiling sugar in water, then reducing the mixture until it becomes syrupy. Widely used in Andalusian confectioneries, which were deeply influenced by eight hundred years of Moorish influence, the original *almibar* was refined by adding all kinds of fruit and flower flavors to make hundreds of varieties of syrup. Interestingly, until the beginning of the sixteenth century, sugar was used in Europe mainly for medicinal purposes. But "it was in the colonies of the New World," wrote Brillat-Savarin, that sugar as cuisine "was really born."

This vehicle for sugar adds a little jazzy sweetness to any number of desserts.

1 vanilla bean, split lengthwise

1 cup sugar

1 cup water

1 cinnamon stick

1 tablespoon grated orange zest

2 tablespoons fresh orange juice

Combine all the ingredients in a saucepan, bring to a boil, and simmer, uncovered, for 15 to 20 minutes, or until slightly golden and syrupy. Remove the vanilla bean and cinnamon stick. Refrigerate the syrup and reheat as you need. (This will keep for up to 2 months.)

vanilla-cinnamon almibar

Substitute lime juice for the orange juice, and omit the zest. Combine all the ingredients in a saucepan, bring to a boil, and simmer, uncovered, for 15 to 20 minutes, or until slightly golden and syrupy. Remove the vanilla bean and cinnamon stick. Refrigerate the syrup and reheat as needed. (It will keep for up to 2 months.)

cajeta

(Goat's Milk Caramel)

MAKES 1 3/4 CUPS

This caramel is traditionally made from a combination of cow's milk and goat's milk—which is available in health food and specialty markets. It's worth hunting for, as it adds dimension to this syrup, which is delicious on *Churros* (page 234). It also can be used to stuff *buñuelos* or as a dip for cookies.

You can buy jarred *cajeta* these days, but like most commercial products, it has the taint of food coloring and preservatives. It is quite easy to prepare and will make your kitchen smell very inviting.

1/4 teaspoon baking soda
1 tablespoon warm water
2 cups canned evaporated goat's milk
2 cups whole milk
1 cup sugar
1 cinnamon stick

In a small cup, dissolve the baking soda in the water; set aside.

Combine the milks, sugar, and cinnamon stick in a medium saucepan and bring to a boil over medium heat. Stir in the baking soda and water—the mixture will bubble and foam; if it looks as if it will overflow, briefly take it off the heat. Continue to stir over medium heat for 1 minute or so, then cook, stirring occasionally, for 35 to 45 minutes, until the *cajeta* becomes a light amber color and is thick enough to coat the back of your spoon. Stir constantly for 10 minutes more.

Remove from the heat and let cool slightly; remove the cinnamon stick. Refrigerated, this keeps for 3 to 4 days. If it is too thick when you warm it, you may want to add a little milk. Serve warm or at room temperature.

calabaza caramel
(Sweet Squash Caramel)

MAKES 1 ³/₄ TO 2 CUPS

When you're preparing anything that caramel might be good on or in, think of this recipe. A drizzle of *calabaza* caramel transforms even a humble pound cake.

1 ¹/₂ cups sugar

1 vanilla bean, split lengthwise

12 ounces *calabaza*, peeled and cut into ¹/₂-inch dice

¹/₂ teaspoon ground cinnamon

3 tablespoons fresh orange juice

¹/₂ cup heavy cream

Preheat the oven to 350 degrees.

Spread a couple of tablespoons of the sugar on a plate. With the back of a knife, scrape out the vanilla seeds from the bean and mix the seeds into the sugar, making sure they separate. Reserve the vanilla bean.

In a baking dish, combine the *calabaza* with the rest of the sugar, the vanilla sugar, and cinnamon. Drizzle the orange juice over the top. Bake for about an hour, or until the squash is soft and the cooking liquid has turned syrupy.

Remove the *calabaza* from the oven, and drain the liquid into a saucepan; reserve the squash. Add the reserved vanilla bean to the liquid. Cook over high heat until it reaches a temperature of 250 degrees.

Meanwhile, in a separate saucepan, heat the heavy cream until very hot but not boiling. Whisk it into the syrup and remove from the heat. Discard the vanilla bean pod, and add the *calabaza*.

dulce de leche

MAKES 1 ²/₃ CUPS

One 14-ounce can sweetened condensed milk
One 12-ounce can evaporated milk
2 cinnamon sticks, broken in half
1 vanilla bean, split lengthwise

In a medium saucepan, combine the two milks and the cinnamon sticks. Using the back of a knife, scrape the seeds from the vanilla bean. Add to the saucepan and stir well to combine. Bring to a simmer over medium-high heat, then reduce the heat to medium-low; keeping the liquid at a slow simmer, stir slowly and constantly—with a wooden spoon so that it does not burn—for 20 to 30 minutes, until it has the consistency of soft caramel.

Take off the heat and remove the cinnamon sticks and vanilla bean. Serve warm. (Refrigerated, this keeps for 3 to 4 days. Reheat gently before serving.)

the larder

A larder is a place where food is stored, but I think of it not so much as a place as a source of ideas: my "culinary tool chest," in which I have on hand infused oils and vinegar, spice rubs and chutneys, roasted garlic mash, and homemade meat and chicken stocks. With these ingredients I can take whatever I've picked up at the market in the morning, improvise, and make something special for whomever I am feeding. When I conduct cooking classes at the restaurant, I enjoy showing the students my tool chest. Their eyes light up at the notion of possessing some of this power for themselves.

I love to explore food markets in search of new foods; I love to discover new tastes and textures and to get to know the cultures from which these foods come. When traveling in Mexico, South America, or the Caribbean, I pick up whatever I can; I've been accused of looking a little like a mad scientist with his potions when I get back home and put my treasures in the larder. Rare spices are combined with more familiar ones and made into rubs; herbs are dried and put into oils for infusions. Beans and legumes from all over the world wait for the muse to strike. Each ingredient and each preparation tells a story of people, the way humankind finds magic in food. The larder inspires my guests, students, and those who eat at the restaurant to realize that they too can create beautiful food in their homes.

The paradox of the larder is that while it's the laboratory that produces many of the complex and delicate tastes in this book, its components are very easy to make. In this chapter, you'll learn how to prepare the building blocks of my cuisine. Yes, you can buy infused oils and canned or jarred stocks in the store. But the flavor of homemade staples is so superior and the labor so minimal that I entreat you to create your own larder, starting here.

ancho-cumin oil

Two of the most revered ingredients in Latin American cuisine unite here with olive oil, creating a lusty staple of New World cuisine. Dip bread in a bowl of the stuff, or drizzle the oil on just about anything.

2 ancho chiles, stemmed and seeded
¹/₄ cup cumin seeds
3 cups virgin olive oil

Put the anchos and cumin in a heavy saucepan and toast over medium heat until fragrant. Add the oil and heat until moderately warm. Pour the oil, anchos, and cumin into an airtight container. Stored in a cool, dark place, this will keep for 6 months.

annatto oil

The ochre hue characteristic of so many dishes of the Caribbean and Latin America comes from annatto. Annatto seeds, also known as *achiote*, deliver a mildly pungent flavor, but not a spicy one. Use this infused oil when cooking rice, or brush it on chicken or fish before you put them on the grill.

¹/₂ cup annatto seeds
2 cups pure olive oil

Toast the annatto seeds in a heavy saucepan until they just start to smoke. Add the olive oil. When the oil begins to simmer, remove from the heat and allow to cool. Strain the oil and store in an airtight container in a cool, dark place for several months.

roasted garlic oil and roasted garlic

MAKES 2 ²/₃ CUPS GARLIC OIL AND ¹/₂ CUP GARLIC MASH

Few foods metamorphose as dramatically or alluringly as garlic when it is roasted. Hardly a savory recipe exists in which one could not imagine this substance: Potato Tacos (page 26), *Pipián*-Stuffed *Empanadas* (page 30), *Camarones al Ajillo* (page 40), Tropical Tuber Hash (page 209), Black Bean, Sweet Pea, and Cilantro Rice (page 201). I always have these garlic preparations on hand.

3 large heads garlic, cut horizontally in half
3 cups pure olive oil
4 sprigs thyme
1 ¹/₂ teaspoons black peppercorns, toasted
    (see page 9)

Preheat the oven to 300 degrees.

Put the garlic heads cut side down in a small casserole or ovenproof pot and pour the olive oil over them. Add the thyme and pepper. Cover with a lid or foil and bake for 45 minutes to 1 hour, until the garlic is soft enough to mash.

Remove the garlic from the oil and set aside.

Strain the oil into a bowl and let cool, then pour into an airtight container. The oil will keep for at least a month.

To make the garlic mash, squeeze the cloves out of their papery husks into a bowl. Mash the roasted garlic with a fork. Store mash in an airtight container in the refrigerator for up to 1 month.

roasted garlic oil
and roasted garlic

Two items you'll find in my kitchen every day of the year come from the same culinary effort: roasting garlic in olive oil. Roasted garlic, widely believed to be one of the healthiest foods on the planet, can be used in an endless array of dishes, as can the oil.

Garlic was very important to the ancient Romans and the Greeks; in fact, there was a section in the Athens food market called *ta skorda,* or "the garlic." Garlic was believed to give strength to workers and soldiers. The Egyptians were said to have fed it to the Hebrew slaves who built the Pyramids.

You may have heard of, or tasted, the French dish Chicken with 40 Cloves of Garlic. It seems inconceivable to serve guests so many cloves of garlic, but that's what you do . . . and it is delicious. *Allium sativum,* so powerful in its raw state, takes on an entirely different character when the cloves are left whole and tamed through slow cooking. The more finely you cut or mince garlic, the stronger it becomes. That is why I abhor the garlic press and I prefer to slice garlic razor-thin, rather than mince it, for many of my preparations.

Note: Whenever a recipe calls for Roasted Garlic Oil, you can substitute pure olive oil or an olive oil/canola blend, but the oil is so easy to make, I urge you just to try the recipe once. You'll be glad you did.

chipotle vinegar

MAKES 1 3/4 CUPS

Making chipotle vinegar is about as difficult as making a cup of tea. It is a fantastic tool to have in your repertoire when you want to add acidity with smoke in one easy pour. Use it in your favorite salads or anywhere you want to add smokiness.

2 chipotle chiles, stemmed, halved, and seeded
1 3/4 cups Spanish sherry vinegar

In a small pot, toast the chipotles over medium heat for 2 minutes. Add the vinegar, bring to a simmer, and simmer for 2 to 3 minutes. Remove from the heat and pour into an airtight container. Allow the vinegar to sit for at least 24 hours before using. Stored in a cool, dark place, this spicy vinegar will keep for 6 months.

golden pineapple chutney

MAKES 4 CUPS

The word *chutney* comes from the Hindustani *chatni*, which means "strong spices." The sweet juiciness of golden pineapples—much more intensely flavored than ordinary pineapples—balances the spices with the lusciousness that only tropical foods possess. But you can substitute regular pineapple if you cannot find the golden variety, and the chutney will still be complementary. Serve it with Jerked Pork Chops (page 153) or any grilled meat.

$1/2$ cup sugar
$1/2$ medium red onion, diced
1 $1/4$ cups diced mango
1 $1/2$ cups diced golden pineapple
1 Granny Smith apple, peeled, cored, and diced
1 Asian pear, peeled, cored, and diced
$3/4$ cup diced papaya
1 tablespoon ground allspice
$1/4$ cup peeled and finely chopped ginger
2 tablespoons Caribbean hot sauce
　　(your favorite)
$1/2$ teaspoon kosher salt
$1/2$ teaspoon freshly ground black pepper
3 tablespoons allspice berries, toasted
1 cup apple cider vinegar or white wine vinegar

In a large bowl, combine all of the ingredients except the allspice and the vinegar. Allow to stand for 30 minutes.

Meanwhile, toast the allspice berries in a small saucepan until they just begin to smoke. Add the vinegar, bring to a simmer, and reduce to $1/4$ cup. Strain, and discard the allspice berries.

Combine the reduced vinegar with the fruit mixture in a large heavy saucepan and simmer over medium heat, stirring occasionally, for 20 to 30 minutes until the liquid is almost syrupy. Refrigerated, this will keep for up to 3 months.

curry spice rub

Spice rubs may emanate from Mexico, Central America, and many other places—cumin and black pepper rub comes to mind—but a curry spice rub is a natural progression in New World cooking. This recipe imparts beautiful color and flavor to whatever you rub it on. And when the food comes into contact with heat, a third player enters the stage: aroma. Use this to prepare *Mojo Curry Chicken* (page 141).

¹/₄ cup Madras curry powder
¹/₄ cup freshly ground black pepper
2 tablespoons sugar
1 ¹/₂ tablespoons kosher salt

Combine all the ingredients in an airtight container. Stored in a cool dark place, the rub will keep for 6 months.

escabeche spice rub

Escabeche comes to us via the Spaniards. The word means "spiced pickled fish," and it surely derives from the Spanish *pesca,* or "fish." At my restaurant, I interpret *escabeche* more broadly as a spice rub. I use it in such dishes as Tuna *Escabeche Caliente* (page 119), *Masa*-Crusted Chicken (page 44), and *Vaca Frita* (page 166), to name a few.

2 tablespoons cumin seeds
2 tablespoons black peppercorns
1 tablespoon sugar
1 tablespoon kosher salt

In a dry skillet, toast the cumin and peppercorns over medium heat until fragrant, 30 to 60 seconds. Cool the spices, then finely grind them in a spice mill or with a mortar and pestle. Pour into an airtight container, add the sugar and salt, and mix well. Stored in a cool, dry place, the rub will keep for 6 months.

chicken stock

MAKES 7 CUPS

If there were just one stock I'd encourage you to make, this is it. Why? Because it is the foundation of more soups and sauces than any other stock I use.

For this recipe, you'll need a large stockpot, a colander, and a fine-mesh strainer (or a colander lined with cheesecloth).

3 tablespoons unsalted butter
1 tablespoon virgin olive oil
3 large carrots, peeled and roughly chopped
1 large onion, roughly chopped
3 large stalks celery, roughly chopped
1 head garlic, cut horizontally in half
8 ounces mushrooms, roughly chopped
1 cup dry white wine
6 sprigs thyme
6 sprigs Italian parsley
6 basil leaves
2 bay leaves, broken in half
1 tablespoon black peppercorns, toasted
    (see page 9)
3 to 4 pounds chicken bones, wings, backs,
    and/or necks
10 to 12 cups water, or enough to cover

Heat the butter and olive oil in a large stockpot over medium heat. When the butter begins to foam, add the carrots, onion, celery, garlic, and mushrooms. Sauté the vegetables, stirring occasionally, until golden brown, about 10 minutes.

Add the white wine and stir, then add the herbs, peppercorns, chicken bones, and water and bring just to a simmer. Turn the heat to low, skim off any impurities that have risen to the surface (don't stir, or the stock will be cloudy), and simmer, uncovered, for 2 1/2 hours.

Strain the stock first through a colander, then through a fine-mesh strainer (or cheesecloth-lined colander) into a stainless steel bowl or container. Chill the stock in an ice-water bath. (This not only kills harmful bacteria, it prevents you from having to put steaming-hot stock into your refrigerator—and inadvertently heating it and its contents.) Then refrigerate until chilled, or, preferably, overnight.

Skim any fat from the top of the stock, and transfer to airtight containers. The stock will keep for 3 days in the refrigerator, or you can freeze it for up to 6 months.

beef stock

MAKES 3 QUARTS

Many recipes call for veal stock, and a good veal stock is a great thing. But I find this stock—in which I use veal bones as well—more comforting. Beef stock can be made two to three days in advance of when you need it, and in fact it is preferable to make it at least one day beforehand, as it benefits from being refrigerated overnight so you can then easily remove the fat.

For this recipe you'll need two large roasting pans, one or two large stockpots, a colander, and a fine-mesh strainer (or a colander lined with cheesecloth).

4 ¹/₂ pounds beef neckbones
4 ¹/₂ pounds veal bones
¹/₄ cup peanut oil
2 onions, roughly chopped
2 large carrots, peeled and roughly chopped
4 large stalks celery, roughly chopped
2 heads garlic, cut horizontally in half
6 to 8 quarts water, or enough to cover
3 bay leaves, broken in half
20 sprigs thyme
20 sprigs Italian parsley
1 tablespoon black peppercorns, toasted (see page 9)

Preheat the oven to 425 degrees.

Put the bones into two large roasting pans and splash with the peanut oil; it is important not to crowd the meat, or it will not brown properly. Place the pans side by side in the oven for 30 to 45 minutes. (If your oven isn't large enough for both pans to fit on one rack, you'll need to rotate the pans between upper and lower racks so that the meat on the bones cooks evenly.) Once the meat is nicely dark, remove the pans from the oven and give the bones a stir. Return them to the oven and roast 10 minutes more.

Add the chopped onions, carrots, celery, and garlic, dividing them evenly between the two pans, and stir to coat with the peanut oil and beef juices. Roast for 40 to 60 minutes: be sure to check the pans frequently, as you don't want the vegetables to get any more than slightly blackened. Transfer the contents of both pans to a large stockpot, or divide evenly between two large pots.

Pour a cup or two of water into each roasting pan. Place the pans on the stovetop over medium-high heat and, using a wooden spoon, scrape loose the dark bits of meat and bone stuck to the bottoms. Spoon this good stuff over the bones and vegetables stockpot(s).

Cover with the remaining water and bring to a slow simmer, skimming the fat and impurities that rise to the surface. (Don't stir, or the stock will be cloudy.) Once the broth remains clear, add the herbs and peppercorns. Simmer, uncovered, for 3 hours. Let cool slightly.

Strain the stock through a colander, then strain through a fine-mesh strainer or a cheesecloth-lined colander into another container. Chill the stock in an ice-water bath. (This not only kills harmful bacteria, it prevents you from having to put steaming-hot stock in your refrigerator and inadvertently heating it and its contents.) Then refrigerate until chilled, or, preferably, overnight.

Skim any remaining fat from the top of the stock, and transfer to airtight containers. Refrigerated, the stock will keep for 2 to 3 days; frozen, it will keep for up to 6 months.

pork stock

MAKES 5 TO 6 CUPS

The late, great James Beard is considered the father of American gastronomy. His favorite meat was pork, and he kept pig statues and other paraphernalia in his New York City kitchen, garden, and dining room—a veritable embarrassment of porcine riches.

For this recipe, you'll need a large roasting pan, a stockpot, a colander, and a fine-mesh strainer (or a colander lined with cheesecloth).

4 pounds meaty pork bones (unsmoked)

2 fresh pigs' feet (unsmoked)

$^1/_4$ cup peanut oil

$^1/_3$ cup pure olive oil

2 tablespoons unsalted butter

2 heads garlic, cut horizontally in half

2 ancho chiles, cut in half, stems discarded but seeds left intact

2 medium Spanish onions, roughly chopped

2 carrots, peeled and roughly chopped

6 small stalks celery, roughly chopped

2 leeks, white parts only, thoroughly washed and roughly chopped

8 ounces button mushrooms, quartered

2 tomatoes, cored and roughly chopped

1 tablespoon black peppercorns, toasted (see page 9) and bruised

10 to 12 cups water, or enough to cover

A pinch of kosher salt

6 sprigs Italian parsley

6 sage leaves

A sprig of rosemary

2 bay leaves, broken in half

Preheat the oven to 475 degrees.

Place the pork bones and pigs' feet in a large roasting pan and drizzle them with the peanut oil. Roast for about 30 minutes, or until nicely browned. Transfer them to a bowl or plate and pour off the oil. If there are any unburned bits of meat sticking to the bottom of the pan, add 1 or 2 cups water to the pan, put it over medium-high heat and scrape up the stuck bits with a wooden spoon. Set the pan of liquid aside with the pork bones.

In a large stockpot, heat the olive oil and butter over medium-high heat. When the butter begins to foam, add the garlic, anchos, onions, carrots, celery, and leeks. Cook, stirring often, for 8 to 10 minutes, until the vegetables are well glazed and beginning to caramelize. Add the mushrooms, tomatoes, peppercorns, the bones, and the roasting pan scrapings, then pour in the remaining water and add the salt. Bring to a boil. Skim the impurities and fat off the top as necessary (but don't stir, or the stock will become cloudy). Add the parsley, sage, rosemary, and bay leaves. Turn the heat to very low and simmer, uncovered, for about 3 hours.

Strain the stock through a colander and then through a fine-mesh strainer (or the cheesecloth-lined colander) into another container. Chill the stock in an ice-water bath. (This not only kills harmful bacteria, it prevents you from having to put steaming-hot stock in your refrigerator, which would heat up your refrigerator and its contents.) Then refrigerate until chilled, or, preferably, overnight.

Skim off the fat from the top of the stock, and transfer to airtight containers. Refrigerated, the stock will keep for 3 days; frozen, it will keep for up to 6 months.

note: To make smoked pork stock, simply use smoked pork bones and pigs' feet.

blue crab stock

Blue crab produces a dark and hearty broth, ideal for Fish Chowder (page 61). If you want a clearer, lighter stock, simply substitute various other shell-fish shells such as shrimp or lobster shells for the blue crabs.

$^1/_4$ cup virgin olive oil

2 tablespoons unsalted butter

1 large Spanish onion, roughly chopped

3 stalks celery, roughly chopped

1 large carrot, peeled and roughly chopped

1 leek, white and light green parts only, thoroughly washed and roughly chopped

1 small fennel bulb, cored and roughly chopped

1 head garlic, cut horizontally in half

2 large ripe tomatoes, cored and roughly chopped

6 sprigs Italian parsley

6 basil leaves

6 sprigs thyme

2 bay leaves, broken in half

1 tablespoon black peppercorns, toasted (see page 9)

4 pounds blue crabs, cleaned and split

2 cups dry white wine

4 quarts water

Heat the olive oil and butter in a large saucepan over medium-high heat. When the butter begins to foam, add the onion, celery, carrot, leek, fennel, and garlic. Stir to coat, then cook, stirring occasionally, for 15 to 20 minutes, until the vegetables are nicely golden.

Add the tomatoes, herb sprigs, bay leaves, peppercorns, and crab, and cook, stirring, for 2 minutes. Add the wine and water, increase the heat, and bring to a simmer, skimming off any impurities that come to the surface. Reduce the heat to medium-low and simmer, un-covered, for 1 $^1/_4$ hours. Remove from the heat and allow the stock to cool for about 20 minutes.

Strain the stock through a colander and then through a fine-mesh strainer or a colan-der lined with cheesecloth. Chill in an ice-water bath (this both kills harmful bacteria and prevents you from having to put steaming-hot stock in the refrigerator, which would heat up the refrigerator and its contents) until chilled. Transfer to airtight containers. Refrigerate. This stock will keep for 3 days in the refrigera-tor; it can be frozen for up to 6 months.

simple court bouillon

MAKES 3 ¹/₂ CUPS

Court bouillon is indeed the simplest of the stocks we make at the restaurant, yet it has a pretty sophisticated pedigree. Food histories record the English preparing this stock as early at 1685; they surely learned it from the French, who presumably were cooking with it well before that. It is an uncomplicated, effective way to cook various seafood; I use it in the preparation of *Bacalao* Fritters (page 15), Mussels *Callao* (page 49), and *Arroz con Mariscos* (page 104).

¹/₂ Spanish onion, diced
1 large carrot, peeled and diced
2 stalks celery, diced
1 small head garlic, cut horizontally in half
1 small fennel bulb, cored and diced
12 button mushrooms, quartered
1 tablespoon black peppercorns, toasted
    (see page 9) and bruised
1 tablespoon coriander seeds, toasted
    (see page 9) and bruised
2 bay leaves, broken in half
Zest of 1 lemon removed in strips with a
    vegetable peeler
Zest of 1 orange removed in strips with a
    vegetable peeler
A few sprigs thyme, roughly chopped
A few sprigs basil, roughly chopped
1 small bunch tarragon, roughly chopped
6 cups water
1 cup dry white wine

Combine all of the ingredients in a stockpot and bring almost to a boil. Reduce the heat and let simmer, uncovered, for 30 minutes.

Turn off the heat and allow the stock to steep for at least 2 hours, to infuse it with flavor.

Strain the stock through a fine-mesh strainer or a colander lined with cheesecloth. Refrigerate until ready to use. This stock will keep in the refrigerator for 3 days; transferred to airtight containers, it can be frozen for up to 3 months.

salsas, sauces, *mojos*, marinades, and vinaigrettes

The use of salsas, sauces, *mojos*, marinades, and vinaigrettes in the New World is more akin to the Mediterranean style of cooking than to the intricacies of French haute cuisine. The recipes in this chapter are typically served as a dish's complement rather than being its underpinning rationale.

Perhaps the most ubiquitous illustration of this philosophy is the small but potent battalion of hot sauce bottles arrayed on tables throughout the Caribbean. In Peru you'll find a cousin to these sauces in *ají amarillo;* in Argentina, it is *chimichurri rojo* and *verde.* The classic Cuban *mojo* doubles as a marinade and a vinaigrette. The Mexican *moles* and the African-influenced sauces of Brazil are complex distillations of flavor and history—yet even these are quite simple to prepare.

I've offered tips along the way to suggest how some of the recipes in this chapter can complement other dishes, but I am confident that you'll conjure up many ways to make these your own.

avocado–pumpkin seed salsa

MAKES 3 TO 4 CUPS

This is a simple but refreshing twist on gua-camole. The piquillo peppers sold in jars and cans are one of the most convenient and tasty ways to enjoy roasted peppers. If you serve this with a dish with a bit of fat to it, you might want to up the acidity with more lime or sherry vinegar.

$^1/_2$ cup unsalted raw pumpkin seeds
2 tablespoons fresh lime juice
1 teaspoon Spanish sherry vinegar
$^1/_2$ teaspoon Tabasco
1 clove garlic, minced
$^1/_3$ cup diced jarred piquillo peppers
1 large Florida or 2 Hass avocados, pitted,
     peeled, and cut into $^1/_2$-inch dice
Kosher salt and freshly ground black pepper
     to taste

Preheat the oven to 350 degrees.

Spread the pumpkin seeds on a baking sheet and roast for 12 minutes, or until fragrant. Allow to cool, then coarsely chop.

For the dressing, combine the lime juice, vinegar, Tabasco, and garlic in a small bowl.

In a medium bowl, combine the piquillos, avocado, and pumpkin seeds. Toss gently with the dressing. Season with salt and pepper and serve.

charred corn salsa

I grew up in corn country, the American Midwest. We used to sneak into the farmers' fields at night and eat the kernels raw off the cobs. So I feel right at home with the Latin American love of corn. Serve this simple salsa with all kinds of meats, birds, and fish.

4 ¹/₂ tablespoons unsalted butter
3 ears corn, husked and kernels removed
¹/₂ red onion, diced
1 green bell pepper, stemmed, seeded, and diced
2 jalapeños, stemmed, seeded, and minced
3 cloves garlic, thinly sliced
1 tablespoon Spanish sherry vinegar
3 tablespoons roughly chopped cilantro
Kosher salt and freshly ground black pepper to taste

Melt 2 tablespoons of the butter in a skillet over medium-high heat. Add the corn and cook until it begins to caramelize, 6 to 8 minutes. Transfer the corn to a medium bowl.

Melt the remaining 2 ¹/₂ tablespoons butter in the pan and sauté the onion, bell pepper, jalapeños, and garlic until soft. Add to the corn, along with the vinegar and cilantro, and season with salt and pepper.

herbed *ají* salsa

MAKES 1 ¹/₂ CUPS

Chiles are indigenous to the New World, and the Peruvian Andes are the probable home of the *ají*. Indeed, "the *ají* is so much a part of the diet of natives of Peru," writes Jean Andrews in her groundbreaking *Peppers*, "that it must have seemed natural for the Spanish-trained Indian artist who painted *The Last Supper* for the Cathedral of Cusco to place a dish of *ajís* on the table before Christ and his Apostles." Given the expanding interest in Latin cuisine, North Americans should be more and more able to find the famed *ají* chile in markets. I love this with the Pork Cali-Style (page 154), but don't hesitate to try it on a wide variety of meats and fish.

¹/₂ *ají* chile, stemmed, seeded, and minced (you can substitute ¹/₂ Scotch bonnet or habanero chile)
¹/₂ teaspoon kosher salt
¹/₂ teaspoon freshly ground black pepper
¹/₄ cup Spanish sherry vinegar
1 large ripe tomato, peeled, seeded, and finely chopped
2 tablespoons minced cilantro
¹/₂ small red onion, minced
6 scallions, white and green parts, minced
3 cloves garlic, minced

Combine all of the ingredients in a bowl. Serve at room temperature.

pico de gallo

A zesty tomato salsa that has been around forever, in certain parts of Mexico *pico de gallo* takes another delicious form: a fruit medley sold in paper cups, salted and dusted with red chile powder. I add the tomato version to my Steak and Eggs Salvadoran-Style (page 165); it helps cut the richness of the proteins. *Pico de gallo* literally means "beak of a rooster"—the idea being that the sharp "beak" (the salsa) breaks open the flavors of the foods it accompanies.

2 medium very ripe tomatoes, peeled, seeded, and diced
¹/₃ small Spanish onion, diced
1 jalapeño, stemmed, seeded, and minced
1 teaspoon minced garlic
2 tablespoons minced cilantro
1 tablespoon Spanish sherry vinegar
1 teaspoon fresh lime juice
¹/₂ teaspoon kosher salt
¹/₂ teaspoon freshly ground black pepper

Mix all of the ingredients together in a bowl and let stand for 30 minutes before serving.

pimiento corn relish

This bright relish offers a range of sharp flavor notes. I like it with hamburgers or grilled flank steak, or with meaty tuna, swordfish, and dolphin. I also serve it alongside our Guatemalan-inspired dish *Jocon* (page 127).

If you cannot find fresh pimiento peppers, some good varieties are sold in jars in Spanish and gourmet markets and in many supermarkets.

¹/₄ cup Spanish sherry vinegar
2 tablespoons sugar
³/₄ teaspoon kosher salt
¹/₄ teaspoon ground turmeric
1 ¹/₂ cups corn kernels (from about 2 ears)
¹/₂ Scotch bonnet chile, stemmed, seeded, and minced
¹/₂ small pimiento, roasted, peeled, seeded, and diced (or jarred pimiento, drained and diced)
1 teaspoon freshly ground black pepper

In a saucepan, combine the vinegar, sugar, salt, and turmeric and bring to a boil, stirring to dissolve the sugar. Add the corn and boil for 1 minute more. Remove the pan from the heat and stir in the Scotch bonnet and pimiento, mixing well. Allow to cool, then refrigerate until ready to serve.

pineapple tartar salsa

MAKES 3 CUPS

I created this to go with the Coconut-Almond Snapper Fingers (page 48), but its sweet, pickled richness would complement an array of the crispy-fried seafood dishes we are all guilty of loving.

1 ²/₃ cups finely diced golden pineapple
　　(you can substitute regular pineapple)
¹/₂ cup Champagne vinegar
3 egg yolks
2 tablespoons fresh lemon juice
1 cup virgin olive oil
1 cup canola oil
A few drops of water
2 tablespoons cornichons, finely chopped
2 teaspoons capers, rinsed and minced
1 teaspoon cayenne pepper
1 tablespoon fresh orange juice
¹/₂ teaspoon Tabasco
Kosher salt and freshly ground black pepper to
　　taste

Combine the pineapple and vinegar in a saucepan, bring to a boil, and cook on medium heat until almost no liquid remains, about 10 minutes. Allow to cool.

In the bowl of an electric mixer, beat the egg yolks and lemon juice until pale yellow. Slowly add the oils, drop by drop at first, then in a slow, steady stream. As the mixture thickens, add the water to keep it from becoming *too* thick.

Fold in the pineapple mixture. Add the capers, cornichons, cayenne, orange juice, and Tabasco and season with salt and pepper. Refrigerate until needed; the salsa will keep for up to a week.

chimichurri verde
(Argentine Green Sauce)

MAKES $^2/_3$ CUP

Chimichurri verde is the sauce most favored by Argentines to give zest to meats and other ingredients of the classic *gaucho*-style *asado,* or roast. You could even mix some of this sauce into mayonnaise to add tremendous *Nuevo Latino* style to a sandwich or salad.

$^1/_2$ cup minced Italian parsley
$^1/_2$ cup virgin olive oil
2 tablespoons Spanish sherry vinegar
1 teaspoon cayenne pepper
6 cloves garlic, minced
1 teaspoon freshly ground black pepper
1 teaspoon toasted and ground cumin seeds
   (see page 9)
$^1/_2$ teaspoon kosher salt

Combine all of the ingredients and mix well. Refrigerated, this will keep for up to 1 month.

chimichurri rojo
(Argentine Red Sauce)

MAKES ABOUT 1 CUP

This vibrant sauce/marinade is a nice variation on the classic *Chimichurri Verde*. A sort of Argentine Worcestershire, it is slightly more herbaceous. Try marinating some chicken pieces in this sauce (in a nonreactive dish) for a few hours before cooking them.

$^1/_2$ cup Spanish sherry vinegar or red wine
   vinegar
$^1/_4$ cup virgin olive oil
1 $^1/_2$ tablespoons hot paprika
2 teaspoons cayenne pepper
4 cloves garlic, minced
1 teaspoon freshly ground black pepper
1 teaspoon toasted and ground cumin seeds
   (see page 9)
1 bay leaf, broken in half
$^1/_2$ teaspoon kosher salt

Combine all of the ingredients and mix well. Refrigerated, this keeps for 1 month.

sugarcane marinade

MAKES 4 1/2 CUPS

An all-purpose barbecue-style marinade that is great with chicken, quail, and duck. I like it so much that I use it on the chicken when I make my Tortilla Soup (page 72).

1 1/2 cups dark molasses
3/4 cup Spanish sherry vinegar
6 tablespoons fresh lemon juice
3/4 cup Creole mustard
1 1/2 cups top-quality canned tomato sauce
3 cloves garlic, minced
2 Scotch bonnet chiles, stemmed, seeded, and minced
3/4 teaspoon cayenne pepper
1 1/2 teaspoons peeled and minced ginger
1 1/2 teaspoons grated orange zest
1/8 teaspoon minced fresh thyme
1/8 teaspoon grated nutmeg

In a food processor, combine all the ingredients, and pulse until smooth. Refrigerate until needed; this keeps for 1 month.

sugarcane marinade with tamarind

MAKES ABOUT 1 CUP

This is the marinade we use on the Tamarind Barbecued Duck with Smoky Plantain *Crema* (page 142).

Combine 1 1/4 cups Sugarcane Marinade with 1/2 cup tamarind pulp in a small pot and heat over medium-low heat, stirring to dissolve the tamarind. When the mixture just begins to simmer, remove from the heat and pass through a coarse strainer. Let cool.

toasted cumin vinaigrette

MAKES ABOUT ³/₄ CUP

Cumin is one of the most beloved spices of Latin cooking. Here it is featured in a robust vinaigrette that you can use in a great number of dishes, from meats (like a *mojo*) to salads. I like to drizzle it on tomato-and-goat-cheese toasts.

1 tablespoon minced shallot
1 clove garlic, minced
1 ¹/₂ tablespoons coarsely chopped Italian
    parsley
1 teaspoon toasted and ground cumin seeds
    (see page 9)
¹/₄ teaspoon freshly ground black pepper
¹/₄ cup Spanish sherry vinegar
¹/₂ cup extra virgin olive oil
Kosher salt to taste

Whisk all of the ingredients together in a small mixing bowl. Serve.

classic sour orange *mojo*

MAKES ABOUT 1 ¹/₃ CUPS

Mojos are a classic Cuban preparation, and plenty of bottled versions are now available: avoid them at all costs. Manufacturers have yet to capture the perfection of what you can easily make at home, and the versatility of this Classic Sour Orange *Mojo* is unparalleled. I've used it for years in the restaurant on our Yuca-Stuffed Shrimp, and I cannot tell you how many orders we have made. At home, I use it not only as a sauce but as a marinade for chicken, pork, and steak—particularly flank and skirt steak—as well. I also mix it with mayonnaise-based sauces and even ketchup, for a New World version of that condiment.

6 cloves garlic, roughly chopped
1 Scotch bonnet chile, stemmed, seeded, and
    minced
2 teaspoons cumin seeds, toasted (see page 9)
¹/₂ teaspoon kosher salt
1 cup pure olive oil
¹/₃ cup fresh sour orange juice (you can
    substitute ¹/₃ cup combined regular orange
    and lime juices)
2 teaspoons Spanish sherry vinegar
Freshly ground black pepper to taste

In a mortar, mash the garlic, Scotch bonnet, cumin seeds, and salt until fairly smooth. Scrape into a bowl.

In a saucepan, warm the olive oil over medium heat, until just hot. Pour it over the garlic-chile mix, stirring well. Allow to stand for 10 minutes.

Whisk in the sour orange juice and vinegar. Season with pepper. Refrigerated, this will keep for up to 3 months.

mojos and sour oranges

Many Americans would read the word *"Mojo"* and pronounce it as *mo-joe*. But it's a Spanish word, pronounced *mo-ho*. The word comes from the Spanish verb *mojar,* which means "to wet." (What bluesmen and rock 'n' rollers were referring to when they sang, "I've got my *mojo* working," is a rich subject for speculation, but not here.) Having lived in South Florida for twenty-five years, I've been encountering *mojos* for a long time now. Their growing popularity has a down side: when you look for them in the market, you may be disappointed to discover how many chemically processed, artificially colored, factory-bottled *mojos* are on the shelf. I don't know why anyone would buy them; they're a shadow of the good, homemade version— which is a breeze to make and keeps for months in the fridge.

My classic *mojo* is made with freshly toasted and ground cumin, virgin olive oil, a touch of chiles, some cilantro, garlic, salt and pepper, and freshly squeezed sour orange juice (or equal parts lime juice and orange juice). In Spanish, the sour orange is known as *naranja agría*. A large fruit with bumpy skin, it is believed to be the progenitor of all oranges. The fruit is not eaten fresh because it's far too sour. The sour orange's primary use is in marinades, which is why it's such a fine ingredient in *mojos*.

The chief difference between a classic *mojo* and a classic vinaigrette is that a *mojo* involves cooking. The olive oil is heated, then poured over the garlic and herbs to create a quick infusion. However, the olive oil is a relatively modern turn of events in *mojo* preparation, as these did not originate in olive oil–producing lands. The slave cooks who first prepared them used lard, which had to be melted, or the *mojo* wouldn't flow properly over other foods. The process of heating the fat continues to this day, even though the ingredients have gotten lighter.

I love teaching my students how to make Classic Sour Orange *Mojo*. The moment I pour the hot oil onto the garlic, chiles, and cumin, the kitchen is gloriously perfumed.

curry *mojo*

MAKES ABOUT 2 CUPS

This version of *mojo* takes the Cuban specialty into the kitchens of the West Indies.

3 large cloves garlic, minced
1 Scotch bonnet chile, stemmed, seeded, and
    minced
2 tablespoons Madras curry powder
6 scallions, green and white parts, chopped
3/4 cup Roasted Garlic Oil (page 262) or pure
    olive oil
3 tablespoons apple cider vinegar
1/3 cup fresh orange juice
1/3 cup fresh lime juice

Combine the garlic, chile, curry powder, and scallions in a bowl.

In a small saucepan, heat the oil until warm but not hot. Pour it into the bowl and whisk to combine. Let stand for 15 minutes.

Whisk in the cider vinegar and orange and lime juices. Refrigerate until needed; this will keep for 1 month.

mojo verde

MAKES 1 1/2 CUPS

Tomatillos are the key ingredient in this alluring green sauce. They have an unusual and pleasant tartness that works well with a variety of dishes. I pair this *mojo* with a grand Fish in Foil (page 111). The sauce has the brightness of a lemon with the attendant complexity you'd expect of the other ingredients that go into making it.

2 large poblano peppers
8 ounces tomatillos, papery husks and cores
    removed, and rinsed
Canola oil
1/2 cup virgin olive oil
1 tablespoon Spanish sherry vinegar
1/4 cup Roasted Garlic (page 262)
1/2 teaspoon kosher salt
2 teaspoons toasted and ground cumin seeds
    (see page 9)
1/2 teaspoon freshly ground black pepper

Preheat the oven to 350 degrees. Lightly rub the poblanos and tomatillos with canola oil. Place on a baking sheet, and roast for 20 minutes. Put the poblanos in a bowl, cover tightly with plastic wrap, and let stand for about 15 minutes. Set the tomatillos aside to cool.

Peel the poblanos and remove the stems and seeds.

Combine all of the ingredients in a food processor and puree until fairly smooth. Refrigerated, this will keep for up to 1 month.

red *mole*

Canela, a Latin American cousin of cinnamon, is a leading player in this sauce. Once used by affluent Romans in love potions and perfumes, the spice, derived from the inner bark of a tropical evergreen, is hugely popular in New World cuisine, in everything from soups to desserts.

3 large ripe tomatoes

1 cup peanuts

8 ancho chiles

$^1/_4$ cup canola or peanut oil

1 ripe plantain, peeled, halved lengthwise and then crosswise

1 tablespoon annatto seeds

1 tablespoon allspice berries

1 teaspoon whole cloves

1 *canela* or cinnamon stick, broken into pieces

1 $^1/_2$ teaspoons black peppercorns

3 canned chipotle chiles in *adobo* sauce

$^1/_3$ cup Roasted Garlic Oil (page 262) or pure olive oil

3 $^3/_4$ ounces bittersweet chocolate, finely chopped

1 tablespoon Spanish sherry vinegar

2 cups Chicken Stock (page 267)

Kosher salt to taste

Preheat the oven to 400 degrees.

Slice the tomatoes crosswise in half. Using a small spoon or your fingers, scrape out the seeds. Place the tomatoes cut side down on a baking sheet lined with parchment paper (this keeps the acidic tomatoes from reacting with the pan) and roast for about 20 minutes. Let cool slightly, then remove and discard the skins and cores. Reserve.

Meanwhile, also roast the peanuts on a baking sheet for 10 to 12 minutes. Let cool, then coarsely grind in a food processor. Set aside.

Toast the anchos in a small skillet over medium heat. Soak in hot water to soften, about 20 minutes. Drain, and remove the seeds and stems. Reserve.

Heat the canola oil in a medium skillet over high heat. Add the plantain slices and sauté until well browned and caramelized. Remove from the skillet and drain on paper towels.

In a dry skillet, toast the annatto, allspice, cloves, and peppercorns until fragrant. Let cool, then combine with the *canela* in a spice grinder and grind to a fine powder.

In a blender, puree the anchos and chipotles until smooth. Add the plantains, ground spices, and tomatoes and puree. Reserve.

Pour the garlic oil into a medium pot and heat over medium-high heat. When the oil is very hot, add the puree and simmer for 10 minutes, stirring frequently. Add the peanuts and simmer for another 2 minutes. Add the chocolate and let it melt. Stir in the vinegar and chicken stock and cook for another 5 minutes. Season with salt. Refrigerated, this keeps for 1 month.

sauce au chien

MAKES 1 ¹/₂ CUPS

Chien is French for "dog," and I've been told that this sauce is so named for the little bite it delivers. I use it on dishes that can handle just such a quality, such as *Cachapas* with *Queso Fundido* (page 41).

¹/₂ cup extra virgin olive oil
Juice of 3 limes
¹/₄ cup Italian parsley leaves
¹/₄ cup cilantro leaves
¹/₂ medium red onion, chopped
3 cloves garlic, chopped
1 tablespoon minced chives
1 teaspoon fresh thyme leaves
1 Scotch bonnet chile, stemmed, seeded,
    and chopped
Kosher salt and freshly ground black pepper
    to taste

Combine all of the ingredients in a blender and puree. Refrigerated, this will keep for a week.

sauce créole

MAKES 3 CUPS

Brazilian cooking has influenced and invigorated several other cuisines. Here we have a prime example, a spicy tomato-based sauce that is indelibly stamped with the flavors of New Orleans, but which in various earlier incarnations knew a home in Brazil and, of course, Africa. Use it on soft-shelled crabs, shrimp, and chicken.

1 ounce smoky bacon, diced
1 tablespoon pure olive oil
1 tablespoon unsalted butter
1 Scotch bonnet chile, stemmed, seeded, and minced
2 cloves garlic, minced
1/2 small red onion, diced
1 tablespoon sugar
1 large stalk celery, cut into medium dice
1 red bell pepper, stemmed, seeded, and diced
1 tablespoon Spanish sherry vinegar
1 teaspoon Tabasco
1 bay leaf, broken in half
1/2 teaspoon cayenne pepper
1 tablespoon chopped fresh thyme
1 tablespoon fresh chopped basil
1 cup Chicken Stock (page 267)
1 1/2 cups peeled, seeded, and chopped ripe tomatoes
Kosher salt and freshly ground black pepper to taste

In a heavy saucepan, cook the bacon in the olive oil over medium heat, until beginning to crisp. Add the butter, Scotch bonnet, garlic, and red onion, turn the heat up to high, and cook for about 3 minutes, until the onions are lightly caramelized. Add the sugar, celery, and bell pepper. Cook until the pepper just begins to soften, about 3 minutes.

Add the vinegar, Tabasco, bay leaf, caynene, thyme, and basil, then the stock and tomatoes, reduce the heat to medium, and cook, stirring frequently, for 8 to 10 minutes. Season with salt and pepper. Refrigerated this keeps for up to 1 week.

chipotle-lime *crema*

MAKES ABOUT 1 ¹/₂ CUPS

Use this all-purpose *crema* when you want to add a little bit of richness and heat to a dish. I love it with fried foods, but it is just as good on a baked potato or over grilled meats. If you want a milder version, simply cut back on the chiles.

1 ³/₄ ounces canned chipotle chiles in *adobo* sauce (about 2 chiles)
1 ¹/₂ teaspoons fresh lime juice
¹/₄ cup heavy cream
1 teaspoon Spanish sherry vinegar
1 cup sour cream

Puree the chipotles with the lime juice, cream, and vinegar in a blender or food processor until fairly smooth. Add the sour cream and pulse until smooth. This will keep in the refrigerator for up to 2 weeks.

jalapeño-cumin-lime *crema*

MAKES 1 ¹/₄ CUPS

Here I combine the "holy trinity" of Latin flavors that works so well with so many of the foods in this book. It is a sauce of my own imagination, which I've served at every event from a tailgating party to a sit-down dinner for 100 at the Winter Olympics. (I made friends in both places.)

¹/₄ cup fresh lime juice
1 jalapeño, stemmed, seeded, and roughly chopped
¹/₃ cup roughly chopped cilantro
1 cup sour cream
¹/₂ teaspoon toasted and ground cumin seeds (see page 9)
¹/₂ teaspoon freshly ground black pepper

In a blender, process the lime juice, jalapeño, and cilantro until smooth. Pour into a bowl and stir in the sour cream, cumin, and pepper. Refrigerated, this will keep for up to 3 weeks.

trinities

The power of a trinity lies in the way that it connects human experience to the divine. In Christian symbolism, three circles connected by bands, forming an equilateral triangle, represent the Father, Son, and Holy Ghost. Hinduism, too, has its holy trinity: Lord Brahma, Lord Vishnu, and Lord Shiva. Brahma is the creator, Vishnu the preserver, and Shiva the destroyer.

It's not surprising that cooking, so integral to the rituals of the world's religions, has its own trinities, capable of uplifting and igniting a meal from a state of simple nourishment to the feeding of the soul.

The "holy trinity" of New Orleans cooking is green bell peppers, onions, and celery, which make up the base for many dishes. In Spain, the culinary trinity is bread, oil, and wine.

Agreeing on a single Latin/Caribbean culinary trinity, however, would likely be impossible for cooks of these cuisines, whose passions are so often influenced by their allegiances to their own countries. But we can certainly narrow the field down to a group of apostles. Among them I would include olive oil, coconut milk, beans, various tropical fruits, potatoes, rice, corn, garlic, cumin, chiles, and lime juice. But these last three are, for me, the inspiration behind so many dishes. To them I say, amen and hallelujah.

Matambre (page 186)

Xinxim (page 190)

Beijinhos de Coco (page 232)

Panqueques de Manzana (page 238)

Tropical Fruit *Beignets* (page 236)

Guava Cheesecake with
Ginger Cookie Crust (page 240)

Mama's Mocha Melting Love Cake
(page 243)

Tres Leches (page 248)

smoky plantain *crema*

MAKES 2 CUPS

This is one of my all-time favorite sauces. It is excellent with grilled or roasted poultry or pork dishes. When I travel and cook at various events, I often include this on the menu.

1 chipotle chile

1 tablespoon Chipotle Vinegar (page 264) or Spanish sherry vinegar

2 ¹/₂ ounces smoky bacon, diced

1 tablespoon olive oil

1 poblano pepper, stemmed, seeded, and minced

¹/₂ large red onion, diced

1 carrot, peeled and diced

2 cloves garlic, sliced

1 Scotch bonnet chile, stemmed, seeded, and minced

Kosher salt and freshly ground black pepper

1 teaspoon annatto seeds

1 bay leaf, broken in half

1 teaspoon toasted and ground cumin seeds

¹/₂ cup fresh orange juice

¹/₂ cup Chicken Stock (page 267)

2 cups heavy cream

1 vanilla bean, split lengthwise

1 tablespoon canola oil

¹/₂ very ripe plantain (the skin should be almost black)

Toast the chipotle in a small skillet over medium heat. Remove the stem and seeds.

Combine the vinegar and sherry in a small bowl. Add the toasted chipotle and set aside to soften.

In a medium pot, cook the bacon in the olive oil over medium-low heat until beginning to crisp. Turn the heat up to medium, add the poblano, onion, carrot, garlic, and Scotch bonnet, and season with salt and pepper. Cook until the vegetables begin to soften, about 4 minutes.

Add the annatto seeds and stir. Then add the chipotle-vinegar mixture, the bay leaf, cumin, and 1 teaspoon pepper, and simmer until almost all of the liquid has evaporated, 2 to 3 minutes. Add the orange juice and simmer until only a small amount of liquid remains, 4 to 6 minutes.

Add the chicken stock and reduce almost to a glaze, about 7 minutes (you'll know it is done when the bubbles start getting bigger). Add the heavy cream and vanilla bean, stir, and simmer for 8 to 10 minutes, until the cream is quite thick. Pass the mixture through a fine-mesh strainer; discard the solids. Reserve.

In a sauté pan, heat the canola oil. Add the plantain, season with salt and pepper, and cook over medium heat, turning occasionally, until dark golden brown on all sides. Transfer to a paper towel to drain.

In a blender, puree the plantain with the strained liquid. If any lumps of plantain remain, strain one more time. Refrigerate until needed; this will keep for 4 or 5 days.

cocktails

In the cocktail repertoire of the Caribbean and equatorial Latin America, rum and tropical fruit juices have traditionally taken center stage. From Cuba comes the debonair daiquiri with light and spry Bacardi rum; from Jamaica hails the hefty planter's punch, with its swash-buckling Myers's; and from Barbados, the very cradle of rum, a late arrival is the Bajan Smile, made from flower-scented Mount Gay.

Other more esoteric spirits wait backstage: Peru's pisco, a grape brandy milder than Italy's Old World *grappa;* Mexico's mul-tifaceted tequilas; and *cachaça,* Brazil's national drink. The origin of the pisco sour, sometime in the 1930s, is (like so many New World culinary traditions) shrouded in controversy and mystery. Cocktail purists attribute the drink to Tony Bergna at his elegant Hotel Maury in Old Lima. But the literati swear that Noel Coward concocted it during one of his visits to the fabled Pension Beech, run by an American society lady in the colonial Peruvian city of Arequipa.

Tequila, traditionally drunk in Mexico macho-style (Step 1: salt your hand and lick it; Step 2: down the shot in one gulp; Step 3: suck on a lime half; Step 4: repeat steps 1, 2, and 3) was for years thought to be unmixable. That is, until 1948, when the Mexican heiress Margarita Samas had the bright idea of mixing it with lime juice, crushed ice, and sugar, and, as her pièce de résistance, rimmed the glass with salt. Hence, the margarita was born. The fierce liquor was now tamed, and a slew of ingenious tequila-based cocktails followed.

The next act in this mixed-drink drama may end up being dominated by Brazil's *cachaça*. Though it is distilled from sugarcane, Brazilians refuse to call it rum and prefer to use the more euphemistic "cane brandy." Actually *cachaça* and white rum share the same color, bouquet, and alcohol content (80 proof). But *cachaça* possesses more floral hints than rum. Maybe this is why it blends so well with Brazil's exotic tropical fruit, served in the mixed drink called a *batida*. This liquor, like so many other things Brazilian, seems designed to make life joyous. It originated in Bahía, and more specifically in the Modelo Market's Batida Row, so colorfully described in the novels of the late Jorge Amado. The names of drinks made from *cachaça* are as outlandish as their ingredients: Monkey's Tail, Mother-in-Law's Poison, A Primer of Love, Tigress's Milk, Virgin's Dream, and, in honor of one of Amado's most beloved characters, Gabriela, Clove, and Cinnamon. *Cachaça* is now finding its own niche in the U.S. market as a result of the introduction of the now-popular *caipirinha*—the so-called Brazilian margarita, in which the liquor is combined, in the style of the Cuban *mojito*, with crushed lime and ice. *Batidas* are sure to follow in the *caipirinha*'s footsteps, as exotic fruit juices and purees begin to be more commonly imported from Brazil.

a perfect day

While I am not advocating beginning the day with this cocktail, it is a quick way to perfect one.

2 ounces añejo rum
1 ounce Triple Sec
1/2 ounce Marie Brizard Parfait Amour liquor
2 ounces guava juice or nectar
2 ounces mango juice or nectar
2 ounces papaya juice or nectar
2 ounces guanabana juice
2 ounces grapefruit juice
2 ounces fresh sour orange juice (or 1 ounce
    each lime and regular orange juice)
1/2 ounce Myers's dark rum

In a cocktail shaker, mix all the ingredients except the dark rum (and garnishes) with ice. Pour into a cocktail glass, float the dark rum on top, and garnish, if you like, with blood orange and kiwi slices.

bahamian *batido*

Bahamians' love of rum is well known. So is their love of fruit. The *batido*—a fruit drink served across the Caribbean—is the best of both.

1 1/2 ounces Mount Gay Eclipse rum
1 ounce Midori melon liquor
3/4 ounce Grand Marnier
2 ounces mango juice
2 ounces passion fruit juice
1 ounce Coco Lopez cream of coconut

In a cocktail shaker, mix all the ingredients. Serve on the rocks in a cocktail glass. Garnish with a slice of pineapple and a strawberry, if you like.

bush doctor

SERVES 6

When I visit the Technicolor farmers' markets of St. Thomas on the U.S. Virgin Islands, I am always intrigued by the island ladies who sell a collection of various herbs that they simply call "bush." The medicinal and invigorating properties of these herbs—everything, purportedly, from stimulating sexual appetite to combating depression—remind me of the snake-oil salesmen of the old American West. Thus the name Bush Doctor.

2 ¹/₂ ounces Ron Añejo Pampero Aniversario rum
2 ¹/₂ ounces Bombay gin
1 ¹/₂ ounces Cointreau
1 ¹/₂ ounces apricot brandy
2 ounces sugarcane juice or 1 ounce Suntanned Simple Syrup (page 301)
8 ounces fresh orange juice
1 lime, halved
2 dashes Angostura bitters
2 bottles cold Mexican beer (you can substitute any pilsner)
4 ounces ginger ale

In a pitcher, combine the rum, gin, Cointreau, apricot brandy, sugarcane juice, and orange juice. Squeeze the lime juice into the mixture and add the bitters and beer. Finish with the ginger ale on the top. Pour into large glasses filled with ice cubes.

cachaça sunset

SERVES 1

Cachaça (pronounced *cah-CHAH-suh*) is the brandy of Brazil. It is made from distilled sugarcane juice, which is then concentrated by boiling. *Cachaça* is becoming more popular in North America because of the *caipirinha,* often called the Brazilian margarita.

2 ounces *cachaça*
¹/₂ ounce pineapple-coconut liquor
2 ounces mango juice or nectar
3 ounces guava juice or nectar
¹/₂ ounce Coco Lopez cream of coconut
¹/₄ ripe banana
Crushed ice

Put all the ingredients, including the crushed ice into a blender and mix. Pour into a tall glass and garnish with a pineapple slice and toasted unsweetened coconut flakes.

caribbean *carnivale*

SERVES 1

In late February or early March of each year, the Brazilian city of Rio de Janeiro goes into a four-day, four-night nonstop orgy of ritualistic celebration. It is like Mardi Gras—if Mardi Gras were run by the MTV generation and staged by *zaftig* multiracial cast members from *Oh! Calcutta!*, propelled by rocket fuel and rum laced with aphrodisiacs. While Rio's party is the granddaddy of pre-Lenten festivals—in fact the word *carnivale* derives from the Latin for "flesh" (*carne*) and "farewell" (*vale*)—similarly inspired festivals take place all over the Caribbean. Make this drink at home, and soon you'll be throwing your own party.

1 ¹/₄ ounces Bacardi light rum
¹/₂ ounce Bombay gin
¹/₂ ounce Triple Sec
¹/₂ ounce Amaretto di Saronno
2 ounces pineapple juice
2 ounces fresh orange juice
1 ounce fresh grapefruit juice
A dash of Angostura bitters

Mix all the ingredients in a cocktail shaker. Serve on the rocks in a hurricane glass, garnished with pineapple and orange slices.

copa loca

SERVES 1

Here is a drink that derives its flavors from both the Caribbean and Latin America. When you combine all the ingredients, you get a *copa loca*—one crazy cup.

Blue Curaçao to rim the glass
Sugar to rim the glass
A dash of grenadine
Crushed ice
¹/₂ ounce sugarcane juice or ¹/₄ ounce
    Suntanned Simple Syrup (page 301)
2 ¹/₂ ounces passion fruit juice
2 ¹/₂ ounces mango juice or nectar
1 ¹/₄ ounces *cachaça*
³/₄ ounce Grand Marnier
Añejo rum to float on the top

Pour a bit of Blue Curaçao onto one small plate and some sugar onto another. Dip the rim of a large hurricane glass in the liqueur, then quickly dip it in the sugar. Pour the grenadine into the glass. Add enough crushed ice to cover the grenadine. Pour in the sugarcane juice and add a little more ice. Pour in the fruit juices and add a little more ice, then the *cachaça* and ice, and then the Grand Marnier and more ice. Finally, float the rum on top. You should have achieved a layered effect. Garnish with a pineapple slice and whole strawberry, if desired.

cosmo *carioca*

SERVES 1

The people of Rio de Janeiro are known as *carioca*. I model this cocktail on the classic Cosmopolitan but give it Brazilian style with *cachaça* and other temptations.

1 ¹/₄ ounces *cachaça*
¹/₄ ounce Bacardi Limón
¹/₄ ounce Bacardi Orange
¹/₄ ounce Marie Brizard Parfait Amour liquor
1 ¹/₂ ounces cranberry juice
¹/₂ ounce fresh sour orange juice (you can substitute ¹/₄ ounce each lime and regular orange juice)

In a cocktail shaker, mix all of the ingredients. Serve straight up in a martini glass, garnished with a twist of orange peel.

dulce noche
(Sweet Night)

SERVES 1

The English translation of this Latin-inspired cocktail is "sweet night," and so it will be—as long as you resist the temptation to have more than one!

¹/₂ ounce Myers's dark rum
¹/₂ ounce Malibu coconut rum
¹/₂ ounce Godiva white chocolate liquor
¹/₂ ounce white crème de cacao
1 tablespoon *dulce de leche* ice cream (see page 251)
A double espresso
1 ice cube

Put all the ingredients in a blender and mix well. Serve in a port glass and top with foamed milk, with a sprinkling of nutmeg on the top.

green-eyed lady

I named this for the song, which I first heard while living in Hawaii many years ago. After two of these drinks, the spirit of the melody and the times revisits me.

1 ½ ounces Jose Cuervo gold tequila
½ ounce Blue Curaçao
1 ½ ounces sugarcane juice or ½ ounce
    Suntanned Simple Syrup (page 301)
2 ounces passion fruit juice
2 ounces *Guarapo de Piña* (recipe follows)

In a cocktail shaker, mix all of the ingredients together. Serve in a large cocktail glass over ice.

guarapo de piña
(Fermented Pineapple Juice)

MAKES 4 CUPS

Guarapo is the juice extracted from sugarcane. Here I make a version with pineapple, sugar, and water. It is used to make my Green-Eyed Lady (at left), but alone, it makes a simple syrup with a real kick. And after a few weeks' rest, the *guarapo* begins to take on some fascinating wine-like qualities.

In Venezuela, where this drink originates, the locals call it by its slang name, *guarapo e piña*, dropping the "d" altogether.

The peel of 1 pineapple
½ cup sugar
4 cups water

Combine the ingredients in a bowl and cover tightly with plastic wrap. Let ferment at room temperature for 3 to 4 days. Strain and store in a Mason jar in the refrigerator, where it will keep for 2 to 3 months.

libardo's pisco sour

SERVES 1

The pisco sour is one of the greatest of the Latin-based cocktails. Our barman, Libardo Salazar, hails from Venezuela. I consider his a nearly lost profession, and he deserves to have his own book on cocktails—this drink is just one reason why.

1 ¼ ounces Don Cesar pisco
¾ ounce apricot brandy
4 ounces fresh orange juice
½ ounce passion fruit juice
½ ounce sugarcane juice or ¼ ounce
    Suntanned Simple Syrup (page 301)

Mix all ingredients in a cocktail shaker. Serve on the rocks in a cocktail glass, garnished with a slice of blood orange and a slice of lime.

levantamuertos
(Raise the Dead)

SERVES 6

When you are on the beach in some parts of South America, children carrying plastic cups sometimes greet you. Often they are the youngsters of local fishermen, and they have made a concoction of their fathers' catches—chopped oysters, clams, shrimp—mixed with minced *cachucha* pepper, the idea being that if you are on the beach, you may be hung over from the previous night's events and in need of a powerful restorative. *Levantamuertos* generally does the trick.

1 ½ ounces spiced gin, such as Bombay
    Sapphire
6 ounces *Nueva María* Mix (page 301), chilled
Raw oysters, raw clams, and/or steamed
    shrimp or other fish bits, chilled, as desired

Combine the gin and the *nueva maría* mix in a pitcher. Spoon the seafood into individual shot glasses. Top off with the gin and mix and serve with limes on the side, if you like.

nueva maría mix

This is our basic Bloody Mary mix. I use it when I make any kind of Bloody Mary, but it is especially good with *Levantamuertos* (page 300).

One 46-ounce can V-8 juice
2 ounces Spanish dry sherry (optional)
3 tablespoons Pick a Peppa Sauce
1 ¹/₂ teaspoons kosher salt
1 ¹/₂ teaspoons toasted and ground cumin
  seeds (see page 9)
1 ¹/₂ teaspoons freshly ground white pepper
¹/₄ teaspoon chili powder
2 tablespoons fresh lime juice

Mix all the ingredients in a large pitcher. To make Bloody Marys, use 1 ¹/₂ ounces vodka and 6 ounces mix per drink. Serve with a squeeze of lime over ice.

suntanned simple syrup

White sugar is almost universally used to make the simple syrups that are the staple of cocktails, but I prefer raw sugar, and I don't mind its slightly darker color. Hence our "suntanned" simple syrup.

2 cups raw sugar
2 cups water

In a saucepan, combine the sugar and water over medium-high heat, stirring until the sugar dissolves. Let cool, and store in an airtight container. Refrigerated, this keeps for 3 months.

twisted *mojito*

SERVES 1

The *mojito* is to Cuba what the martini is to New York and London—quite simply, the classic cocktail. The twist in this *mojito* is the orange rum.

4 sprigs mint
Juice of ¹/₂ lime
1 ³/₄ ounces Bacardi Orange
3 ounces sugarcane juice or 2 ounces
    Suntanned Simple Syrup (page 301)
Ice
Club soda

In a tall glass, with the back of a spoon, gently mash 3 of the mint sprigs with the lime juice. Add the rum and sugarcane juice and stir. Fill the glass about three-quarters full of ice. Add club soda until the drink is the strength you desire, and stir to blend. Garnish with the remaining mint sprig.

glossary

One of the most interesting aspects of writing a glossary of terms for a book like this is that language varies from region to region; what is called one thing in Cuba is called another in Mexico and another entirely in Puerto Rico. For example, if I were to hold up to the chefs at NORMAN'S a kind of squash we frequently cook, I'd be told emphatically, and diversely, that I was holding a *mirliton,* a *christophine,* a *chayote,* a *chocho,* a vegetable pear, a custard marrow, a *pepinella,* or a *xuxu.* Or, if I asked them, "What is a *caldo?*" I'd see them all look at one another, and soon they would be going to a vote. (The more diverse the population, the less quickly goes the vote.)

This glossary is not meant to be definitive—I'm not sure that's even possible, given the culinary-cultural nuances and rivalries in Latin America and the Caribbean. It *is* meant to be helpful to anyone who wishes to make his or her own way through New World cuisine.

Acarajé (ah-car-ah-ZHAY): These are an unusual fritter in that they get their consistency from a mash of beans called *fradinho* in Brazil. I substitute the more widely available black-eyed peas.

Achiote (ah-chee-OH-tay): See *annatto.*

Ají amarillo (ah-HEE ah-mah-REE-yo): Native of Peru, these are fresh banana-shaped chiles typically 4 to 6 inches in length and ranging in color from bright yellow to deep orange. They are a staple of Peruvian cuisine and are used extensively in *ceviches* and *tiraditos.* Dried whole, *ají amarillo* are called *cusqueño* (sometimes spelled *cuzqueño*), but typically one buys them pureed. *Ají amarillo* are becoming more available in the United States through such purveyors as

LatinGrocer.com (see Source Guide, page 310). Scotch bonnet or habanero chiles can often serve as substitutes.

Legend has it that on the last day before Christopher Columbus returned home to Europe from his first journey, he happened upon his first chile peppers. Because the Spanish royal court had financed his voyage on the premise that he come back with spices, he probably thought hot peppers would put him in good graces with his patrons. He called the chiles *ajís.*

Al ajillo (al ah-HEE-yo): Refers to cooking food with garlic, a mainstay of Latin American cuisines.

A la parilla (ah lah pah-REE-yah): Refers to cooking or broiling over a bed of hot embers. *Parilla* means "grill."

A la plancha (ah lah PLAHN-chah): Refers to cooking on a hot plate or a griddle. A *plancha* is a flat metal griddle.

Ancho (AHN-cho): A dried poblano chile; its flavor is smoky and earthy.

Anise seed: The Greeks were using this aromatic spice, with a delicate licorice-like flavor, in the fourth century, and the Romans followed suit.

Annatto: Also commonly called *achiote,* this is the small seed of a tropical tree native to the West Indies. It is used predominantly to add a red hue to foods.

Arbequina (ar-bay-KEEN-ah): Small, softly flavored olives that originated in Arbeca in the Lérida province of Spain. You can usually substitute Niçoise olives.

Arepas (ah-RAY-pahs): Rich, cheese-topped cornmeal cakes common in Colombian and Venezuelan cookery.

Arepa flour: The preferred flour for making *arepas,* also called *masarepa* or *harina de pan,* or referred to by the brand names Masarepa and Areparina. A processed, precooked cornmeal flour, it is available in Latin American markets and some supermarkets. The extraordinary food writer Elisabeth Lambert Ortiz says, "*arepas* are unique in the world of bread since they are made with cooked flour. Dried corn kernels are boiled with lime (to loosen the skin), then the kernels are drained and ground, and, if not for immediate use, are dried and packaged as flour. Though the method of cooking the corn is the same for tortillas and *arepas,* the result is very different because of the varied types of corn used—and the fact that the flour is cooked. The corn for *arepas* has very large kernels, giving a rather starchy flour."

Arroz (ah-ROSE): Spanish for "rice."

Asopao (ah-so-POW): A Puerto Rican descendant of the classic Spanish dish paella, but soupier. Also called *asapado* in genteel Spanish.

Bacalao (bah-cahl-OW): Salt cod, one of the most important staples in the world. Cod fillets are salted and air-dried to preserve

them. Before cooking, the flesh is soaked for at least 24 hours in several changes of water to remove all of the curing salt. Salt cod is called "salt fish" in the Caribbean, *bacalhau* in Brazil, and *morue* in France.

Batido (bah-TEE-doh): A beverage typically made with blended tropical fruits, sweetened milk, and crushed ice cubes, often mixed with rum or *cachaça.* In Brazil, they call it a *batida.*

Boniato (boh-nee-AH-toh): A white sweet potato common in the Caribbean. In Colombia it is known as *batata,* and in Peru it is called *camote. Boniato*'s starchy consistency makes it ideal for mashes.

Cachaça (kah-CHA-sah): Rum distilled from sugarcane rather than the molasses commonly used. In Brazil, where it has been popular for more than four hundred years, this liquor is also called *aguardente de cana. Cachaça* bars serve the drink from small barrels, each flavored differently: ginger, fennel, coconut, cashew, orange, etc. If you have ever had a *caipirinha,* you have had *cachaça.*

Caipirinha (kye-peer-EEN-ah): A popular drink made with *cachaça,* fresh lime juice, and sugar. If other fruit juice is added, such as pineapple, mango, or passion fruit, the drink is called a *batido.* If a molasses-based rum is substituted for *cachaça,* the drink is

called a *caipirissima;* if vodka is used, it becomes a *caipiroska.*

Cajeta (cah-HAY-tah): Similar to butterscotch, this cousin of *dulce de leche* is made from goat's milk and is popular in Mexico. (Do not use the word *cajeta* in Argentina, where it is slang for a female sexual organ.)

Calabaza (ka-lah-BAH-zah): A squash that also goes by the names West Indian pumpkin and *zapallo.* It is commonly available in Latin and Caribbean markets; if you cannot find *calabaza,* you can substitute *kabocha,* butternut, or acorn squash.

Caldo: In its narrowest definition, a *caldo* is a soup broth or bouillon, rather than the meaty part. That definition is not always tightly adhered to, as is the case in *Caldo Gallego.*

Callaloo: Refers to various tropical green leaves used for making the eponymous Caribbean soup.

Cancha: A Peruvian variety of dried corn that is often toasted and served as a snack at *cevicherías,* or *ceviche* bars, the Latin American answer to sushi bars.

Canela (cah-NEY-lah): Sweet-hot Mexican cinnamon, softer than regular cinnamon. It's available in any good Mexican grocery, but if you cannot find it, it is usually fine to substitute ordinary cinnamon. The word *canela* has another meaning in Spanish: "exquisite thing."

Caramelizing: The technique by which the natural sugars in many vegetables are extracted through steady high heat.

Cardamom: An aromatic spice that is a member of the ginger family. The plant's small pods contain tiny seeds, which are usually used ground in this country, but in India, the whole pods are frequently used to flavor dishes; the pods are not eaten but rather removed, like bay leaves.

Carnitas (car-NEE-tahs): Literally, "little meats," in Mexican cookery, the word *carnitas* also refers to meats cooked in a braising liquid until the liquid reduces to the point that only some fat remains and the meat lightly fries, becoming nicely crispy. Generally refers to pork.

Ceviche, cebiche, or seviche (suh-VEECH-ay): Marinated raw fish, very popular in Latin America, the Caribbean, and the South Pacific. Fish and shellfish are cut into pieces, then "cooked" in a variety of acidic marinades. Peruvians are masters of the technique, making delicious rustic and sophisticated *ceviches* alike.

Chayote: A member of the squash family native to Mexico, this has a thin green skin and is shaped like a small avocado. The flavor is like a zucchini with a touch of apple and pear. It also

goes by the names *mirliton, christophine, xuxu, chocho,* vegetable pear, custard marrow, and *pepinella.*

Chiles molidos (moh-LEE-dohs): Literally "mixed chiles," this is a mixture of ground dried chiles. It makes a better bowl of chili than is possible with conventional store-bought chili powder. *Chiles molidos* is available in gourmet and Latin American specialty markets.

Chimichurri: (cheemy-choori): A sort of Argentine pesto made

with olive oil, vinegar, garlic, and herbs. It is almost always served with grilled steaks but can also be served on seafood and chicken.

Chipotles (chee-POTE-lays): Smoked jalapeño peppers, sold dried in packages or canned in a smoky red puree called *adobo.* Available in Latin American markets and good grocery stores.

Chorizo (cho-REET-zoh): A Spanish or Mexican pork sausage with a nice level of spicy heat. The Spanish is often dried and aged, while the Mexican is generally fresher and soft in texture.

Chuño (CHOON-yo): A method devised by the Incas to preserve potatoes by freeze-drying them. Over a period of several days, the tubers are frozen in the cold Andean air, stamped on to squeeze out all the moisture in them, and then thawed in the potent mountain sun. This turns the frozen mash into a powdery dehydrated product, which can be stored and then reconstituted in the hard winter months.

Churrasco (choor-AHS-co): Generically used to describe any steak or similar cut of beef grilled over wood or charcoal embers. It may also refer to skirt steak that is marinated and then broiled.

Cilantro: The grassy, lemony leaf of the coriander plant. Also called Chinese, Thai, or Mexican parsley, or fresh coriander.

Cocido (co-SEE-do): A Latin stew somewhat similar to the classic French *pot-au-feu.*

Colombo (co-lum-bow): A West Indian meat, fish, and vegetable stew seasoned with a spice mixture of the same name. Similar to curry powder, the mixture contains coriander, chiles, cinnamon, nutmeg, saffron, and garlic.

Conch (konk): A very large mollusk found in Caribbean waters, which has a sweet, exotic, clam-like flavor. Farm-raised conch is now becoming available in the United States; typically, it is ground before cooking (see Source Guide, page 310).

Congri (con-GREE): Stewed black or red beans mixed with rice.

Coquitos (co-KEE-tos): These nuts come from a Chilean palm that takes up to fifty years to start production, but which produce for hundreds of years. They are the size and shape of marbles, and have a surface resembling wood and a soft, white interior flesh. The taste is similar to a nutty coconut. They are sold shelled and can be eaten right from the container without being peeled. Store in an airtight container.

Croqueta (cro-KAYT-ah): The Spanish word for "croquette." Served as snacks, *croquetas* are typically cylinder-shaped and crispy-fried.

Cuchuco (koo-CHOO-co): A soup from the Colombian Andes, made with barley, wheat, or dried corn. Its protein source is usually the spine of pork, and it is garnished with fava beans, green peas, and other local vegetables.

Deglaze: To use a liquid, such as wine or liquor, water, or stock, to dissolve the caramelized food particles and drippings left in a pan after roasting or sautéing.

Dendé (den-day): A type of palm oil important in Brazilian cooking, especially among Brazilians of African descent. Extracted from the nuts of African oil palms *(Elaeis guineensis),* it is extremely high in saturated fat—and for that reason, I typically use annatto or olive oil in its stead.

Dried shrimp: Sun-dried small peeled shrimp used to add an aromatic shellfish flavor to fried rice, pad Thai, and other Asian and Latin dishes. In Spanish, they are known as *camarones secos.* They can be found in Latin and Asian markets.

Dulce (DUL-say): "Sweet" in Spanish.

Dulce de leche (DUL-say deh LAY-chay): A sweet caramel confection made with cow's or goat's milk, originally created as a way to preserve milk. It is also called *manjar blanco* in Chile and *are-quipe* in Colombia. Used as a dipping sauce for fruit or cookies, it can also be the base for intensely flavored ice creams. See also *cajeta.*

Empanada (em-pah-NAH-dah): A wide variety of savory or sweet small pastries are known as *empanadas* (or *empanaditas,* when made in smaller versions). Sometimes they are baked, but more often these little delicacies are fried. In Brazil, they are often called *empadas.*

Escabeche (es-cah-BAY-chay): Literally, "pickled," but its meaning extends to the spices used in the pickling process to make the dishes also referred to as *escabeches*.

Estofado (es-toh-FAH-doh): Spanish for "braised" or "stewed."

Garam masala (gare-um mah-SAH-la): Meaning "a mixture of hot spices" in Hindustani, this spice mix arrived in the New World with the Indian immigrants who came to the Caribbean. Like curry spice mixes, *garam masala* varies according to region. The mixes prepared by southern Indians are likely to incorporate chiles and cumin, while northern Indians use more floral spices.

Golden pineapple: An intensely flavorful variety of pineapple, it is becoming more widely available here. Look for it in good supermarkets.

Guarapo (gwah-RAH-poh): Sugarcane juice extracted by a machine that puts an amazing level of pressure on the canes and squeezes out the sweet juice.

Guava (gwah-vah): Unless you live in South Florida, the Caribbean, or Asia (or have access to an excellent produce market), the guava you'll find is rarely the ripe, perfumed subtropical fruit it should be. For that reason, it is more often found in the form of marmalades and jellies. The Aztecs called guavas "sand plums" because of their many small but edible seeds. I think guava's appeal comes from its sweet-sour "one-two punch."

Habanero (ah-bah-NEHR-oh): Although habanero and Scotch Bonnet chiles are of the same species, they are not of the same cultivar. Habaneros are named after the city of Havana but originate in the Yucatán. Scotch bonnets are used throughout the Caribbean and are also known as "Goat Pepper" in the Bahamas. Both chiles are some of the hottest on the planet. I buy them interchangeably, looking for the fresher of the two.

Harina de pan (AH-reena-day-pahn): See *arepa flour*.

Jerk spices: Common in the cuisines of Jamaica, Trinidad, and Tobago, jerk spices are a standard seasoning rub or paste used on pork and chicken. The mixtures typically contain allspice, Scotch bonnets, cumin, and cinnamon.

Jicama (HEE-cah-mah): The large turnip-shaped, light-brown-skinned root of a native Mexican root vegetable. It has a sweet-bitter apple flavor. Look for firm, unblemished ones, which will have crisp, crunchy flesh.

Kabocha (kah-BOH-chah): A Japanese squash, *kabocha* is now available in the United States and it works well as a substitute for *calabaza* squash.

Mace: A spice that comes from the nutmeg tree, mace is actually the lacy material that surrounds the seed, or nutmeg.

Malanga (mah-LAHN-gah): A shaggy-looking tuber also known as *yautía*, in Puerto Rico. Found in good produce markets alongside the potatoes and sweet potatoes, yams, and yuca, *malanga* should be firm to the touch; it is best stored in a cool, dry place, but not the refrigerator. Its flavor is similar to but less sweet than that of a sweet potato. *Malangas* are most commonly made into chips and fritters. The tuber may have come to Cuba with Nigerian slaves.

Manchego (mahn-CHAY-go): A cheddar-like sheep's-milk cheese produced in the plains area of Spain made famous by Cervantes' *Don Quixote de La Mancha*. Spain's most famous cheese, it is typically sold at three ages: *fresco*, the youngest; *curado*, which is the most common; and *añejo*, which is aged from six months to a year and sometimes sold packed in olive oil. (Archaeological discoveries tell us that sheep rearing and cheese making date back to the Iron Age in La Mancha.)

Masarepa: See *arepa flour*.

Masa harina (mah-sah hah-REEN-ah): Finely ground dried corn used in preparing tortillas and tamales. *Masa* means "dough" in Spanish.

Mojito (moh-HEET-oh). The famous cocktail invented in Cuba, made with rum, lime, sugar, soda water, and, for the most authentic rendition, with a touch of the herb *yerba buena*. Mint is the best substitute.

Mojo (mo-ho): A sauce similar to a vinaigrette, from the Spanish word *mojar,* which means "to wet." Cubans use a recipe that originally came from the Canary Islands and invariably employs olive oil, garlic, cumin seeds, and vinegar or citrus juice; it is most commonly enjoyed with yuca, meats, and poultry. In Puerto Rico, *mojo* refers to a sauce made with tomatoes and olives. *Puertorriqueños* would use the more specific *mojo de ajo* when referring to the Cuban garlic *mojo.*

Mole (mo-lay): A word used to describe a whole collection of uniquely Mexican sauces, ranging from red chile sauces to sauces thick with nuts and seeds to sauces redolent of herbs and spices. It's a misconception that a *mole* always contains chocolate. *Mole poblano,* a Pueblan specialty, and *mole de olores,* or "fragrant mole," do, however, use chocolate.

Muñeta (moon-YEH-tah): Pureed black beans.

Palillo (pah-LEE-yo): Literally "stick"; in culinary terms, a Latin American spice very similar to turmeric.

Papa: Spanish for "potato."

Papas secas: Dried potatoes native to Peru, found in specialty Latin markets. See also *chuño.*

Papelón (pah-pay-LONE): A type of Latin American brown sugar. *Papelón* is sold as brick-like blocks, made from sugarcane juice that is boiled and reduced until it turns a dark brown. It is then shaped into bricks, or cones. Its distinct taste gives the popular dish *Asado Negro* (see page 184) its unique identity.

Pastelillo (pahs-tay-LEE-yo): Ever the rugged individualists, *Puertorriqueños* have their own word for what, in most of Latin America and the Caribbean, is an *empanada.*

Pavo (pah-vo): Spanish for "turkey."

Pepitas (pay-PEE-tahs): Small green pumpkin seeds sold salted or unsalted, roasted or raw, frequently used in Mexican cooking. Look for them in Latin markets and health food stores.

Picadillo (pee-cah-DEE-yo): A homey dish common to Cuban cooking, often made with ground turkey but sometimes with other meat. It's like a Sloppy Joe in consistency, but with the addition of olives, raisins, capers, and, occasionally, nuts.

Pipián (pee-pee-AHN): A paste made of pumpkin seeds and

chiles. The paste can be turned into a sauce and is good in that guise to flavor cooked meats and various starches. In Colombia, ground peanuts are used instead of pumpkin seeds.

Piquillo (pee-KEE-yo): These deep red sweet peppers are found in Latin markets in jars and cans. If you find fresh ones, you'll most likely be roasting and peeling them.

Plantain: A variety of banana, sometimes referred to as a cooking banana; in Spanish, they are called *plátanos* (PLAH-tah-nos). *Plátanos verdes* are green plantains; *plátanos pintones* are just beginning to turn black and are often boiled; and *plátanos maduros* are almost totally black and very ripe and sweet. *Plátanos burros,* which hail from Hawaii (where they are called *hua moa),* are much fatter than the Latin varieties. Plantains are always eaten cooked. They ship well while still in their green phase; bananas are *not* a good substitute.

Poblano (poh-BLAH-no): A fairly mild green fresh chile pepper, widely available in America.

Queso blanco (kay-so BLAHN-co): A Latin American white farmer's-style cheese that generally has a slightly bouncy, slightly salty character.

Relleno (ray-YAY-no): Spanish for "stuffed," as in *chiles rellenos.*

Roti (roh-tee): A West Indian staple, unleavened flatbread found especially in Guyana, Trinidad, and Tobago. Typically *roti* are served stuffed and rolled, similar to Mexican burritos.

Saffron: A spice that is actually the dried stigmas of the *Crocus sativus* flower. They must be painstakingly hand picked: it takes 100,000 fresh flowers to yield 5 kilos of stigmas, which, when dried, yield 1 kilo.

Scotch bonnet: See *habanero*.

Sofrito (soh-FREE-to): A seasoning mixture that is similar to the French *mirepoix* and the Italian *soffritto* in that it is used extensively at the beginning of the cooking of stews, sauces, soups, and other dishes. Typically, a *sofrito* is made from garlic, onions, and peppers, and sometimes tomatoes, cooked in lard, olive oil, butter, or bacon fat.

Sour oranges: Called *naranja agria* in Spanish, the sour orange is believed to be the ancestor of all oranges. It is a large fruit with a bumpy skin. The flesh is not eaten out of hand because it is far too sour. Its primary use is in a marinade or as a component of

a recipe such as the Cuban *mojo de ajo.*

Star anise: Although it is not related to the anise plant, the flavor of this seed pod is also licorice-like. The star-shaped spice is probably native to China.

Tamal (tah-mal, singular), tamales (tah-MAL-ays, plural): A side dish or small plate made of endless varieties of filling enclosed in cornmeal dough, wrapped in corn husks or banana leaves and steamed.

Tamarind: *Tamarindus indica,* a tropical tree that originated in India, produces large brown seed pods. The seeds inside each brittle pod are embedded in a sticky, brown pulp with a tart flavor, which is used in making sauces both savory and sweet, marinades, and juices.

Tomatillo (to-mah-TEE-yo): A small green husk-wrapped fruit that looks like a small green tomato but is not related. It is particularly important in Mexican and Central American cooking. Tomatillos are almost always at least slightly cooked except in some salsas.

Turmeric: A spice, and coloring agent, obtained from the rhi-

zomes of *Curcuma longa,* an herbaceous perennial plant native to India and Southeast Asia, often substituted for the much more expensive saffron. It is one of the typical ingredients in curry powder, providing the characteristic ochre hue.

Vatapá (vah-tah-PAH): African in origin, this dish is more often associated with Brazil. It is a thick stew made with *manioc (cassava or yuca)* flour, coconut, and *dendé* (palm oil), often spiced with ginger and thickened with ground nuts such as peanuts or cashews.

Xuxu (zhoo-zhoo): See *chayote.*

Yuca (YOO-kah): Cuba's native Siboneyes Indians were the first to cultivate this filling tuber. It is called *cassava, casabe, caçabi,* and *manioc* in various parts of the Caribbean. Yuca is cooked in many of the ways potatoes are prepared. Its flavor is like that of a baking potato crossed with chestnuts. It has a tough, nearly bark-like skin that must always be removed: cut the yuca lengthwise in half and remove any woody or fibrous core, and then peel. It is often sold frozen, already peeled and cleaned and ready to boil.

source guide
Where to Buy New World Ingredients

I live in Miami, where it's easy to find ají *amarillo* and West Indian pumpkin in the many thriving markets of the city. Even the big grocery stores here carry many of the ingredients I use in this book. That's not a surprise, given the ethnic makeup of the population of South Florida. What is surprising, perhaps, is that you can find these so-called exotic ingredients all over the country. Thanks to the revolution in American food tastes, and the twin miracles of the Internet and overnight shipping, you can get most of the ingredients I call for in this book, wherever you live. To prove the point, I asked my friends and colleagues, from Paula Wolfert to Douglas Rodriguez, from Alice Waters to Charlie Trotter and Emeril Lagasse, to recommend the places they shop for New World cuisine ingredients. If anyone knows where to buy good food, these people do. The following markets and Internet purveyors are my recommendations, with a little help from my friends.

INTERNET PURVEYORS

chocolates-elrey.com
Best bittersweet chocolate in South America (made in Venezuela); will ship to North America.

deananddeluca.com
One of the pioneers in gourmet and ethnic ingredients in New York now delivers to other cities via the Internet.

friedas.com
If you can't visit the store in Los Angeles, you can order online.

ethnicgrocer.com (also known as Querico.com)
Douglas Rodriguez of New York's Chicama likes this outfit, as do I. Ethnicgrocer.com sells a multitude of ingredients from all over the world. Great quality and reliable shipping.

tienda.com
All types of fine products from Spain. Jose Andres of Jaleo in Washington, D.C., and I recommend this place. Rumor has it that next year Tienda.com will be the first purveyor to sell *jamon Iberico* in the United States.

ARIZONA

Native Seeds/Search
526 North Fourth Avenue
Tucson, AZ 85705
www.nativeseeds.org
Barbara Pool Fenzl of Les Gourmettes Cooking School in Phoenix, Arizona, and I love this outfit, which stocks approximately two thousand species of traditional crops. You can find an additional forty-eight species of crops and wild crop relatives here, among them wild beans, chiles, corn, garbanzo beans, and fava beans.

CALIFORNIA

Casa Lucas
2934 24th Avenue
San Francisco, CA 94132
415–826–4334
Author Joyce Goldstein says Casa Lucas is a great place to get yuca, plantains, and other typical Latin produce.

El Camaguey Meat Market
10925 Venice Boulevard
West Los Angeles, CA 90034
310–839–4037
Recommended by Douglas Rodriguez of Chicama in New York City, El Camaguey sells excellent meats as well as Latin ingredients.

Frieda's
Los Angeles, CA
800–241–1771
www.friedas.com

This market carries a great selection of fresh and dried chiles, as well as a wide variety of tomatillos, jicama, *xuxu*, cactus pears, avocado leaves, yuca, *piloncillos,* and other New World ingredients.

La Palma
2884 24th Street
San Francisco, CA 94110
415–647–1500
Joyce Goldstein loves La Palma, a grocery, tortilla factory, and take-out *taqueria.* The potato chips are fried in lard, cut very thick and supremely crisp and flavorful. La Palma is famous for its squadron of Central American ladies who prepare several kinds of *masa* behind the take-out area.

La Specialty Produce
16633 East Gale Avenue
City of Industry, CA 91745
877–569–5100
Recommended by Emeril Lagasse. La Specialty supplies Emeril's restaurants with very interesting and hard-to-find produce. He also purchases fresh chiles and plantains here.

Melissa's Specialty Produce
Los Angeles, CA
800–588–0151
Douglas Rodriguez of Chicama, author Steven Raichlen, and I recommend Melissa's for its great variety of chiles, fruits, herbs, and Latin foods, among them *xuxu* squash, cocktail avocado, Jamaica hibiscus pod, jicama, *malanga, tamarillo,* tamarind, and a lot more.

Mo Hotta Mo Betta
P.O. Box 4136
San Luis Obispo, CA 93403
800–462–3220
Fax: 912–748–1364
Paula Wolfert recommends this market for its wide variety of chiles.

Tierra Vegetables
13684 Chalk Hill Road
Healdsburg, CA 95448
888–784–3772
"The most amazing delicious chiles," says Alice Waters of Chez Panisse. The fifty varieties available here at this Bay Area treasure trove are pesticide-free.

Grand Central Market
317 South Broadway
Los Angeles, CA 90013
213–624–2378
More than thirty-eight merchants are here offering their finest selections of produce, meats, fish, exotic herbs, and spices from a world of many cultures. Recommended by Mary Sue Milliken and Susan Feniger of *Border Grill* in Santa Monica.

Latino Market (three locations)
Hiro Sone and Lissa Doumani of Terra Restaurant in Napa Valley recommend these comprehensively stocked Latin food markets in three California locations.
2993 Jefferson Street
Napa, CA 94558
707–257–7188
1500 Monument Boulevard
Concord, CA 94520
925–825–2468
1022 Broadway

Seaside, CA 93955
408–394–7294

White Mountain Farm
8890 Lane 4 North
Mosca, CO 81146
800–364–3019
www.whitemountainfarm.com
Great source for quinoa and for russet, red, yellow, purple, and fingerling potatoes.

Ferraro's Market
664 Grand Avenue
New Haven, CT 06511
www.ferrarosmarket.com
Recommended by Jacques Pépin, who purchases chitterlings, offal, lungs, poultry parts, pigs' ears, and pigs' feet from Ferraro's.

Bongiorno Supermarket
288 West Avenue
Stamford, CT 06902
203–324–1054
Recommended by Jacques Pépin.

Todito Grocery
1813 Columbia Road, NW
Washington, DC 20009
202–986–5680
Ann Cashion of Cashion's Eat Place recommends Todito for chiles, yuca, *horchata, queso fresco,* and more.

Sun Ray Seafood
6150 NW 153rd Street
Miami Lakes, FL 33014
305–819–8327
Fax: 305–819–4447

Some of the best clams in America. Sun Ray sells wholesale to most local markets and across the country.

Buford Highway Farmers Market
5600 Buford Highway
Doraville, GA 30340
770–455–0770
Recommended by Ian Winslade of Atlanta's Bluepointe Restaurant. An excellent source of both fresh and dry Latin American products.

Caribbean American Food Market
4467 Glenwood Road
Decatur, GA 30032
404–286–9990
Another favorite of Ian Winslade for its fresh and dry island products.

The following four recommendations come from author and Latin food expert Linda Bladholm.

International Farmers Market
5193 Peachtree Industrial Boulevard
Atlanta, GA 30341
770–455–1777
You can find a vivid array of fresh vegetables here, including baby zucchini with blossoms and *nopales*.

Caribbean Grocery Traders
467 Circle 85
Atlanta, GA 30349
404–766–2082
Where Linda goes for green plantains and plantain flour, cassava bread, concentrated cordial syrups, and hot sauces galore.

Coisas Do Brazil
1480 Terrel Mill Road
Marietta, GA 30067
770–541–2004
A good source for pantry items such as dried beans for *feijoada*, and exotic fruit concentrates.

Inter-Latin Mexican Grocery
3973 Lawrenceville Highway
Tucker, GA 30084
770–414–0219
An excellent place to find not only Mexican but also pan-American items. You can find fresh tortillas and tortilla presses, Mexican chocolate, *horchata* powders, sweet bread, and *panela* here.

Mercado De La Raza
1315 South Beretania Street
Honolulu, HI 96814
808–593–2226
A favorite of chef Roy Yamaguchi, owner of Roy's. It's the only store of its kind in Hawaii, purveying a wide variety of food and products from Mexico, Central and South America, and the Caribbean.

Frankie's Nursery
41–999 Mahiku Place
Honolulu, HI 96795
808–259–8737
Roy Yamaguchi shops at Frankie's for exotic products. Some examples of products offered are rambutan, sapodilla, star fruit, and jujube.

The Poi Company, Inc.
749 Kopke Street
Honolulu, HI 96819
808–847–4764
Recommended by Alan Wong of Alan Wong's in Honolulu. Chef Wong buys *taro (malanga)* here and many other tropical tubers.

Midwest Foods
3100 West 36th Street
Chicago, IL 60632
773–927–8870
www.mwfoods.com
Recommended by Carrie Nahabedian of Chicago's NAHA for its consistently beautiful, high-quality produce, as well as exotic and tropical fruits. A favorite of Charlie Trotter.

George J. Cornille & Sons, Inc.
60 South Water Market
Chicago, IL 60608
312–226–1015
Recommended by Charlie Trotter of Chicago's Charlie Trotter's.

El Sol, Inc.
1514 Monroe Street
Gretna, LA 70053
504–362–6888
Recommended by Emeril Lagasse of Emeril's restaurant. Emeril swears by El Sol's authenticity. In particular, he buys fresh corn and flour tortillas here.

Union Supermarket
4129 South Carrollton Avenue
New Orleans, LA 70119
504–482–5390
Recommended by Susan Spicer

of Bayona in New Orleans for its guava paste, chipotle peppers, *chicharrones,* plantains, yuca, and dried chiles.

MARYLAND
Casa Veiga
8709 Flower Avenue
Silver Spring, MD 20901
301–587–7747
Recommended by author and Latin food expert Linda Bladholm. Products from El Salvador (the owners come from there), Central and South America, and the Caribbean.

MASSACHUSETTS
88 Supermarket
50 Herald Street
Boston, MA 02118
617–423–1688
Jasper White of Boston's Summer Shack recommends 88 Supermarket: "Great, a class by itself, you'll find everything from Latin foods, Caribbean to Asian." Ming Tsai of Blue Ginger near Boston buys his banana leaves, mangoes, papayas, and chiles here.

Maria & Ricardo's Tortilla Factory
30 Germania Street
Jamaica Plain, MA 02130
617–524–6107
Todd English of Boston's Olives recommends Maria & Ricardo's for its wealth of tortillas: flour, corn, fat-free tortillas, wraps, chips, tostadas, and *harina* to make tamales or tortillas.

Tropical Foods, Inc.
201 Washington Street

Boston, MA 02108
617–422–7439
Recommended by Jasper White of Summer Shack.

MINNESOTA
Earthy Delights
4180 Keller Road, Suite B
Holt, MN 48820
517–699–1530 or 800–367–4709
Recommended by Charlie Trotter of Charlie Trotter's.

NEW JERSEY
The CMC Company
P.O. Box 322
Avalon, NJ 08202
800–262–2780
www.thecmccompany.com
CMC carries most Latin products, such as *achiote* paste, *masa harina,* all types of chiles, and Mexican oregano, among many other ingredients.

NEW MEXICO
Los Chileros De Nuevo Mexico
P.O. Box 6215
Santa Fe, NM 87502
505–471–6967
Exotic chiles and New Mexican chiles.

Coyote Café General Store
132 West Water Street
Santa Fe, NM 87501
800–866–4695
The store, attached to Mark Miller's excellent New Mexican cuisine Coyote Café, sells dried beans, chiles, *masa harina,* spices, and other items. When he is in Santa Fe, Douglas Rodriguez of Chicama stops here.

NEW YORK
Abarrotera Central Wholesale
97–03 43rd Avenue
Corona, Queens, NY 11368
718–507–4542
Edward Brown of New York's Sea Grill recommends Abarrotera for its tremendous variety of Latin foods.

Balducci's
424 Sixth Avenue
New York, NY 10011
212–673–2600
The extremely crowded Manhattan mothership of gourmet and ethnic produce, ingredients, spices, you name it.

Kalustyan's
123 Lexington Avenue
New York, NY 10016
212–685–3451
Alfred Portale of New York's Gotham Bar and Grill loves Kalustyan's, and so do I. Alfred says the market has a good selection of fresh, exotic ingredients

and a huge selection of international spices, beans, and chiles.

OHIO
The Chef's Garden
9009 Huron-Avery Road
Huron, OH 44839
800–289–4644
The Chef's Garden grows, picks, and delivers the finest gourmet fruits and vegetables, herbs, lettuces, edible flowers, heirloom tomatoes, peppers, *coquitos,* specialty potatoes, micro-greens, exotic mushrooms, dried and fresh beans, and dried and fresh fruit, with more than 450 items available. Will ship anywhere in the United States.

OREGON
Becerra's Spanish Groceries
3022 NE Glisan Street
Portland, OR 97232
503–234–7785
Jody Denton of Portland recommends Becerra's for its Mexican and Latin American foods.

PENNSYLVANIA
Eckerton Hill Farm
130 Far View Road
Hamburg, PA 19526
610–562–2591
An assortment of Latin products is available here, from chiles to *ají* to some of the best tomatoes I've ever tasted.

TENNESSEE
Farmers Market
900 Eighth Avenue North
Nashville, TN 37208
415–880–2001
Recommended by restaurant critic Thayer Wine for its assortment of authentic produce and spices.

TEXAS
Generation Farms
1109 North McKinney Avenue
Rice, TX 75155
903–326–4263
This produce purveyor near Dallas is recommended by Paula Lambert of Mozzarella Company for its organic herbs, which they cut in the middle of the night so they'll be fresh the following day.

Mozzarella Company
2944 Elm Street
Dallas, TX 75226
800–798–2954
Recommended by chefs such as Stephen Pyles, Dean Fearing, Scott Cohen, and me, Mozzarella Company is an excellent source for ancho chile, *caciotta, jocoque, queso* Oaxaca, and other Latin cheeses.

VIRGINIA
Glebe Market
300 North Glebe Road
Arlington, VA 22203
703–527–7212
Korean-owned Latin market with goods from Bolivia, Peru, and Mexico.

WASHINGTON STATE
El Mercado Latino
1514 Pike Place, Suite 6
Seattle, WA 98101
206–623–3240
Recommended by Tom Douglas of Seattle's Dahlia Lounge for its extensive selection of Mexican, Caribbean, and South American ingredients.

The Spanish Table
1427 Western Avenue
Seattle, WA 98101
206–682 2827
Recommended by Robbin Haas, consulting chef of Seattle's Baleen. Food, wine, and tableware from Spain, Portugal, Cuba, and Brazil.

WISCONSIN
Penzeys Spice House, Ltd.
West 19362 Apollo Drive
P.O. Box 924
Brookfield, WI 53008
800–741–7787
Douglas Rodriguez of Chicama and I love Penzeys, which stocks spices from all over the world.

Asia Mart
1125 Old World Third Street
Milwaukee, WI 53203
414–765–9211
Recommended by Sanford D'Amato of Sanford Restaurant for its full, fresh stocks of American and Caribbean vegetables.

bibliography

Books that have taught and continue to inspire me.

Andrews, Jean. *Peppers*. New York: Macmillan, 1993.

Bayless, Rick. *Authentic Mexican: Regional Cooking from the Heart of Mexico*. New York: Morrow, 1987.

Botafogo, Dolores. *The Art of Brazilian Cookery*. New York: Hippocrene Press, 1994.

Cox, Beverly, and Martin Jacobs. *Spirit of the Earth*. New York: Stewart, Tabori & Chang, 2001.

Custer, Tony. *The Art of Peruvian Cuisine*. Peru S.A., 2000. In 1998, Custer created *Aprendamos Juntos*, a program that installs special classrooms with full-time therapists to help children with learning disabilities in Lima's poorest schools. All proceeds from the book go to the program; for further information, contact <facuster@cpg-peru.com.pe>.

Davidson, Alan. *The Oxford Companion to Food*. Oxford: Oxford University Press, 1999.

DeMers, John. *The Foods of Jamaica*. Singapore: Periplus Editions, 1998.

Fussell, Betty. *Crazy for Corn*. New York: HarperPerennial, 1995.

Gelber, Irwin. *The International Kitchen: Mexico, Central America, South America, and the Caribbean*. New York: John Wiley & Sons, 1993.

Harris, Jessica. *Sky Juice and Flying Fish*. New York: Fireside, 1991.

Idone, Christopher. *Brazil: A Cook's Tour*. New York: Clarkson Potter, 1995.

Kennedy, Diana. *Recipes from the Regional Cooks of Mexico*. New York: HarperCollins, 1978.

Martinez, Zarela. *The Food and Life of Oaxaca*. New York: Macmillan, 1997.

Miller, Mark Charles; Pyles, Stephan; and John Sedlar. *Tamales*. Berkeley: Ten Speed Press, 1997.

Morgan, Jinx and Jefferson. *The Sugar Mill Caribbean Cookbook*. Boston: Harvard Common Press, 1996.

Ortiz, Elisabeth Lambert. *The Book of Latin American Cooking*. reprint. New York: Ecco, 1994.

———. *The New Complete Book of Mexican Cooking*. New York: Ecco, 2000.

Peterson, Joan and David. *Eat Smart in Brazil*. Madison, WI: Ginkgo Press, 1995.

Presilla, Maricel E. *The New Taste of Chocolate*. Berkeley: Ten Speed Press, 2001.

Raichlen, Steven. *Steve Raichlen's Healthy Latin Cooking*. Emmaus, PA: Rodale Press, 2000.

Randelman, Mary Urrutia. *Memories of a Cuban Kitchen*. New York: Macmillan, 1996.

Rodriguez, Douglas. *Latin Ladles*. Berkeley: Ten Speed Press, 1998.

Rojas-Lombardi, Felipe. *The Art of South American Cooking*. New York: HarperCollins, 1991.

Sokolov, Raymond. *Why We Eat What We Eat*. New York: Summit Books, 1991.

Van Waerbeek-Gonzales, Ruth. *The Chilean Kitchen*. New York: Berkeley, 1999.

index